P9-DEE-474

Only Humans
Need Apply

Also by Thomas H. Davenport

Big Data at Work
Keeping Up with the Quants
Judgment Calls
Analytics at Work
Competing on Analytics
Thinking for a Living
What's the Big Idea?
The Attention Economy
Knowledge Management Case Book
Working Knowledge
Mastering Information Management
Mission Critical
Information Ecology
Process Innovation

Also by Julia Kirby

Standing on the Sun

Only Humans Need Apply ✓

Winners and Losers
in the Age of Smart Machines

THOMAS H. DAVENPORT
AND JULIA KIRBY

HARPER
BUSINESS

HarperCollins books may be purchased for educational, business, or sales promotional use. For information, please e-mail the Special Markets Department at SPsales@harpercollins.com.

FIRST EDITION

Designed by Nicola Ferguson

Library of Congress Cataloging-in-Publication Data has been applied for.

ISBN: 978-0-06-243861-4

16 17 18 19 20   ov/rrd   10 9 8 7 6 5 4 3 2 1

Both of us dedicate this book to our kids—Hayes and Chase in Tom's case, and David, Jane, and Ted in Julia's. Julia has confidence that hers, in their very human and different ways, will make the world a better place. Tom is similarly sure that his will continue to find interesting and useful work, and hopes they provide him with grandchildren so that the theories in this book can be fully tested over the long run.

CONTENTS

6. Stepping In   *131*

People who make the machines productive will rely on them to make
routine decisions but will know when to correct their mistakes and
how to tweak them for better performance—and how to explain their
automated logic to other people.

7. Stepping Narrowly   *153*

People who hyperspecialize will hold on to decision-making by gaining
deep expertise in areas that are so narrow they don't make economic
sense for anyone to automate.

8. Stepping Forward   *176*

People who build the next generation of smart machines will be
entrepreneurial as well as technically brilliant. No one will ever go broke
automating the intelligence of the knowledge worker.

9. How You'll Manage Augmentation   *201*

For managers, augmentation is the only viable enterprise strategy, given
the competitive imperative for constant innovation and the very fast
following of any software-based advantages.

10. Utopia or Dystopia? How Society Must Adapt
to Smart Machines   *225*

An emphasis on augmentation has implications for education policy, job
creation policy, and more.

Only Humans
Need Apply

INTRODUCTION

In the bucolic outskirts of tiny Talcott, West Virginia, stands a statue of a man who succeeded—however briefly—in beating a machine that threatened to take his job. John Henry, a steel driver working for the Chesapeake & Ohio Railway in 1870, was part of a crew carving a mile-long tunnel through Big Bend Mountain when management brought in a steam-powered drill. Henry said he could outdo the drill and he did, only to die soon after from the exertion. *Roadside America,* a guide to "offbeat tourist attractions," sums things up: "As an inspiring tale for the working everyman, his story obviously leaves something to be desired."

We might wonder why it was so important to Henry to beat the machine. There is a bigger question, though: Why does his victory over the machine still resonate with the rest of us? Why the folktale and why the statue? Why do we still teach schoolchildren to sing his ballad?

Anxiety about machines encroaching on the work of people runs deep. Some sixty years before the Great Bend Tunnel, the Luddites (possibly named after an early machine smasher, Ned Ludd) reacted more destructively to the stocking frames, spinning frames, and power looms that were making textile workers redundant. Some eighty years after John Henry, in 1955, Ford Motor Company workers rose up against unprecedented automation of the assembly lines in Brook Park, Ohio. Their wildcat strikes were blessed by local union leader Alfred Granakis, who called the automation of manufacturing an "economic Frankenstein."

The aftermath has always been far more positive than folks imagined. We could cite any number of economic studies giving the lie to what economists call the "Luddite fallacy." They show that productivity gains have in fact always led—eventually if not immediately—to more jobs, not fewer. True, many tasks leave the hands of humans, but the technologies simultaneously usher in plenty of new, higher-order tasks for people to do instead. There has always been higher ground to which humans could retreat. Job losses due to "skill-biased technical change" are therefore real, but temporary. Even today, as an Oxford University study claims that 47 percent of total U.S. jobs are at risk of termination because of computerization in the near future, economists (and plenty of technology vendors) offer assurances that the same will happen again.

But what if, this time around, things play out differently? What if there is no higher ground? It's important to note that the type of work being displaced today is of a different kind than in the past. In fact, we can easily trace three eras of automation, based on the types of work they have brought machines forth to challenge. First, machines relieved humans of work that was manually exhausting and mentally enervating. This was the story of the late industrial revolution, which, having pulled all those workers off farms and into factories, proceeded to make most of them unnecessary with contraptions like the flying shuttle, the spinning jenny, and the power loom. And it's a process that continues around the world. Consider Foxconn, the Chinese manufacturing subcontractor to global electronics brands like Apple. Starting in 2011, it started putting robots on the lines to perform welding, polishing, and such tasks—ten thousand of them that first year. In 2013, Chairman Terry Gou noted at Foxconn's annual meeting that the firm now employed over a million people. But, he was quick to add: "In the future we will add one million robotic workers."[1]

If that goal is realized, it will mean, of course, that some hundreds of thousands of human workers will never get hired—a loss of jobs for the local economy. But at the level of the individual worker, it might feel like less of a loss, because the particular tasks that are being taken away are generally not cherished. In Amazon's gargantuan warehouses, for example, it's tough for workers to pick and pack customer orders if they have to do the running from one end of the building to another—so tough that journalists working there undercover have published scathing articles about the inhuman demands placed on them. So now the company uses Kiva Systems (now Amazon Robotics) robots to bring shelves to the workers, allowing humans—who still have strong advantages in spotting the specific items and packing them appropriately—to stay in one place. Does it make the job easier? Without a doubt. Does it mean Amazon needs fewer people to fulfill a given number of orders? You bet.

The second era of automation followed workers to the higher ground they'd headed for when machines took the grunt work. For the most part, this wasn't the realm of the dirty and dangerous anymore. It was the domain of dull. Think, for example, of the 1960s-era secretary toiling away in a typing pool, translating scribbled or spoken words into neat memos. Some might call this "knowledge work," since it calls on brain rather than brawn, but it clearly stops short of decision-making. After computers were invented, it was easy territory for machines to make more productive.

For some secretarial tasks, here's how far that process has gone. In the midst of working on this section, Tom was planning to meet a friend for coffee later in the week. The friend is an independent consultant, so it was slightly surprising to learn, by being cc'd on an email, that he employed an assistant, "Amy." He wrote:

Hi Amy,

Would you please send an invite for Tom and me for Friday 9/19 at 9:30 A.M. at Hi-Rise Cafe in Cambridge, MA. We will be meeting in person.

Thanks,

Judah

Curiosity getting the best of him, Tom looked up the company in Amy's email extension, @x.ai. It turns out X.ai is a company that uses "natural language processing" software to interpret text and schedule meetings via email. "Amy," in other words, is automated. Meanwhile, other tools such as email and voice mail, word processing, online travel sites, and Internet search applications have been chipping away the rest of what used to be a secretarial job.

Era Two automation doesn't only affect office workers. It washes across the entire services-based economy that arose after massive productivity gains wiped out jobs in agriculture, then manufacturing. Many modern jobs are transactional service jobs—that is, they feature people helping customers access what they need from complex business systems. But whether the customer is buying an airline ticket, ordering a meal, or making an appointment, these transactions are so routinized that they are simple to translate into code. You might well know someone—a bank teller, an airline reservations clerk, a call center representative—who lost his or her job to the new reality of computerized systems enabling self-service. At least, you feel the absence of them when you contact a company and encounter a machine interface.

Just as Era One of automation continues to play out, so does Era Two. There is still plenty of work currently performed by humans that could be more cheaply and capably performed by machines—increasingly smart ones in particular. Think, for example, of the loneliness of the long-distance trucker—a job, by the way, that didn't exist in the early industrialization era but was created by technological progress. Human drivers are still kings of the road, but perhaps not for much longer. Tom recently asked a senior FedEx executive whether he thought that his company would switch anytime soon to self-driving trucks. His casual response— "Well, not on the *local* routes"—is perhaps not what the drivers' union would want to hear.

It occurs to us that every type of low-level service task the two of us did during our college summers could probably be done better today with automation—Tom's floor sweeping at a steel mill by a high-powered Roomba, for example, and Julia's retail clerking by a self-service kiosk. Even Tom's best days working at a service station might soon be surpassed by the robotic gas pumps undergoing regulatory testing now.

And this brings us to Era Three, with automation gaining in intelligence and (excuse us while we check our mortgage balances) now breathing down our necks. Now computers are proving in various settings that they are capable of making better *decisions* than humans. As the technology research firm Gartner notes, this will make the next two decades the most disruptive era in history, one in which computer systems "fulfill some of the earliest visions for what information technologies might accomplish—doing what we thought only people could do and machines could not."[2]

As with other dramatic technology advances, Era Three will bring both promise and peril. The good news is that new cognitive technologies will help to solve many important business and societal problems. Your local doctor will have the expertise of an international specialist. You'll be guided effectively through mazes of online products and services. Whatever your job, you'll have the knowledge at your fingertips to perform it productively and effectively.

If you have a job, that is. The obvious peril in Era Three is more job loss. This time the potential victims are not tellers and tollbooth collectors, much less farmers and factory workers, but rather all those "knowledge workers" who assumed they were immune from job displacement by machines. People like the writers and readers of this book.

Knowledge Workers' Jobs Are at Risk

The management consulting firm McKinsey thinks a lot about knowledge workers; they make up essentially 100 percent of its own ranks as well as its clientele. When its research arm, the McKinsey Global Institute, issued a report on the disruptive technologies that would most "transform life, business, and the global economy" in the next decade, it included the automation of knowledge work. Having studied typical job compositions in seven categories of knowledge workers (professionals, managers, engineers, scientists, teachers, analysts, and administrative support staff), McKinsey predicts dramatic change will have already taken hold by 2025. The bottom line: "we estimate that knowledge work automation tools and systems could take on tasks that would be equal to the output of 110 million to 140 million full-time equivalents (FTEs)."[3]

Since we'll continue to use the term "knowledge workers" quite a bit, we should pause to define who these people are. In Tom's 2005 book, *Thinking for a Living*, he described them as workers "whose primary tasks involve the manipulation of knowledge and information."[4] Under that definition, they represent a quarter to a half of all workers in advanced economies (depending on the country, the definition, and the statistics you prefer), and they "pull the plow of economic progress," as Tom put it then. Within large companies, he explained, the knowledge workers are the ones sparking innovation and growth. They invent new products and services, design marketing programs, and create strategies. But knowledge workers don't only work in corporate offices. They include all the highly educated and certified people who make up the professions: doctors, lawyers, scientists, professors, accountants, and more. They include airline pilots and ship captains, private detectives and bookies—anyone who has had to study hard for their job and who succeeds by their wits. And every one of these jobs has significant components that could be performed by automated systems.

It's a category that's fuzzy around the edges. Does it, for example, include London taxi drivers—who famously have to acquire "the Knowledge" to be licensed? Does it include a translator? A filing clerk? A tour guide? For the purposes of this book, we can leave those as questions. Where exactly we draw the line is not all that important because, when we think about what work is threatened, it's all of the above.

Why Worry About Less Work?

Machines are becoming so capable that, today, it is hard to see the higher cognitive ground that many people could move to. That is making some very smart people worry. Massachusetts Institute of Technology (MIT) professors Erik Brynjolfsson and Andy McAfee, for example, in their acclaimed book, *The Second Machine Age*, note that the anticipated recovery in labor markets has been just around the corner for a long time. The persistence of high unemployment levels in Western economies might mean that the dislocation caused by the last wave of skill-biased technical change is permanent. Paul Beaudry, David Green, and Benjamin Sand have done research on the total demand for workers in the United States who are highly skilled.[5] They say demand peaked around the year 2000 and has fallen since, even as universities churn out an ever-growing supply.

Income inequality is a growing concern in an economy that has fewer good jobs to allocate. There is already evidence that the big payoffs in today's economy are going not to the bulk of knowledge workers, but to a small segment of "superstars"—CEOs, hedge fund and private equity managers, investment bankers, and so forth—almost all of whom are very well leveraged by automated decision-making. Meanwhile, labor force participation rates in developed economies steadily fall. Silicon Valley investor Bill Davidow and tech journalist Mike Malone, writing recently for *Harvard Business Review*, declared that "we will soon be looking at hordes of citizens of zero economic value."[6] They say figuring out how to deal with the impacts of this development will be the greatest challenge facing free market economies in this century. Many seem to agree. When the World Economic Forum (WEF) surveyed more than seven hundred leading thinkers in advance of its 2014 annual meeting in Davos, Switzerland, the issue they deemed likeliest to have a major impact on the world economy in the next decade was "income disparity and attendant social unrest."

Explaining that "attendant social unrest," WEF's chief economist, Jennifer Blanke, noted that "disgruntlement can lead to the dissolution of the fabric of society, especially if young people feel they don't have a future."[7] And indeed, various studies have shown that idle hands really are the devil's playground. (Perhaps the best was a 2002 analysis by Bruce Weinberg and his colleagues that looked at crime rates across an eighteen-year period in the United States.[8] All the increases, they discovered, could be explained by rising unemployment and falling wages among men without college educations.)

It isn't only that people become disgruntled when they lack the income that flows from a good job. They miss having the job itself. This was what economics Nobel laureate Robert Shiller had in mind when he called advancing machine intelligence "the most important problem facing the world today." He elaborated:

> It's associated with income inequality, but it may be more than that. Since we tend to define ourselves by our intellectual talents, it's also a question of personal identity. Who am I? Intellectual talents are being replaced by computers. That's a frightening thing for most people. It's an issue with deep philosophical implications.[9]

Jobs bring many benefits to people's lives beyond the paycheck, among them the social community they provide through having coworkers, the satisfaction of setting and meeting challenging goals, even the predictable structure and rhythm they bring to the week. In 2005 Gallup began conducting a global opinion survey called World Poll. Analysis of the responses reveals that people with "good jobs"—which Gallup defines as those offering steady work averaging thirty or more hours per week and a paycheck from an employer—are more likely than others to provide positive responses about other aspects of their present and future lives.

Another World Poll question presents "aspects of life that some people say are important to them" and asks respondents to categorize each as to whether it is something essential they could not live without, very important, or useful but something they could live without. Gallup chairman Jim Clifton says that by 2011, "having a good quality job" had reached the top globally—putting it ahead of, for example, having a family, democracy and freedom, religion, or peace.[10]

Knowledge workers aren't wrong, then, to fear the prospect of losing their jobs. As machines push past the work that is dirty, dangerous, and dull and begin encroaching on the work of decision-making, workers must contend with the loss of territory that is much nearer to their core identity and sense of self-worth. It's dispiriting to think that, even if we can find ways to share the wealth of a tremendously productive system, we might not find ways for many humans to contribute value to it, and derive meaning from it.

But that's why we're publishing this book: because we *can* still see ways for humans to win in what Brynjolfsson and McAfee call the "race against the machine." Our observation is that the experts engaging in the current debate about knowledge work automation tend to fall into two camps— those who say we are heading inexorably toward permanent high levels of unemployment and those who are certain new job types will spring up to replace all the ones that go by the wayside—but that neither camp suggests to workers that there is much they can do personally about the situation. Our main mission in the next couple hundred pages is to persuade you, our knowledge worker reader, that you remain in charge of your destiny. You should be feeling a sense of agency and making decisions for yourself as to how you will deal with advancing automation.

Over the past few years, even as every week brings news of some breakthrough in machine learning or natural language processing or visual image recognition, we've been learning from knowledge workers who are thriving. They're redefining what it means to be more capable than computers, and doubling down on their very human strengths. As you'll find in the chapters to come, these are not superhumans who can somehow process information more quickly than artificial intelligence or perform repetitive tasks as flawlessly as robots. They are normal people who like their work, and bring something special to it. And in the modern struggle to remain relevant in the midst of powerful machines, they offer real inspiration. They—and you—are the new John Henrys.

1

Are Computers Coming After Your Job?

Even if you have never actually visited the New York Stock Exchange, you've probably seen it as a backdrop on financial news shows. It's a telegenic image, with a series of kiosks for each trading firm, and the company logos of the stocks each firm trades on their walls. Electronic screens with fast-changing prices abound. Traders in bright blue jackets gather around market specialists and wave bits of paper or stick fingers in the air to represent the price they will pay to buy. Often we see them clasping their foreheads on days when stock prices take a nosedive. It's the picture of capitalism.

Or is it? The last time we visited, in 2014, the visible action was a bit desultory, and we hear that's the new norm. In 1980 there were 5,500 traders; now there are about 500. A trader could make more than a million dollars a year in the good years; now they struggle to pay back the $40,000 annual cost of a seat on the floor.

During our visit, the few traders we saw who were standing around didn't seem to have much to do, and did have plenty of time to chat. When we asked why they seemed so relaxed, they explained that the great majority of trading is done on computers in a New Jersey data center. One told us that he no longer works on Mondays or Fridays. Even though the NYSE is one of the last "open outcry" exchanges with human traders, there's not a lot of outcrying anymore. That's why it's so well suited to television broadcasts.

This situation is even further along at other exchanges; almost all equities are traded electronically. The Chicago Mercantile Exchange switched to automated trading of commodities in early 2015. Even bond trading, which has resisted automation because of the complex pricing and trades, is about half-electronic now. Algorithms and digital matching of buyers and sellers have replaced human traders. The result is fast and efficient—so much so that the profit margins from stock trading have been dramatically eroded. Human trading is likely to fully disappear within a few more years.

In addition to being the picture of capitalism, the NYSE trading floor is also the ideal image of automation. Time-lapse photography would show it becoming less populated each year. The jobs ended not with a bang, but with an extended whimper over forty years. Will your job still be around in 2055?

Let's be clear: Humans are problematic as workers. First of all, they're expensive, and they only get more so. On top of their basic wage, they cost their employers a third again more in payroll taxes, paid time off, health insurance, 401(k) contributions, and other perks. Think that's all? Ask any facilities manager. Humans need ergonomic workspaces, heat, and light. Plumbing. All this is expensive, but it gets uglier. Ask any corporate counsel if humans like to bring lawsuits. Ask any security officer if embezzlement happens. Ask any inventory managers if they know about shrinkage. Ask any human resource executive what percentage of employees are engaged in their work (the average is 13 percent in the U.S.). But the trouble with human workers is a bigger deal than even that. As we'll discuss in Chapter 2, technologies get smarter and cheaper all the time, but humans as a group don't. You can't simply download preexisting knowledge to a human. Every human starts at square one.

That trading floor is therefore a chilling scene. But at the same time it's too comforting. It implies that "jobs" remain intact and the only problem is that some can now be taken by machines. That's a source of solace to all of us who can name the reasons our own jobs can't be accomplished by machines. But the truth is that jobs are not irreducible. All jobs are really amalgams of tasks, and every job today has some parts that can be effectively automated. The fact that no machine will ever be able to decide, as the executive director of the Pantone Color Institute does, that the design community will embrace "marsala" as 2015's color of the year, or to predict, as executives must in an acquisition opportunity, whether the top talent of the targeted company will thrive or wilt in the proposed merged culture, or to compose a sentence, as we are doing, that rivals late novelist David Foster Wallace's in its ability to remain grammatical while becoming remarkably convoluted does not mean that machines can't take over the large proportions of a knowledge workers' days that are not devoted to such rarefied tasks.[1]

As computer programs focus on the tasks they can do, it's those pieces of jobs that are taken away. The encroachment happens one task at a time, meaning that a job that is only 10 percent automatable doesn't go away. It's just that, now, nine holders of that job can do what used to be the work of ten. This is why, outside *The Twilight Zone*, you've seen virtually no one being summoned into an office and introduced to the computer who will now be doing his job. Instead, they're just nudged, nudged, nudged toward the door.

And again, as with the manual workers who were tired of the dangerous, dirty, and dull aspects of their day, those nine people who continue to do a job are usually more than happy to see that particular 10 percent of their work go. There are loads of tasks they would rather not spend their time doing. The bane of a lawyer's existence, for example, is "discovery"—the tedious process of sifting through documents and deposition transcripts in search of nuggets pertaining to a lawsuit. When "e-discovery" and "predictive coding" arrived on the scene, allowing much of this text review to be automated, few shouted their objections. All of us want to have our skills leveraged. In our work, we are all like Sherlock Holmes: We abhor the dull routine of existence.

As part of this, most workers eagerly embrace the machines that save them from the day-in and day-out chores of their jobs that take up time and add nothing to their net knowledge. If it were otherwise, companies' IT departments wouldn't be dealing with the scourge of "BYOD"—the growing practice of employees' bringing their own favorite computers and other devices to the office. People want the extra productivity they get from state-of-the-art tools because it frees up capacity for them to take on more interesting challenges. They want that so much that they are willing to buy the tools for themselves.

So automation of one task after another tends not to be seen as the infiltrating enemy by employees. And neither is it seen as a problem by most customers. When a task can be performed well by a machine, they prefer it, too. Obviously, paying customers appreciate when higher productivity means that prices go down; while some people might cherish paying higher prices to enjoy artisanal products and services, most go for the product that does the job at the lowest price possible. But beyond price, automation often improves quality, reliability, and convenience. When ATMs arrived, customers didn't complain about the automated option. By now, few could imagine life without them.

So if all of our jobs have parts that are succumbing to automation, which parts will we keep? We might like to think it will be the parts that it took us a long time to learn to do or that we have some special capability to perform. In other words, it will be the same parts that originally gave us the edge over all the other candidates for our jobs. But it isn't as simple as that. Instead, the parts of our jobs we'll keep are just the parts that *can't be codified*. By that we mean that it can't be reduced to known contingencies and clear steps. Codified tasks can be specified in rules and algorithms, and hence automated.

This is a theorem we will return to again and again in this book: If work can be codified, it can be automated. And there's also the corollary: If it can be automated in an economical fashion, it will be. Already we're seeing a rapid decomposition of jobs and automation of the most codifiable parts—which are sometimes the parts that have required the greatest education and experience.

Take the job of "physician advisor," a role important in hospital administration and insurance. In medical settings, physicians see patients and come up with treatment plans for what ails them—but they are expected to do this with an eye to the hospital's need for sound resource management. Extraneous tests or overnight stays use up limited resources and may not be reimbursed by insurers—and by the way, also take their toll on the patient. The physician advisor is there to review the doctors' submitted treatment plans and suggest changes if they seem off base in any way. Can you imagine how much knowledge this person needs to have acquired to second-guess highly educated physicians? Beyond that, the role requires diplomacy. A medical newsletter describes the job profile as follows: "[A] skilled physician advisor must learn to manage by influence rather than by authority. This requires a delicate balance between collegiality and firmness relative to the issues at hand. It also requires the ability to provide reasonable alternatives rather than indicating what can't be done."[2]

It sure doesn't sound like a role a computer could take on. Yet IBM's Watson and other automated systems are now being used at health insurance companies like Anthem to weigh in as physician advisor. And the point to note is that the most cognitive part of the job—the "ability to provide reasonable alternatives" based on extensive knowledge of similar cases in the past—is the part being automated here. No doctor could possibly hold in memory more prior cases than Watson can. But that is also probably the part in which the doctor takes most pride—certainly it's what those hard-earned diplomas framed on the wall attest that she can do. Does Watson get rid of the human in the physician advisor job altogether? No, at least not yet. But by supplying that precious knowledge base, it allows the recommendation task to be done more quickly, or by a less credentialed person—perhaps a nurse. Presumably this means the hiring manager for the role now focuses on the other aspects important to success—like that ability to achieve "a delicate balance between collegiality and firmness." That is undeniably a rare talent, but it's probably not something anyone explicitly trained for, let alone did a residency in.

We should pause here to mention the threat of "deskilling," since the physician advisor's evolution is such a prime example of it. The term, first coined by the Marxist sociologist Harry Braverman, is commonly used to describe both what automation does to jobs and what it does to the labor force. The jobs are deskilled when technologies are introduced that no longer require workers to have formerly necessary skills—meaning that semiskilled or unskilled workers can now hold those jobs. In turn, the labor force is deskilled when, enough machines having taken over a particular task, the skill becomes a "lost art" to people. A simple example courtesy of a 2014 survey of Britons: 40 percent of them admitted to relying completely on autocorrect technology to get their spelling right in daily correspondence—and more than half of those say if they were forced to go without spellcheck, they would "panic." Yet 90 percent say it is still "absolutely crucial" for children to learn to spell properly.[3] For Braverman, and many thinkers since, deskilling is a very dangerous phenomenon. As early as 1974, he was already predicting its inevitable creep into knowledge work, and worrying about the emergence of a "white collar proletariat."

We do expect deskilling to accelerate as computers take on more knowledge work tasks. Imagine the art of teaching, for example. Today a teacher in an elementary grade performs a number of important educational functions. One is to determine what content students have already mastered and what they still need to learn. Another is to actually transmit the content to the students. A third is to maintain discipline and cultivate a love of learning in the classroom. It's unlikely that computers will be able to maintain a calm and quiet demeanor among a group of twenty-five or so fourth graders, but many of the other functions that teachers perform can be carried out by computers, and in some cases this is happening today.

Computers are better than many teachers, in fact, at diagnosing what each student needs to learn, and customizing the educational content to the student's needs. Given traditional classroom sizes, these decisions are just too tailored and time-consuming for many teachers to make effectively. Computers are also good—at least when the educational software is well crafted—at transmitting educational content to students, and knowing when they have mastered it. We could imagine, then, that the human roles in highly computerized schools could be reduced to monitoring and discipline, and being occupied by people who look more like "teachers' aides" and proctors than professionals with deep knowledge of pedagogy and subject matter. This isn't a popular idea with teachers' unions, but that might be the only reason the wholesale shift hasn't happened already.

Will a Computer Take *Your* Job?

Is it starting to feel to you like your highfalutin knowledge worker job might not be so invulnerable? To read the signs a little more, let's consult the radiology profession. Radiologists are another highly educated group whose jobs are being deconstructed, with the parts they trained longest and hardest to do being the very ones that are automated. And note here that, not long ago, we would not have said the ability to study an X-ray or MRI and render a diagnosis could be codified. This is, after all, the profession that loves its "Aunt Minnie." That's a term, reportedly first used by a Cincinnati radiologist named Ben Felson in the 1940s, that honors tacit knowledge. As a radiologist gains practical experience, some diagnoses become possible at a glance, because the same image has come up so many times before. In Felson's words, the radiologist is presented with "a case with radiologic findings so specific and compelling that no realistic differential diagnosis exists." Over time, the radiologist learns: If it looks like your Aunt Minnie, then it's your Aunt Minnie.

Radiology isn't just a specialty requiring a long education; it has been one of the highest-paid medical specialties in the United States. The explosion of imaging technologies over the past couple of decades made doctors who can read such images the "cash cows" of hospitals and medical practices. But in recent years their numbers have been decreasing and incomes falling. It's instructive to look at the three-step process that brought this about. First, the image-reading work was outsourced and offshored to radiologists overseas, because that allowed a greater volume of images to be processed. This could only happen when the images were digitized and could be sent across an ocean in an instant. Second, the discovery of the much lower cost of those offshore physicians' time caused more work to flow their way. And all that shifting of work off-site from hospitals forced administrators to codify it more, in order to monitor the quality of work being done remotely. Finally, that thorough codification has made it more possible to take the ultimate step, to automation.

There are already technologies that can read CT scans and MRIs and seize upon the likely lesions that may mean cancer. They highlight the suspicious spots with prominent brackets so that any doctor or nurse can see the problem. Looking ahead, as the prices of imaging devices continue to fall, the day will come when every family doctor's office has one—thoroughly deskilling the interpretation of radiologic findings. Aunt Minnie is rolling over in her grave.

Not surprisingly, the number of medical students applying for radiology internships in the United States has been dropping steadily over the past several years. But again, there are still parts of what is today a radiologist's job in a hospital setting that no machine can perform. There is an art to getting a nervous patient properly positioned for imaging, for example (though this task is often performed by technicians, not radiologists). "Interventional" radiologists, moreover, must be able to read images in real time as they direct minimally invasive instruments through tissue. That is a skill that is still a very long way from being automated. It's digital, but still in the sense that involves fingers.

The process we're describing, of machines taking the high-end cognitive parts of work and turning people into a sort of human user interface, is occurring across many professional realms. Actual decision-making roles have been ceded to computers—and they are doing pretty well in those roles, despite some occasional hiccups. "Program trading" (also known as high-frequency, algorithmic, or quantitative trading) of equities and fixed-income investments, for example, is widespread on Wall Street and around the financial world. It's one of the reasons why the New York Stock Exchange is so quiet today. Decisions about which stocks and bonds to buy for what price used to be made by human traders but are now largely made by computer. Likewise, decisions that used to be made by human pricing analysts are now arrived at automatically. What price should an organization charge for perishable goods like airplane seats and hotel rooms? That depends—and depends on more factors than the human mind can process in time to make the sale. With thousands of flights per day and hundreds of prices per flight, the result is literally millions of airline price changes per year; one analysis found that the lowest-price ticket on one flight changed 139 times based on seat availability and demand.

It goes on. Who now makes the business decisions of whether to give someone a mortgage or credit card, the premium to charge for an insurance policy, or which ad to show to a media consumer? All require chewing through massive amounts of data, intense analytics, and strict adherence to rules. Very few humans need apply for these jobs. At the level of setting the rules and writing the code that automates that decision-making, a few people still have very important roles. But on a day-to-day basis, these relatively structured and quantitative tasks are today no longer performed by wetware.

Ten Reasons to Look over Your Shoulder

We've always loved the line in H. G. Wells's classic *The War of the Worlds* when the narrator rues the fact he did not react sooner to the arrival of an "intelligence greater than man's"—in his case, Martians landing on earth. Comparing himself to a comfortable dodo in its nest, he imagined those ill-fated birds also dithering as hungry sailors invaded their island: "We will peck them to death to-morrow, my dear."

And what about you? As intelligent technologies take over more and more of the decision-making territory once occupied by humans, are you taking any action? Are you sufficiently aware of the signs that you should? To help you get the head start you may need, here are the signs that it's time to fly the nest. All of them are evidence that a knowledge worker's job is on the path to automation.

1. There are automated systems available today to do some of its core tasks.

The strongest evidence that automation will increasingly threaten a job is the existence of an automated system today that performs all or part of its core function. If we were radiologists or pathologists, for example, we'd be worried about the computer-aided detection systems that read images and detect signs of problems in mammography images or Pap smears. If we were IT operations engineers, we'd be worried about the systems at Facebook that let one engineer run 25,000 servers. These systems haven't achieved broad penetration yet, but they probably will in ten years.

2. It involves little physical contact or manipulation of things.

If you don't have to touch your work or see your customer face-to-face in order to perform your job, there's less reason not to automate it. If you deal primarily in documents (as real estate and many other types of attorneys do, for example) or images (again, like radiologists), systems can digest that content and determine its meaning. If your job requires you to wrestle with something physical in unpredictable ways, it's not going away very soon. An anesthesiologist friend, for example, says he often has to move patients around a lot to clear airways, so he doubts robots will put him out of work.

3. It involves simple content transmission.

To the extent your work has you transmitting existing content to other humans, you may be in trouble. Think about teachers: They figure out what content students need, and transmit it to them through generally manual methods (lectures, demonstrations, and so forth). But there are already "adaptive learning" systems from companies like Amplify, McGraw-Hill Education, and Knewton that diagnose what content a student needs to learn, and many online repositories for educational material, such as Khan Academy. There are some functions that computers can't perform in such educational settings, like managing a classroom and maintaining discipline in class, but they don't necessarily require knowledge workers to perform them.

4. It involves straightforward content analysis.

"Cognitive computing" systems like IBM Watson have already demonstrated that they can do an amazing job of analyzing and "understanding" content. While people will be needed to program and modify such systems, the tasks of analyzing vast amounts of content—as, for example, pharmaceutical researchers and medical diagnosticians do—will increasingly be given over to machines. Lawyers are at risk here as well, because a large component of legal work involves document analysis. Now "e-discovery" tools, through such capabilities as "technology-assisted review" and "predictive coding," can read through thousands of documents, find key terms and phrases, identify the documents that need a human review, and even judge the likelihood of a case's success.

5. It involves answering data-dependent questions.

We already know that analytics and algorithms are better at creating insights from data than most humans. They have already replaced some insurance policy underwriters and financial planners. They'll probably replace more, since this human/machine performance gap will only increase. For example, a company called Kensho Technologies has created an intelligent software system called Warren, which can already answer questions like, "What happens to the share prices of energy companies when oil trades above $100 a barrel and political unrest has recently occurred in the Middle East?" The company stated that by the end of 2014 its software would be able to answer 100 million different distinct financial questions involving complex data.

6. It involves doing quantitative analysis.

One might think that quantitative analysts would be immune from job loss in the "Age of Analytics," but there are technologies that place their jobs at risk, too. Many quantitative analysts' jobs will be replaced—or at the least heavily augmented—by machine-learning systems. Machine learning is probably best used to augment human analysts and improve their productivity in analysis and model development. But in some settings, such as online advertising, it is virtually impossible not to employ machine-learning approaches to generate models at the necessary pace. The number of models needed to target a particular consumer and a particular advertising opportunity easily ranges into the thousands per week, and the likelihood of a successful conversion (say, the customer buying the advertised product within a week) is about one in a thousand at best—meaning it's not worth human attention. Models generated through machine learning are the only possibility in this industry and a growing number of other ones. Of course, it takes an expert quantitative analyst to design the machine-learning approach, but one such analyst can ultimately generate millions of models over time. If you're a quantitative analyst who understands machine learning, you may well keep your job. If you don't understand it, you'll probably be replaced by it.

7. It involves tasks that can be simulated or performed virtually.

This is another problem for teachers and other content experts; if a task can be simulated, one of the best ways to teach it is to have the student undergo a simulation. Just ask the few aircraft flying instructors who are left. Now there are also good simulations for training leaders. Perhaps business school professors and executive coaches are at risk, too.

8. Consistency of performance is critical in it.

Computers are unfailingly consistent; that's why they already determine who gets credit in financial services, for example. Where consistency matters in other job domains—insurance claims adjusting, financial stress testing, perhaps even judging crimes and issuing punishments—computers will increasingly take on the task. In insurance claims, for example, "auto-adjudication" can automatically evaluate and approve up to

75 percent of claims. Human claims adjusters are left to approve only the most challenging ones.

9. It involves the creation of data-based narratives.

Jobs involving the narrative description of data and analysis were once the province of humans, but automated systems are already beginning to take them over. In journalism, companies like Automated Insights and Narrative Science are already creating data-intensive content. Sports and financial reporting are already at some risk, although the automation of these domains is on the margins thus far—high school and fantasy sports, and earnings reports for small companies. Other companies, like AnalytixInsight, create investment analysis narratives on more than 40,000 public companies with its CapitalCube service. The job at risk in this case is that of investment analyst. Wealth management in financial services, which already relies on computer systems in many cases to determine the ideal portfolio for a particular type of investor, is also at risk. Wealth managers and brokers today often take automated recommendations and translate them into narratives for their customers. As customers grow more sophisticated and computer-literate, the translation function will be less necessary.

10. There are well-defined formal rules for performing the work.

The easiest domains to automate have always been those with clear, consistent rules. Now rule-based systems can handle increasingly complex problems. If we were training for a career in financial auditing, for example, we'd be concerned. There are already some systems that automate key aspects of auditing.[4] In tax preparation—a job that is entirely based on following complex rules—much of the work has already been taken over by systems like TurboTax and TaxCut for consumers and small businesses, and Lacerte, ProSystem, and UltraTax for corporate returns.

Think of these as the attributes of "dodo jobs"—those that are sitting there just waiting to be gobbled up by technology. It may be that we'll be left with fewer of them and not none; the most experienced knowledge workers in careers affected by these technologies may keep their jobs, while no new positions open up for entry-level workers. But for your own well-being, or your children's or grandchildren's, we'd advise you to run from them while you can.

How Job Loss Happens

Many of the attributes we've just described apply to large numbers of knowledge workers. So, yes—computers are going to take away your job as it exists today. They'll do it by stealing away small and then big parts of how you currently spend your day. The more structured tasks will be taken over by machines, or made substantially more productive by them. In this way, jobs will literally be disintegrated. And one of your colleagues will be able to handle the work that ten of you do today.

Even if you are that lucky colleague, here's how it could all go down: Your immensely higher productivity could mean the next generation doesn't get hired. The process has been called "silent firing"—getting rid of the jobs that would otherwise have been filled. In radiology, for example, even where automation hasn't been complete, computerized detection systems for breast and colon cancers are being used as a "second set of eyes" that once might have belonged to a human. This slow-but-steady process doesn't wipe out entire job categories, but it takes over enough of the work to limit the growth in them, leaving new grads with no employment offers and dissuading other smart students from following in their footsteps.

The biggest casualties of silent firing are typically entry-level workers. Even when technologies that support knowledge work are not particularly "smart," increases in productivity that they support can limit the demand for inexperienced employees. In architecture, for example, entry-level architects once did a lot of drafting. A minor change to a blueprint or design might have meant a lot of work to re-create it. Today this type of work is done almost exclusively in computer-aided design (CAD) systems, and productivity for drafting and design work is much higher. This is one of the reasons that recent architecture graduates have struggled to find jobs. A study released in 2012 by Georgetown University's Center on Education and the Workforce placed their unemployment rate at 14 percent, the highest of any major. As a *New York Times* story headline baldly put it, "Want a Job? Go to College, and Don't Major in Architecture."[5]

More generally, the effect of too many people chasing too few jobs is severe downward pressure on wages. Recall that glut of knowledge workers that Paul Beaudry and his colleagues found. It can only mean that some highly educated people will compromise to take jobs below their skill level, which in turn will push less-educated workers even further down. All this spells zero wage growth even for those who stay employed. This will be especially true of any work that is also done by the growing movement of amateurs. It's always been true in music and writing that it's hard to make a decent wage, because so many are willing to do it for the sheer joy of expressing themselves and showing off their chops. Now it's becoming true, too, of documentary filmmaking, conference organizing, sports analytics, and who knows how many more highly creative endeavors.

Finally, there's the problem of whether you'd even want that highly leveraged job as the token human among the machines. Chances are you'd be lonely. This is what they discovered in Japan when heavy adoption of robotics produced the first "lights-out" factories, requiring only a few workers to run. When Frederik Schodt did the research behind his 1988 book, *Inside the Robot Kingdom*, he learned about what was being called "the isolation syndrome of automation." Older workers tended to be proud to be part of such technologically advanced operations, but new employees found it hard to find meaning in jobs stripped of human interaction—jobs in which they themselves "felt like robots" reduced to operating and programming other machinery.

What's Our Time Frame Here?

Paul Saffo, a longtime observer of the tech scene, has a great rule that he offers to others speculating about what the future will bring: "Never mistake a clear view for a short distance." A change can be inevitable and still take a good long while to transpire.

We do think it's going to take a while for widespread dislocation of knowledge workers to take place—although we suspect the view of a changed landscape will fill our windshields within a decade. Encroaching on all kinds of jobs are technologies that can already perform some decision-making tasks better than humans. They haven't taken over whole roles, and in many cases they are still proving the extent of their usefulness. But with each passing year, none of these systems becomes less capable—only more.

Bureaucracies of various kinds might apply some brakes to the progress of automation. For example, insurance companies might refuse to cover automated decision technologies, and regulators might continue to base their rules on past ways of getting things done well. Fears of litigation might also make adoption somewhat cautious; lawyers show a real appetite for suits against organizations that implement automated decision technologies earlier than their peers. There is some evidence in radiology, for example, that malpractice insurance companies have constrained what would otherwise be greater adoption of automated cancer-detection technologies.

On the other hand, there is no organized effort by displaced parties trying to slow things down, in the way that organized labor has often presented obstacles in the past. We could imagine powerful professional associations resisting the replacement of human jobs, either for that specific reason or because automated decisions are deemed of lower or uncertain quality. But while some associations do seem reluctant to embrace productivity-enhancing tools—perhaps to protect their human members—we've seen nothing that looks like organized resistance. Even a momentarily exciting protest at the 2015 South by Southwest conference by a group calling itself "Stop the Robots" turned out only to be a marketing stunt by a tech company with a new app to promote.

With little to slow them down, the automated decision technologies already endangering knowledge workers' jobs will go on to achieve future impacts that are revolutionary. Thus, even professionals who personally feel safe from displacement are predicting real challenges to future generations. As one expert on automated financial audits told us, "I'm not worried about my own job, particularly since I focus on how to improve these systems. But I am worried about what to tell my children about their careers."

We knowledge workers have observed—and commented on—the replacement of other people's labor by machines for many decades. We have

ourselves remained sanguine that computers are not going to take our
own jobs. We think we are different than transaction workers or manual
laborers because our jobs are complex, requiring substantial expertise
and experience. We think our judgment can't be quantified or turned into
rules. We imagine that the combination of art and science we deploy in
our decisions can't be modeled or programmed. We believe that our collaborative work processes are too variable and unpredictable to be computerized. In all this, we are wrong.

A greater degree of automation of knowledge work is inevitable—for
you and for your children and their children. Dramatic change in jobs is
unavoidable, even for the most educated knowledge work roles to which
many of us aspire. And thus, action needs to be taken. One way or another,
as a human in an environment increasingly populated by machines, you
will have to adjust. You'll have to do things that computers don't do well,
or somehow add value to the work that computers have largely taken over.
You'll be more likely to find your way to a job you can love if you understand what relative strengths you still bring to the workplace.

What Are Humans Good For, Anyway?

The question is: for what proportion of your job is it true that a machine
could perform it better? And how can you amp up the part that really
needs you? As we've been discussing, there are undeniably still components of most knowledge work jobs that require specifically human skills.
But they might not be the parts you think—in proportion or in particulars. To find your way of remaining valuable, you should understand what
humans do better at than machines, and expect that not all of this will be
obvious. Also accept that some advantages are temporary; as machines
keep getting better at certain tasks, today's safe ground might be eroding
very quickly under your feet.

The question of what humans are good for is one that has been taken
up by various thinkers since machines first showed glimmers of "intelligence." The legendary Norbert Wiener, who published *The Human Use
of Human Beings* in 1950, established a starting point for the discussion.
While his objective was mainly to show how advancing automation could

and must enable humans to embrace their humanity more, and he wasn't as concerned with defining those human attributes too tightly, he did point to creativity and spirituality as parts of the human condition that machines do not share. He also identified a human strength in the range and speed of our adaptability, in contrast to both other animals and machines.

More recently, economists Frank Levy and Richard Murnane put a finer point on things, saying (in their persuasive book, *The New Division of Labor: How Computers Are Creating the Next Job Market*) that the great strengths of humans are expert thinking and complex communication. The brain's gift for pattern recognition is the key to what they call "expert thinking," which is what allows humans, but not computers, to imagine new ways of solving problems (ways, in other words, that have not already been discovered and spelled out step by step). By complex communication, they mean communication that involves a broader interpretation of a situation than could be gained by the explicitly transmitted information. For example, a doctor hoping to elicit information from a patient during an annual checkup engages in a complex process. As Levy writes in a 2010 working paper for the Organisation for Economic Cooperation and Development (OECD), it involves not only listening to the patient's words, but also his body language, tone of voice, eye contact, and incomplete sentences. He notes, "The doctor must be particularly alert for the famous 'last minute' of an appointment when the patient, on his way out the door, looks over his shoulder and says 'By the way, my wife says I should tell you about this pain I have in my stomach.'"[6]

Levy's MIT colleagues Erik Brynjolfsson and Andy McAfee agree with pattern recognition and complex communication as uniquely human traits, and they add a third: ideation. "Scientists come up with new hypotheses," they write. "Chefs add a new dish to the menu. Engineers on a factory floor figure out why a machine is no longer working properly. Steve Jobs and his colleagues at Apple figure out what kind of tablet computer we actually want. Many of these activities are supported and accelerated by computers, but none are driven by them."

There is a common thread in all these thinkers' categories, and it has everything to do with the codification mentioned earlier. The moment a realm of intellectual activity is codifiable, it ceases to be uniquely human.

The human strengths they point to all involve tacit knowledge and judgment calls that can't be specified in an algorithm—at least, not yet.

But what the past sixty years have shown us is that, as soon as a realm of knowledge can be made explicit, the algorithm becomes possible. At that point, no decisions requiring judgment need to be made—or the few that still do are considered acceptable casualties, because there are only small consequences and costs associated with them if the decisions are made poorly. To elaborate on this last point, we recently heard about the plight of a man who applied to refinance his mortgage just after leaving his most recent job. He was turned down for the loan even though he'd had a steady government job for eight years, and a steady teaching job before that for more than twenty years. Indeed, he was still earning more than enough income from a variety of paying gigs to cover the payments. For the computer making the decision, however, that mishmash of income-earning activity looked too uncertain. Refinancing denied.

That hard-luck case was Ben Bernanke, the former chairman of the U.S. Federal Reserve. If you were in the business of running business conferences, you'd know he commands up to $250,000 per appearance—and if you were in publishing you might have heard of the million-dollar book deal he landed. Obviously, the decision to turn him down for a loan was a dumb one, and would have been made better with human judgment seeing his ability to pay for what it really is. But do the consequences of it really matter much to the company—enough that is, to dial back the reliance on automation and reintroduce more human judgment into all its mortgage decisions? Doubtless, Bernanke eventually got a new mortgage. We are kidding ourselves if we think this kind of occasional goof will keep enterprises from giving computers more power to make high-volume decisions.

So let's accept that all intellectual processes that can be expressed as series of rules or algorithms, specifying actions for all contingencies, are ripe for takeover by computers. Have the thinkers we've been quoting—Wiener, Levy and Murnane, Brynjolfsson and McAfee—left humanity enough of an iceberg to stand on? Keep in mind there are a lot of us. Maybe the overwhelming proportion of the current labor force is capable of expert thinking, complex communication, and ideation. Maybe the world suffers from a tremendous unmet demand for those. But can we be sure of that—especially as computers gain capabilities to take on even these types of intellectually refined tasks?

Perhaps instead, to have a hope of retaining human jobs in large numbers, we need to reframe the nature of the competition. What if the "winners" in the race with machines aren't just the humans who can ascend to these ultimate cognitive heights, and perform the greatest feats of logical rationality? What if, in thinking about job design for human beings, we emphasized some of the traits found in humans that aren't imitated by computers—that we wouldn't program into labor-saving automation even if we could?

Take a hint from the financial advisor we interviewed, who says his job is as much about "psychiatry" these days as about financial acumen. His company had recently implemented a smart system that could, with some basic inputs about a client's income, age, and goals, instantly spit out an optimal investment allocation plan. In response to a question about how vulnerable he felt given this automation, "I'm hearing the footsteps," he admitted. "Our advice to clients isn't automated yet, but it's feeling more and more robotic. My comments to clients are increasingly scripted." The advisor was even more concerned about his firm's agreement to work with a couple of "robo-advisor" companies. "I am thinking that over time they will phase us out altogether," he worries. Wanting to be proactive about the situation, he wondered if he should start planning an entrepreneurial venture, or take some very different types of courses in the MBA he's getting.

Rather than running for the hills, the better strategy for a financial advisor might be to focus on that part of his current job that automation isn't threatening: the hand-holding he does with clients who, for example, know they could be earning higher returns but have trouble stomaching any level of risk. "Reading scripts is obviously something that a computer can do; convincing a client to invest more money requires some more skills," he argued. "I am already often more of a psychiatrist than a stockbroker."

If you believe your ability to add value depends on your ability to outthink the computers (in this case, to devise a more optimal allocation of investment assets), you are on the John Henry track. Whatever performance level you are now achieving, a year from now the computer will achieve, and you will have to step up your game. Unfortunately, that's been our collective strategy in the knowledge-based economy. And how's that working out for us? With each year, more are left behind—because more education is required to even get in the game. More education generally means more wealth required. We're left with quite an irony: The rich are taking all the work.

The point we want to make here is simple. The question of "what are you good for" as a human worker has an answer that is much richer than your most easily codified intelligence. Therefore, the question of "what are you paid for" should be reexamined as well. The authors of the Oxford study we referenced earlier—the one that says 47 percent of U.S. jobs are about to go the way of the passenger pigeon—manage to conclude their report with a ray of hope. They predict that "occupations that involve complex perception and manipulation tasks, creative intelligence tasks, and social intelligence tasks are unlikely to be substituted by computer capital over the next decade or two." Although we could debate the 47 percent conclusion (and how it will translate to actual jobs lost), that sounds right to us, and we'll amplify it a bit further. Work that involves courage and counterintuitive ideas won't be taken away from humans. People will still be uniquely able to inspire other people to act, and they will still have a monopoly on empathy, diplomacy, and ambition. Our pursuits will still be the only ones marked by passion, humor, joy—or, for that matter, good taste. And machines, up to now the brawn to our brains, can become the brains to our brio.

Stepping into Post-Automation Human Work

The big problem with the punditry to date is that it doesn't give those of us with mortgages much to go on. Are we remaining knowledge workers just going to tend the computers and ensure they are doing a good job of the work formerly done by humans? Once a knowledge worker, now a type of cyborg? The advice on avoiding that fate has been noticeably thin. For the most part, the experts boil it down to a single, daunting task: Keep getting smarter.

That may be an option for some, but it doesn't seem like it could work for everyone. Indeed, even though one book from such experts is titled *Race Against the Machine*, you may really be racing against other humans. Those humans who get smarter and smarter are relatively likely to grab one of the diminished number of jobs left, which reminds us of an old joke. When you and your friend are confronted by the bear of automation, you don't have to outrun the bear to avoid losing your job—you just have to outrun your friend.

We're going to argue that there are other strategies, all of them featuring "augmentation" of human work by machines. They fall into five categories. For shorthand, we like to say that, as they increasingly work with machines, people can step up, step aside, step in, step narrowly, or step forward. (The last step involves building the machines themselves. We have to remind ourselves that smart machines are still built by smart humans, albeit a relative few of them.)

The other widely discussed option is to somehow convince a cash-strapped government to guarantee you an income if you lose your job to automation. We don't deny that it's important for governments at every level to address this pressing issue. But government bureaucracies have always been slow to notice problems and address them with serious interventions, and some (particularly the U.S. government) are seeming particularly slow and ineffective right now. We think it's important for individual workers to assess to what degree their jobs are at risk, and to begin now to think about how they fit into a world in which decisions and actions are powered by smart machines. If governments end up helping out—and we encourage them to do so, in the last chapter of this book—so much the better.

The strategies we lay out in the coming chapters will work for those humans who are willing to work to add value to machines, and who are willing to have machines add value to them. Those humans—and it's impossible to know just how many there are of them—will be the ones who read this book, burn the midnight oil to improve their own skills, and either make friends with smart machines or find a way to do things they can't do. Complacency is not an option. But despondency isn't required, either.

The same attitude of optimistic concern is appropriate for how we think about the capabilities of technology. Just as we've tried to impress upon you in this chapter that technology will take over some aspects of our jobs, in the next chapter we'll argue that cognitive technologies are fully up to the task. Then, after scaring you for a couple of chapters, we'll try to comfort you a bit with the possibilities for new and better jobs that work alongside these powerful technologies.

2

Just How Smart Are Smart Machines?

In order to understand what technology may do to your job, it's pretty important to know just how smart are smart machines. And the answer is smart—really smart. Smarter than us already on many narrow intellectual tasks, and probably eventually much smarter than us in general.

Because thinking about the capabilities of smart machines is a bit abstract, we often resort to the depictions of them in books and movies. Take, for example, Ava—the artificial intelligence at the center of the 2015 science fiction movie *Ex Machina*. Ava has it all—she's gorgeous, diabolically clever, emotionally engaging, and even capable of self-repair. She has definite yearnings, if not for love then at least for freedom from the lovely but confining home in which she's imprisoned. She deftly manipulates her human Turing-tester in order to achieve her objectives. Here, in one package, is all the intelligence and autonomy needed to outwit human beings at every turn.

We know it isn't true as of now. What most of us don't know is how much of it could *become* true, and over what time frame. Which of Ava's strengths will develop quickly and which won't arrive, if ever, till a long, long time from now? For that matter, which are already reality, becoming commonplace in the world of smart machines? It's important to understand all this because, in our work alongside cognitive technologies, we will need to keep adjusting to their evolving capabilities. To be able to anticipate how our own roles will change, we must be able to predict the pathways from today's state of the art to future possibilities.

In this chapter we'll suggest a way to do that by mapping the prog-

Figure 3.1. Types of Cognitive Technology and Their Sophistication

Level of Intelligence

TASK TYPE	HUMAN SUPPORT	REPETITIVE TASK AUTOMATION	CONTEXT AWARENESS AND LEARNING	SELF-AWARE INTELLIGENCE	
Analyze Numbers	Business intelligence; data visualization; hypothesis-driven analytics	Operational analytics, scoring, model management	Machine learning; neural nets	Not yet	
Digest Words, Images	Character and speech recognition	Image recognition, machine vision	Watson; natural language processing	Not yet	The Great Convergence
Perform Digital Tasks (Admin and Decisions)	Business Process Management	Rules engines, robotic process automation	Not yet	Not yet	
Perform Physical Tasks	Remote operation	Industrial robotics, collaborative robotics	Fully autonomous robots; vehicles	Not yet	

ress of intelligent machines along two key dimensions: their *ability to act* and their *ability to learn.* Beyond basic computation, a good definition of growing intelligence would involve both of these. Plot them together and they create a matrix. (See Figure 3.1.) The upper left of it consists of territory already conquered by machines. The lower right—most of the tasks on the far right, for that matter—is territory that is still far away. All the ground spilling across the middle represents territory that is or will be in contention in the near term.

For simplicity, we'll look at machines' *ability to act* as proceeding through four levels. The most basic tasks, at the first level, consist of computation, or simply *analyzing numbers.* The second level involves the harder analytical task of *digesting words and images.* In terms of action, these first two are limited purely to performing the analyses that yield good decisions. The latter two move into the realm of executing those decisions. Thus the third level is *performing digital tasks* or, in other words, actions that can be accomplished through purely digital means (such as providing you with a new password). The fourth level involves *performing physical tasks* that require some manipulation of objects in space (as in the use of robotics). These latter two types of tasks are pretty easy when they are repetitive and structured, but combining them with learning and complex human interactions is not yet possible.

At the same time, we'll portray the *ability to learn* as escalating through various levels. At the first level of pure *human support*, the machine has no inherent intelligence and the only learner is the human, who by using it becomes informed by better data processing or retrieval. At the second level, *repetitive task automation*, the machine has been "taught" how to perform a task reliably, but its knowledge cannot grow any further based on its experience or in response to changing conditions. At the third level, the machine is able to observe the effects of its performance or results of its analysis and make adjustments to what it knows, perhaps by experimenting with other possibilities that might perform better. Yet at this level of *context awareness and learning* it can't question anything above the inputs it has been told to consider in its optimization, let alone the objective. That power only comes with the fourth level of learning capability, the much vaunted *self-awareness* level. Here the machine gains the ability to consider the goal and to find other routes toward it—and ultimately to question the goal. This is a strength strongly associated with the move from "narrow" to "general" artificial intelligence (AI), and the potential for machines to slip beyond human control.

With progress happening constantly along both these dimensions, the most astonishing machines built at any point tend to be the ones that combine current, high levels of capability on both dimensions. These convergences surprise us in ways that we aren't surprised when we track the incremental advances taking place along one dimension; they strike us as step changes in progress. And, back to Ava, the most spine-tingling visions we tend to form of future machine intelligence combine the ultimate of both lines of progress. We might call it the Great Convergence: a self-aware machine that is able not only to make decisions based on its own defined goals, but to carry them out in the physical world. When Ava is a reality, we'll be there.

Tracing all the steps between where we are now and that great convergence is a valuable exercise, because it helps to reveal the workplace realities that are most likely within the spans of our own careers. As we'll see, there will remain plenty of opportunities to work with smart machines that don't yet have it all.

Ode to AI Spring

For the sellers of smart machines, if we may slightly paraphrase Gerard Manley Hopkins, nothing is so beautiful as AI spring. The observation that artificial intelligence has its seasons of enthusiasm and also (in AI winter) of despair has become commonplace; by most accounts, the term "AI winter" was first coined as an allusion to nuclear winter, a level of devastation that seemed analogous when a slew of AI-related companies that had been founded in the 1970s all went bust in the early 1980s. By later in that same decade, a thaw was beginning. (In 1988, for example, *Time* magazine had AI back on its cover with an in-depth story called "Putting Knowledge to Work.") Since then, the seasons of hype have come and gone.

But the reality is that there has never been an actual regression in the technology. As Ray Kurzweil writes in his mind-bending book *The Singularity Is Near*: "I still run into people who claim that artificial intelligence withered in the 1980s, an argument that is comparable to insisting that the Internet died in the dot-com bust of the early 2000s. The bandwidth and price-performance of Internet technologies, the number of nodes (servers), and the dollar volume of e-commerce all accelerated smoothly through the boom as well as the bust and the period since. The same has been true for AI."[1]

Smart machines have been steadily advancing through every season—and, it is worth reminding ourselves, at a much faster rate than our own species has. Perhaps even more dramatically than the science, the practical use of AI blossomed in recent decades as more and more companies quietly began implementing the tools to do useful things.[2] During that time frame, computer programs began to analyze data or exercise predetermined rules to make sound judgments on such matters as what are the key facts in a document, how to diagnose and treat a patient's illness, or what price to charge for a product to make maximum profit—all with little or no human help. In narrowly specified domains, we reached the point where computers often made better decisions than people.

It's clear, then, that the cycles have to do with enthusiasm and expectations, not functionality. Like sap, hype runs freely in the spring. People get overexcited and assume more change in the near term than is actually possible. Once those expectations are disappointed, winter sets in. And what accounts for the timing of those seasons? We would suggest that the framework laid out in this chapter helps to clarify that, too. Spring has tended to arrive when a new level was reached in machines' ability to learn—the most challenging of the two dimensions of progress. Once an advance is made in machines' ability to build on their own knowledge, that advance plays out relatively quickly across the other key dimension, the machines' ability to act by executing decisions in the real world. This abundance of new AI development and implementation generates much excitement—and fills everyone with feverish anticipation for the still greater capabilities that will come with higher powers of learning. Those, however, turn out to be a long time coming, and the temperature drops.

Where It All Began

Today, someone using the term "smart machine" could be talking about any number of technologies. The term "artificial intelligence" alone, for example, has been used to describe such technologies as expert systems (collections of rules facilitating decisions in a specified domain, such as financial planning or knowing when a batch of soup is cooked), neural networks (a more mathematical approach to creating a model that fits a data set), machine learning (semiautomated statistical modeling to achieve the best fitting-model to data), natural language processing or NLP (in which computers make sense of human language in textual form), and so forth.

Wikipedia lists at least ten branches of AI, and we have seen other sources that mention many more.

To make sense of this army of machines and the direction in which it is marching, it helps to remember where it all started: with numerical analytics supporting and supported by human decision-makers. While early systems for full-blown decision-making were seen as impractical for use in business, as early as the 1970s, companies began to employ tools that augmented the intelligence of managers and analysts. Tom's first nonacademic job in the 1980s was for a consulting firm whose stock in trade was "decision support."

These computer systems excelled at analyzing structured (in nice rows and columns) numerical data and reporting the results. This left the tasks at the front end (framing problems and posing questions) and the back end (interpreting results and making business decisions) to the human analyst and decision-maker. Although many decision-support tools had the potential to yield novel, sophisticated statistical insights into business problems, most required special skills to use. Therefore, if you were a business manager, you weren't likely to encounter those unsought insights; instead you formulated hypotheses for others to test. A separate class of professional data analysts—and later, more sophisticated "data scientists"—became necessary to do the analytical work. Together the human components of the process might take weeks or even months to complete, even if the computers themselves did their analyses in seconds.

Moreover, these smart tools were usually not connected to any of the other software used in a business's operations. Every analysis was ad hoc. Having used them to make some decision, managers had to execute that decision as a separate project, perhaps using other software applications. For these and other reasons, such tools didn't catch on as much as other computer systems designed to integrate basic transactions. Even as the twenty-first century dawned and companies got very excited about "analytics," the machines were very much relegated to crunching data and performing quantitative or statistical analysis that would spur insights and inform decisions by people. More integrated systems enabled revelatory visual displays of data, some of them updating in real time, and even predictive analytics. But a human was still required to create and interpret the analysis.

That's why, when you look at the matrix in Figure 3.1 you see in the upper-left corner a cell that represents the intersection of "human support" and "analyzing numbers." When we map the progression of smart machines across the decades, the story starts here. Chances are, if you are a decision-maker in a large organization, you have found yourself working with business intelligence software, data visualization tools, and hypothesis-driven analytics. In the overall pattern by which automation comes to knowledge work, such tools represent square one.

Unfolding from that point to the squares farthest from it on the horizontal is the history and future of smart machines, moving from the least to the greatest of their increasingly unnerving capabilities.

Newer Ways to Support Humans

We won't march through every cell of this matrix; we trust you get the idea of it well enough to fill in some of the blanks in our narrative. But perhaps we should run down its first column, to make clear just how much humans have come to be supported by machines increasingly capable of executing the decisions their analyses yield.

The first step beyond purely numerical analysis was for machines to gain the power to digest words and images. Determining the meaning and significance of these has always been the province of human beings— and a key aspect of human cognition. But now a wide variety of tools are capable of it, too. Words are increasingly "understood"—counted, classified, interpreted, predicted, etc.—through technologies such as machine learning, natural language processing, neural networks, deep learning, and so forth. Some of the same technologies are being used to analyze and identify images. Humans are still better able to make subjective judgments on unstructured data, such as interpreting the meaning of a poem, or distinguishing between images of good neighborhoods and bad ones. But computers are making headway even on these fronts.

Meanwhile, intelligent applications that already combine text, image, and speech recognition offer very welcome "human support" by making it easier for us to communicate with computers. As you probably know, it is very difficult for machines to deal with high levels of variation in speech accents, pronunciation, volume, background noise, and so forth. If you use Siri on your iPhone or have an Amazon Echo device, you know both the joy and the frustration. Yet even if the progress is not as fast as we would like, these systems are getting better all the time—as are tools for recognizing handwriting and identifying facial images.

This brings us to the next hurdle for smart machines: actually performing some of the tasks implied by their analysis rather than leaving them for humans to execute. Of course this is easiest when the task itself is purely digital. An example would be the task of tracking the work done and decisions made in a standard business process. So-called business process management (BPM) tools help people maintain control over complicated operations by monitoring workflows, measuring output, and analyzing performance. "Intelligent business process management" can even go so far as to intervene according to programmed rules to improve performance. But humans are still the ones designing the work processes in the first place and writing the rules for machines to enact.

Finally, some machines are able to execute tasks that go beyond the digital environment and require manipulation of objects in the physical world. This brings us to the realm of robots, which are capable of doing manual work in support of humans—whether that work requires greater strength or finer precision of movement. The human supervision might be remote or direct. Remote supervision of robotic devices often makes sense to keep human workers safe and healthy. For example, at Codelco, the Chilean national copper mining company, broad adoption of "telecommand" rock hammers and other devices keeps more workers aboveground (an enlightened approach we'll explore more in Chapter 9). Or think of the remotely piloted drone aircraft becoming so popular in the U.S. Air Force—or the robotic surgeries being increasingly performed in hospitals. Many invasive procedures are now being performed with less trauma thanks to "telemanipulators" guided by surgeons moving knobs as they gaze at video displays on monitors. Catherine Mohr, a surgeon who works with robots made by Intuitive Surgical, noted in an interview: "I think of it as giving the surgeon superpowers, things like better vision and finer dexterity. . . . When the surgeon makes a motion with their hands, this tiny instrument becomes a surrogate hand inside the body, doing exactly the same motion."[3]

Health care in general has been such a booming field that, thus far, the use of advanced technology has served purely to augment human clinicians. Even in radiology, increasingly automated detection of potentially cancerous lesions has not yet displaced radiologists, but rather been introduced as a "second set of eyes." In anesthesiology, automated administration of anesthesia may be overseen by non-anesthesiologists, but it is at least overseen by some type of physician. "Human support" remains the role for smart machines.

However, hospitals might quickly discover that surgeons with superpowers can handle far greater caseloads than in the past. With robots allowing them to do precision work faster, and screens and knobs making distance from the table irrelevant, surgeons in one place (perhaps in a large urban hospital) could also perform procedures on patients prepped elsewhere (in satellite hospitals across a whole region). "In this way," technology journalist Farhad Manjoo speculated, "surgeons could suffer the same fate as pharmacists who will be able to work through telepharmacies—one surgeon could perform the work that currently occupies many."[4]

In this section, we have walked down the first vertical column of our matrix, and named tools that are typical at four levels of human support. But we don't mean to claim that the advancement of labor-saving technology has been as clean and sequential as our matrix implies. Developers of robots to perform physical tasks, for example, were already achieving impressive things at the same time that AI scientists were meeting their early objectives for word and image processing. Much of this work has been simultaneous. However, as a broad-brush statement, one line of progress in smart machines has been their move from analysis to action in support of humans. And, going forward, as they learn to work increasingly autonomously, we will see them broadly advance from analysis to action again.

Higher Learning for Machines

Over the same period in which machines have gained the ability to execute decisions, they have also gained abilities to make better ones for themselves, based on growing knowledge bases. An important move in this respect (now shifting horizontally to explore the second column of our matrix) was to gain the amount of decision-making autonomy required for *repetitive task automation*—meaning they had the knowledge resident in them to choose among strictly limited options.

We have already said about the use of analytics by firms—or extensive data-crunching in support of better decision-making—that, in its early days, it was an ad hoc batch activity. Analysts and decision-makers would typically meet to frame an analysis, analysts would gather data and perform the analysis, and results would be presented to the decision-maker—who might or might not actually use the analysis in his or her decision process. The whole cycle might take weeks or even months.

Today, however, companies are increasingly embedding analytics into operational systems and processes so that logical decisions are made automatically and on a repetitive basis. This is what is going on when, for example, Ben Bernanke—or any of us—applies for a loan, or credit card, or insurance policy. The analytical models that decide whether we should be granted these financial wishes are embedded into well-structured systems and processes. Such models tend to "score" individual customers based on a whole range of variables. The same kind of scoring is behind the personalized coupons and offers you often receive from retailers, especially online. When you see one, it's because some algorithm has sized you up as a likely prospect for that deal—and it is likewise tailoring other offers for other customers, automatically and repetitively, all day long.

Where originally there would have been human analysts, computers now run on their own in an automated or semiautomated fashion. And in their narrow realms, these systems turn in results that are dramatically better than any human could achieve. (Indeed, since the algorithms or decision logic are often buried within systems and process workflows, it may be difficult for people to monitor or even understand them.) When they first started to come online, the promise of repetitive task automation suddenly revealed itself to all kinds of smart managers. A new spring began. By now, heavy use of embedded analytics, or operational analytics, has given rise to what Tom has elsewhere called "Analytics 3.0," a new era in which data drive the workings of organizations at dramatically greater speed and scale.[5] Gartner, the IT market research firm, recognized "advanced, pervasive, and invisible analytics" as one of its "ten strategic technologies for 2015."[6] Bill Franks, the chief analytics officer of Teradata, is referring to the same transformation in his book on operational analytics called *The Analytics Revolution*.

If you are already weary of the buzzwords "big data" and "the Internet of things," this is why; both represent fire hoses of data that become extremely valuable when the computing power is in place to find patterns and make decisions to capitalize on them. Already today, the Internet connects more smart objects than people (and has thus become an Internet of things); by 2020, Cisco estimates, the number of devices connected to the Internet will rise to 50 billion.[7] As they transmit data in near-real time, fast computers are able to make frequent decisions based on continuous analysis. Sensors in a jet engine, for example, collect and transmit data on heat, vibration, and other conditions, allowing a smart machine to schedule service as needed, or to advise a pilot to shut it down as soon as possible.

Repetitive task automation makes sense for any tactical decisions a business must make frequently that involve data analysis. (If the need is only occasional, it might not be worth the effort to create the program and process.) And the data analysis need not be confined to number-crunching. Machines are also increasingly capable of taking autonomous action based on their processing of words and images. This might involve translating words across languages, understanding questions posed by people in plain language, and answering in kind, or "reading" a text with sufficient understanding to summarize it—or create new passages in the same style.

Machine translation has been around for a while, and like everything else digital, it gets better all the time. Written language translation has progressed much faster than spoken language, since no speech recognition is necessary, but both are becoming quite useful. Google Translate, for example, does a credible job of it using "statistical machine translation," or looking at a variety of examples of translated work and determining which translation is most likely.

IBM's Watson is the first tool to be broadly capable of ingesting, analyzing, and "understanding" text to a sufficient degree to answer detailed questions on it. Since it's so well known, it's worth a brief digression on its strengths and weaknesses. Watson searches and analyzes English text (and recently added a translation module for some other languages), but it doesn't deal with structured numerical data (there are "Watson Analytics" tools that do that, but they are not in the same set of programs as Watson). It doesn't understand relationships between variables and can't make predictions. It's also not well suited for applying rules or analyzing options on decision trees. It is only starting to work with images. Given IBM's good job of marketing Watson, one gets the feeling that it can leap tall buildings in a single bound. And certainly the company (and increasingly, external app developers it considers part of its ecosystem) are hard at work applying Watson's cognitive computing capabilities to a variety of business and social domains, of which health-care problems like cancer treatment are the most prominent. But so far the notable success stories for Watson have been in less ambitious applications, partly because each new application domain requires a considerable amount of customization and implementation.

There are more and more examples of such systems beyond Watson. Most of them were developed for very particular applications—their versions of Watson's *Jeopardy!* challenge—and are slowly being modified to handle other types of cognitive situations. Digital Reasoning, for example, a company that previously developed cognitive computing software for national intelligence purposes, has now begun to market intelligent software for employee fraud in financial institutions. Like Watson, it reads and understands words. The company's goal, as a *Fortune* magazine article put it, is to "analyze every shred of digital traffic coursing through their networks to hunt down and expose potential rogue traders, market manipulators, and SEC rule violators within their own ranks." (We'll have more to say about Digital Reasoning and its CEO in Chapter 8.)

Another company, IPsoft, is known for its intelligent customer agent, Amelia. Amelia's job is to analyze spoken language to understand a customer's service issue and, when possible, resolve it for them. If Amelia can't accomplish the fix or (more rarely) can't understand what the customer wants, the call is forwarded to a human service rep.

Amelia, Digital Reasoning, and Watson all use similar components, including:

- Language classification—identifying nouns, verbs, and other parts of speech in a passage;
- Entity extraction—identifying the key entities in a text passage;
- Relationship extraction—identifying relationships between key entities;
- Fact extraction—identifying stated facts in a passage;
- Relationship graph—showing the relationships between entities and facts in a graphical diagram (for human review);
- Trade-off analytics—links entities and relationships with your objectives, and tells you which are most closely connected.

In most of the software offerings these different services are inextricable from the whole system, but IBM has made all of them available as distinct services in its "Bluemix" cognitive cloud offering. The company has announced more than thirty services as we write, and has plans for up to fifty within a year. The "Q&A" capability that let Watson beat its human opponents at *Jeopardy!* is only one of these. Other vendors are taking this modular approach as well. CognitiveScale, an Austin, Texas–based cognitive technologies company founded by several former Watson developers (including Manoj Saxena, the first general manager of the Watson business unit at IBM), offers a "cognitive cloud" that integrates a variety of cognitive applications. It views this capability as a "cognitive operating system" that would function like Windows for a variety of cognitive apps. All of these apps employ machine learning to improve the quality of the results over time.

Other systems that handle text take a "computational linguistics" approach, and focus on understanding the underlying grammatical structures of sentences and paragraphs. RAGE Frameworks, a company that also has tools for rapid development of a wide variety of computer applications, has tools that use computational linguistics to understand, for example, a wide range of information about companies and their operational and financial performance. The objective is to churn through documents on companies, identify the key statements in them, and diagnose the implications for investors or analysts.

This category of application is best suited for situations with much more—and more rapidly changing—codified textual information than any human could possibly absorb and retain. Diagnosing and recommending treatment protocols for cancer is an illustrative example. There are more than four hundred different types of cancer, and digesting research findings and understanding the relationships between symptoms, genome patterns, drugs, and therapies is beyond any human brain. Memorial Sloan Kettering Cancer Center is one of Watson's development partners, and researchers there report progress (if not full success yet, even for a single type of cancer) in the system's ability to recommend treatments. Meanwhile, it's important to point out the Memorial Sloan Kettering and other medical institutions are using other cognitive technologies besides Watson to make similar types of diagnoses, and they're making progress on those, too.

Of course, disease diagnosis isn't only about technical capabilities. Researchers have been working on automated diagnosis and treatment protocols at least since the 1970s (the MYCIN expert system, developed at Stanford in that decade, was focused on identifying and treating blood infections). It has often been proven in research studies that such systems provide more consistent and accurate advice than clinicians, but implementation has never taken off. Resistance by physicians, fears of malpractice suits, and lack of awareness are probably the major reasons. Perhaps cognitive technologies will be sufficiently powerful and visible enough to overcome these barriers—or perhaps health care is too difficult a field to totally conquer.

It's worth noting, however, that it doesn't take the vast resources of a big company to create a useful cognitive computing tool in health care. Brittany Wenger, while a high school senior in Sarasota, Florida, created a science project to classify a type of minimally invasive breast cancer biopsies as malignant or benign. Using nine key variables in a neural network model, her analysis successfully identified malignant cancers in more than 99 percent of the cases studied. Wenger won the Google Science Fair prize in 2012 and hopes that her diagnostic model will be used on real patients someday.

Image identification and classification is the other key activity in this category. It's not new, either; "machine vision" systems from companies like Cognex have been locating parts in production lines and reading bar codes for decades. That type of system uses a geometric pattern-matching technology, which is good at rudimentary vision tasks like knowing whether a part is in the right spot for a drill press.

Today, however, many companies are interested in more sensitive vision tasks: recognizing faces, classifying photos on the Internet, or assessing the collision damage to a car. This sort of automated vision requires more sophisticated tools to match particular patterns of pixels to a recognizable image. Our eyes and brains are great at this, but computers are just starting to get good at it. Machine learning and neural network analysis is the most promising technology for this application.

One branch of machine learning, for example, is particularly well suited to analyzing data in multiple dimensions. Images and video are an example of this type of data—any individual pixel has x and y coordinates, color, intensity, and in videos, time. "Deep learning" neural network approaches have been developed to deal with data in multiple dimensions; the "deep" refers not to "profound," but rather to a hierarchy of dimensions in the data. It's this technology that is letting Google engineers identify photos of cats on the Internet. Although it's difficult to imagine more important tasks than that, perhaps in the near future it will let smart machines watch video taken by drones and security cameras and determine whether something bad is happening.

A lot of smart humans are developing new tools in this category, and improvements are pretty rapid. We are generating enough volumes of text and images that there aren't enough humans to deal with it all; we have little choice to use smart machines if we want to make sense of all the big data out there. And we have to remember that humans make mistakes looking at large numbers of images, too. It won't be long at all before there is no competition between machines and humans in terms of speed and accuracy of image analysis.

With repetitive task automation showing its power to relieve humans of difficult analyses of numbers, words, and images, it was perhaps inevitable that it would also come to relieve them of some of the task work they had done as a result of such analyses. Purely digital administrative tasks are now being performed routinely by smart machines. This is the category in which "rule engines" excel. Given a structured task (processing an insurance policy application, for example) with clearly defined rules, a rules engine can churn through massive amounts of work. Human intervention is typically only required for exceptions. Progress consists of reducing the number of exceptions and in revising the rules to keep up with changes in the economy and in customer behavior. In health insurance companies, for example, the automated processing of medical claims (known as "auto-adjudication") went from 37 percent in 2002 to 79 percent in 2011— and it's probably well over that figure now.[8] While this sort of automated decision-making can be done with paper documents, it's a lot easier if the information is all digitized.

More recently, companies have begun to employ a technology related to business rules and BPM called "robotic process automation." This technology has the following traits:

It does not involve robots, contrary to its name;
It makes use of workflow and business rules technology;
It is easily configured and modified by business users;
It deals with highly repetitive and transactional tasks;
It doesn't learn or improve its performance without human modification;
It typically interfaces with multiple information systems as if it were a human user; this is called "presentation layer" integration.

Examples of settings in which this technology is popular include banking (for example, for back-office customer service tasks, such as replacing a lost ATM card), insurance (processing claims and payments), IT (monitoring system error messages and fixing simple problems), and supply chain management (processing invoices and responding to routine requests from customers and suppliers).

There are substantial benefits from this type of automation, even though it is one of the less exotic forms of intelligent technology. Case studies compiled by process automation vendor Automation Anywhere suggest that 30 to 40 percent reductions in the cost and time to perform a process are not atypical.

When implemented broadly across an organization, process automa-

tion can yield dramatic performance gains. A study of process automation at Telefónica's O2—the second-largest mobile carrier in the United
Kingdom—found that as of April 2015, the company had automated more
than 160 process areas involving between 400,000 and 500,000 transactions.[9] Each of the process areas employed software "robots" from vendor
Blue Prism. The overall ROI of this technology was between 650 and
800 percent. That's a better payoff than most companies achieved from
other approaches to process improvement, including reengineering and
Six Sigma.

There is certainly organizational and behavioral change involved with
this form of technology, and it may eventually lead to layoffs. But most of
the companies we've observed have redeployed workers to other roles.
Human employees' initial mistrust of automation tools gives way to relief
that boring work is being done by a machine. At Xchanging, a process
outsourcing company in the United Kingdom, the Blue Prism "robots"
were given cute names like Poppy (after the poppies people wear in that
country on Remembrance Day, when the machine went live) and Henry.[10]
The anthropomorphizing of these smart machines suggests that workers
didn't find this form of technology particularly threatening.

We'll finish our exposition of our matrix's second column by looking
at how repetitive task automation applies to the performance of physical
tasks. This, of course, is what robots are all about. That's exactly what
they do—both traditional industrial robots, and the more recent collaborative robots. The only real difference is how easy it is to teach the robots
new repetitive tasks, and whether they can work in close cooperation with
humans or not.

Because traditional robots take a lot of work to train—each movement
has to be carefully specified in a vendor-specific robotics programming
language such as RAPID or Karel, for example—they are well suited to
highly repetitive and heavy-lifting industrial tasks that don't change at
all. If you have many different products, or if your products change frequently, you probably won't find it a good technology.

Collaborative robots are much easier to train and to change programming, but they aren't perfect, either. They tend to be for relatively light-
duty applications—typically tasks like picking up light parts and moving

them somewhere else. If your production work requires a high degree of precision, collaborative robots may not supply it.

John Dulchinos, vice president of global automation at contract manufacturer Jabil Circuit, told us in an interview that we will need both types of robots for the foreseeable future. He notes, "Collaborative robots are still a small percentage of the total number. The technology is new, and its capabilities are limited. They don't yet have the precision or stiffness to do things like assembly or stamping. The lion's share of robots today are doing dirty, dull, dangerous tasks involving things like welding and heavy material handling tasks—work that has been dangerous or difficult for humans to do, or both. A good bit of that work will continue, and it won't be done by collaborative robots. The choice between robot types all depends on the type of application."

We expect robots to continue gaining ground in repetitive tasks. What would make them advance more quickly would be combining the industrial robots' ability to deal with heavier work with the collaborative robots' ease of programming. A cross-industry standard for robotics programming languages—and perhaps a popular open-source alternative—would also help to facilitate code reuse and improve productivity.

Like every other kind of smart machine, robots are becoming more autonomous. To some degree robots are already autonomous once programmed, but they are quite limited in their flexibility and their ability to respond to unexpected conditions. More intelligent robots would be able to, for example, look around the proximate area if a part isn't found in the expected location.

As robots develop more intelligence, better machine vision, and greater ability to make decisions, they will become a combination of other types of cognitive technologies, but with the added ability to transform the physical environment (remember the "Great Convergence" toward the right in the chart at the beginning of this chapter). There are already, as we have discussed, systems to understand text and speech, systems to engage in intelligent Q&A with humans, and systems to recognize a variety of images. It's just that they're not yet embedded in the brain of a robot. Jim Lawton, the head of products at Rethink Robotics, commented to us in an interview: "An important area of experimentation today is around the intersection of collaborative robots, big data, and deep learning. The goal is to combine automation of physical tasks and cognitive tasks. For example, a robot could start combining all the information about how much torque is applied in a screw. Robots are, after all, a big bucket of sensors. A truly intelligent robot could begin to see what works in terms of how much torque in a screw leads to field failures. It could combine its own sensor data with warranty data, pattern recognition, and so forth."

There is plenty of evidence that robots are becoming more autonomous at the DARPA (Defense Advanced Research Projects Agency) Robotics Challenge, staged annually since 2012. The robot contestants are expected to complete eight tasks, from driving a utility vehicle to connecting a fire hose and turning a valve. The robots mostly struggle to accomplish all eight tasks, but three entrants completed them all in the 2015 competition, which was won by a South Korean university team. But perhaps illustrating the distance autonomous robots still have to go, the second-place robot, entered by a Florida robotics company, raised his hands and did a little dance to celebrate victory after completing the last task, and promptly fell over.[11]

We will also see more autonomous capabilities in devices that are currently controlled by humans. It's pretty clear, for example, that this will happen with robotic surgeries in hospitals. One robot in Canada in 2010 removed a patient's prostate with no human at the controls— and an automated anesthesia system kept the patient asleep through the same surgery. And a new research center at the University of California, Berkeley, is focused on developing surgical robots that can perform entire operations—at least the repetitive and low-level ones. The usual pattern, of course, is that once automation tackles relatively primitive tasks it moves up the ladder of complexity. We see no reason why this wouldn't happen in surgery over the next couple of decades.

Autonomous vehicles are another area of intelligent technology involving physical tasks—moving and getting things around. These vehicles employ a combination of GPS and digital maps, light radar ("lidar"), video cameras, and ultrasonic, radar, and odometry sensors to generate and analyze a massive amount of data about the vehicle's position and surroundings. We probably don't have to tell you too much about this area, because it gets more than its share of media attention. But it's a good bet that autonomous cars and trucks will be commonplace on our streets within the next decade. If they're not, it will probably be because of slow regulatory change processes, rather than technical limitations.

Context Awareness and Learning
Are Already Here—Sort Of

With smart machines moving quickly beyond simple human support to become capable of some autonomous task performance, as we've been describing, human workers have had to adjust. Their adjustment will have to be much greater as more machines come on line that feature the next level of capability in knowledge accretion: context awareness and learning. We are still in early days of growth of this capability, but already the excitement about it is generating more than a hint of spring in the air.

Context awareness and learning sounds very human, but the extent to which that is true depends on the task at hand. If we're only talking about the task of "analyzing numbers," for example, it doesn't mean that computers can think things like, "I am tired, so I had better pay special attention to this data set," or "After many years of analysis I have learned that gender is not a good predictor of purchase behavior for clothing, because women often buy clothes for men."

In analyzing numbers, context awareness is as much about data and speed of analysis as anything else. As data flows more continuously and voluminously, we need analytical approaches that make sense of it in real time—detecting anomalies, noticing patterns, and predicting what will happen next. The context of which a smart machine is aware might include a location, a time, or the identity of a user. The context is put to work in the form of recommendations or predictions from a model that take contextual factors into account. A context-aware model might compute, for example, the best route to work based on the time of day, traffic levels, the driver's preference for highways or back roads, etc.

As in the route recommendation example, context-aware recommendations must often be made in real time to be of any value. Finding out after you get to work what would have been the best route—had you only been smart enough to take it—is of limited utility. Fortunately, big data analytics make real-time recommendations on a wide variety of contextual factors quite easily. You know this if you have used Google's Waze app for traffic-sensitive route recommendations, for example.

Learning in this context is becoming aware of a pattern, and applying it to predict or classify something. The machine-learning models in this context may be "supervised"—that is, they are trained on a training data set, and they do the same type of analysis on other data after being trained. Or they may be unsupervised, in which case they are not trained on what to look for and simply try to find some pattern in the data other than random noise.

At this point we're beginning to see some of the convergence of the two lines of progress. The most sophisticated forms of cognitive technology tend to deal with multiple types of problems and data. For example, in addition to dealing with numbers, machine-learning models also deal with text (or at least numerical representations of text). A context-aware machine learning program, for example, might be used to predict what words you are fumbling toward on your iPhone or Android phone (called autocomplete or autosuggest). The statistical and mathematical models are still manipulating numbers, but it's pretty trivial to convert words into numeric expressions.

Many of the systems we've mentioned in the previous section are capable of "learning" in that their decisions get better with more data, and they "remember" previously ingested information. Watson, for example, can be fed more and more documents as they become available over time; that's what makes it well suited for keeping track of cancer research, for example. Other systems in this category get better at their cognitive task by having more data for training purposes. As more documents that have been translated from Urdu to Hindi become available to Google Translate, for example, it gets better with its machine translations across those languages.

What differentiates cognitive technologies in this category is "context awareness." Most of the systems we've described above don't have this yet, primarily because they are designed to perform a single cognitive task. Watson, for example, may be able to ingest and digest thousands of documents about leukemia (as it is doing, for example, at MD Anderson Cancer Center in Houston), but as yet it can't combine that information with a patient's smoking status or family history of leukemia (though IBM and the Cleveland Clinic are working on this capability). A system for facial recognition in a retail store may be able to identify likely shoplifters from a database of known shoplifters' photos (as does FaceFirst, a company selling software in this application area). However, it can't integrate with your customer loyalty program or your human resources database to recognize good customers or your own employees coming to work.

In order for context awareness to become widespread, companies will need to tie together their traditional systems with their cognitive systems. In health care, electronic medical record systems will have to be linked to automated diagnosis and treatment recommendation tools. In manufacturing, robots will need to have access to information in material requirements planning (MRP) systems. This can be accomplished by breaking down cognitive systems into a series of modular components (as we will point out later in this chapter that several vendors are doing) or by traditional systems vendors adding cognitive capabilities to their existing offerings (which is also under way). The former approach seems the more likely to be successful, although these are the early days for this sort of integration.

Why Self-Awareness Is Such a Big Deal

Perhaps it is clear by now why the next step in machine-learning capability will be a momentous one and will undoubtedly bring forth the AI spring to end all vernal flowerings. A major advantage that the human brain still enjoys over automated systems is its breadth—the ability to do a lot of things pretty well. We can read, add and subtract, recognize images, understand words, move with grace (some of us, anyway), pick up and put down fragile items, and so forth. A computer might be trainable to do any of these things as well as or better than us, but it will be a while before it can do all of them. Computers may be able to do depth well, but they can't match us in breadth—yet. Systems are usually very specialized; they address one narrowly defined problem—how to diagnose a certain type of cancer, for example, or how to identify an optimal investment portfolio. Even leading-edge AI experiments have this problem. As Ramón López de Mántaras, a longtime AI researcher and director of the Spanish National Research Council's Artificial Intelligence Research Institute, charmingly put it, "We have machines that are very good at playing chess, for example, but they cannot play domino too."[12]

For the most part, intelligent word and image systems aren't yet self-aware. They don't initiate analyses on their own, they don't understand the larger purpose of what they're doing, and they don't tell you when they aren't up to the task at hand. As Mike Rhodin, the head of IBM's Watson business unit, noted, "Watson doesn't have the ability to think on its own," and neither does any other intelligent system thus far created.[13]

There is some progress, however, in the area of telling humans whether the output of smart machines should be used and trusted. The statistically based systems used for analyzing words and images are increasingly capable of this latter task. In fact, it should be a requirement that all such systems tell you when you should and shouldn't trust their results, and some already do this. You may recall, for example, that when Watson dominated the *Jeopardy!* game in 2011, the program displayed a "confidence bar" ranking the top three answers and its confidence level in each one. Generally it wouldn't buzz in unless its confidence level in an answer was more than 50 percent. This confidence bar was something of an afterthought for Watson's creators, and it was added only at the last minute. But it turns out to be a really important capability for Watson and other smart machines.

For example, Watson's biggest goof during the match was on the "Final Jeopardy" challenge at the end of the second day. The answer for which it was trying to create the right question (the confusing way in which *Jeopardy!* works) was, "Its largest airport was named for a World War II hero; its second largest, for a World War II battle." Watson was confused and lamely supplied "What is Toronto?" as its response (Chicago is correct, of course, and both human contestants wrote it in). But Watson's level of confidence was only 30 percent, and were it not a Final Jeopardy question (to which a response is required), it would not have answered at all. And it made only a small bet ($947) that its answer was correct.

In augmentation-oriented systems and processes, it's important for humans to know the confidence level of a recommendation before deciding whether to trust and accept it. Of course, humans evaluating such recommendations would need to have some idea of how the level of probability was assigned. But if, for example, a lung cancer diagnosis arising from the KRAS gene had 90 percent confidence, that would give a doctor a very different feeling than he or she would have about a 30 percent level diagnosis.

The real-time nature of some decision contexts will preclude a reporting of the confidence of some decisions. In Google Translate or Skype Translator, for example, it won't help much to know the confidence level for each word or phrase in a translation. In general, however, knowing and reporting the level of confidence for an automated answer or decision is an important step for smart machines. It will help us know when to trust these systems. We don't often know that with human decisions, and it's one of the reasons why their outcomes are often poor.

This category of self-aware systems, as you will see in our matrix, is not filled out yet. We can only try to provide some glimpses of the capability and some further examples of what it might look like as it develops over the next decade or so.

Most dramatically, self-awareness has not come to robots yet. The robot that fell down in the DARPA Robotics Challenge after congratulating itself (presumably the congratulatory gestures were programmed in or remotely controlled by its human masters) didn't feel embarrassed or question why it ever entered the contest. That may never happen, but we could imagine some degree of self-awareness in devices that perform physical tasks. A truly smart robot, for example, might determine that it could be more effective if it were at a different place in the production process, and then move itself to that spot and train itself on a new operation. Such capabilities may not be that far off as various cognitive technologies converge; IBM Watson's brain, for example, has already been embedded in several different robots on an experimental basis.

This is also the goal of some new initiatives at Fanuc, a Japanese company that is one of the world's largest robot makers. Fanuc acquired part of a Japanese deep-learning software company, and hopes to make its robots more autonomous using the learning capabilities. As one article put it, "Preferred Networks' expertise should allow Fanuc's customers to link their robots in new ways. It should also enable the machines to automatically recognize problems and learn to avoid them, or find workarounds in conjunction with other machines."[14]

This somewhat scary prospect of robots working together to solve problems may not come true for a while, but it does suggest that autonomy and awareness are long-term destinations for devices that perform physical tasks, and that the worlds of artificially intelligent software and robots are converging.

In the meantime, we could be in for a long winter.

Where Do Humans Fit In?

The answer to the question of "just how smart are smart machines?" is clearly evolving. Algorithms and techniques get better, computers get faster and more networked, and underlying software is able to deal with more and different types of information—and this happens continuously. As the machines march on, remarkably steadily, they get better and better at making decisions and taking autonomous actions. Recently, Stephen Wolfram, the founder of analytics software company Wolfram Research, commented about the long-standing hurdle of image recognition and the fact that neural networks were now capable of it:

> This has been a recent thing that for me is one of the last major things where it's looked like, "Oh, gosh! The brain has some magic thing that computers don't have." We can go through all kinds of different things about creativity, about language, about this and that and the other, and I think we can put a checkmark against essentially all of them at this point as, yes, that component is automatable.[15]

The result is that the quality of decisions made and actions taken by computers and robots gets better all the time.

The usefulness of mapping the progress along these two dimensions is not just that it helps clarify why such disparate technologies and tools are talked about under the same heading of smart machines. It also reveals the very positive truth that there are still plenty of settings and use cases where people must be part of value creation.

The four-by-four matrix we've been discussing yields sixteen cells, and the overwhelming majority of them involve human work. Indeed, even at the ultimate level, no matter how smart these machines get, there is still some potential value from human augmentation. Humans not only would create these autonomous, self-aware systems, but they would also need to monitor and improve them over time. It would also be a human who would decide that such an intelligent system had been surpassed in capability by another such machine, and engineer a switch of them.

We're not going to keep reverting to the language of this chapter as we go on to discuss the possibilities. But the point is worth underscoring: winning in the age of smart machines will take many forms, because it will involve working with them in many configurations. Each cell of our matrix offers human work of different kinds, just as it features different technologies. When smart machines like *Ex Machina*'s Ava do arrive—perhaps in forty or fifty years—all bets are off as to how humans will relate to them. In the meantime, however, there are plenty of partnerships in which humans can thrive.

Don't Automate, Augment

L egend has it that Hans Lippershey, a German eyeglass maker plying his trade in 1608 in the town of Middelburg, Netherlands, got his big idea when he glanced over at two children playing with lenses he'd ground. Holding one lens behind another and peering through the shop's window, they exclaimed at how close this made the weathervane on a distant building appear. When Lippershey soon after submitted a patent claim for the first telescope, it was clear what had happened. Human powers of perception and understanding had just been augmented. Within a few years, Galileo was pointing the new device toward the heavens and for the first time seeing the craters and mountains of the moon.

A distant echo of that moment came in 2012, when Francisco Kitaura and his team at the Leibniz Institute for Astrophysics in Potsdam, Germany, developed a new algorithm based on artificial intelligence, called KIGEN, to map the "dark matter" of the cosmos. Dark matter makes up some 23 percent of the universe, compared to just 5 percent "normal matter" of visible stars, planets, dust, and gases—and both are flung across the 72 percent that consists purely of "dark energy." Understanding just where and how the dark matter has been distributed since the Big Bang is essential to gaining deeper knowledge of the universe's dynamics, but the computational task is immense. Summing up the contribution of the new algorithm, Kitaura says: "With the help of AI, we can now model the universe around us with unprecedented accuracy and study how the largest structures in the cosmos came into being."[1]

That is a pretty smart machine—and it's the kind of smart machine we can all love because, again, it is pure augmentation. No astrophysicist loses his or her job the day the KIGEN code shows up to work at the institute. Instead this Bayesian networks machine-learning algorithm allows people to make faster progress in a line of work that literally has no end.

It's a similar story in the search for the cure for cancer. In Framingham, Massachusetts, a company called Berg (named for the billionaire real estate developer who bankrolled it) is defying the usual drug discovery process by having its highly educated pharmacologists and oncology researchers skip the first step of forming a hypothesis about what drug therapy might prove effective. Instead, Berg's powerful computers analyze actual tissue samples of tumors and health history records provided by medical partners like Beth Israel Deaconess Medical Center in Boston and find patterns within them worth investigating further. Berg's president and CTO, Niven Narain, calls the process "interrogative biology," and it didn't take long for it to yield a candidate therapy. In less than half the typical time for a new drug, its promising therapy called BPM 31510 has made its way to Phase Ib and IIb clinical trials.

Deciding on potential drug leads to pursue sounds like a job for well-educated scientists—and therefore a big part of their job to be taken away if a machine can do it better. But Narain points out that the most important thing going away is the immense amount of thinking by those PhDs that was being squandered on blind alleys. Starting from the point when the AI has zeroed in on a truly promising possibility, there is still plenty of work for scientists to work out the "why" of the phenomenon revealed by the data. "Once we finish the *in silico* output of the platform, we go back to a highly coordinated and functional point of validation to ensure that we're looking at what happens in the cell biology," Narain told a reporter from *Bio-IT World*. "What is the mechanism of action? Are we seeing that this target has an effect in the disease we're studying?" The best use of his human talent is in the "wet lab" preclinical studies where a compound is applied to live disease and it's time to figure out just how it could be formulated to treat a patient, with sensitivity to toxicity and dose tolerance.[2]

Both of these are realms where smart machines are on the rise but don't threaten jobs, because the goals are so immense that today's labor supply doesn't begin to match the requirements of the tasks in their unautomated states. There are not enough pharmacologists in Framingham, or indeed the world, to pore over the tens of trillions of data points that Berg's AI system processes in its analysis of tissue samples. All the astronomers ever churned out by the world's universities could not map the dark matter lurking among the 54,000 known galaxies of the universe.

We're guessing that there are no neo-Luddites out there trying to smash any of this machinery. The question is, then: Why don't all applications of smart machines feel as helpful as these? What really is so different about these combinations of humans and machines? If we could pin that down, maybe we could dispel the brewing fear of knowledge work automation, and even mark the path toward more and better jobs for humans in a machine-filled world.

The Answer Is Augmentation

If the effect of the last chapter was to unsettle you with the new awareness that the job-overtaking machines in your rearview mirror are closer than they appear, our job in the rest of this book is to give you hope. We know there are very real downsides to the new wave of smart machines, but the upside potential of the advancing technology is the promise of *augmentation*—in which humans and computers combine their strengths to achieve more favorable outcomes than either could alone.

The reason that many applications of digital intelligence are not as happy as the ones noted above is that they are simply *automation*—uses of machines to do what humans would otherwise do, and therefore do without the humans. Automation and augmentation might sound like two sides of the same coin, and in some cases they are. Yet it's also clearly true that workers love augmentation and hate automation, so it's reasonable to assume that the difference between them is not just rhetorical.

Having looked into a lot of instances where automation has engendered fear and resentment, we think we can sum up the problem with it simply enough: The reason people hate automation is that it involves someone in a managerial position spotting a shortcoming or limitation in employees, or simply a weakness relative to machine performance, and then punishing them for that weakness. Punishment usually takes the form of workforce reduction or pay reduction in real terms.

Indeed, the punishment can extend further than the immediately targeted employees, to their colleagues and even to the enterprise's customers. Take the automation of what has been the work of checkout clerks in
many grocery stores. The worker's weakness was her cost, and automation
punishes her for that by eliminating her position, replacing her with a self-
checkout lane. But the customer also bears the brunt of the replacement,
because now she must perform more work in the transaction than she did
previously. The two of us have spent our share of time in grocery store
lines and can report that we have seen no customer capable of scanning
a cart full of purchases as efficiently as the cashiers we once knew. As a
result, we know no one who, given the choice of either lane with no waiting, opts for the self-checkout. The same kind of punishment is inflicted
in offices where administrative assistants have been removed after their
tasks were automated. The executives they once supported don't come out
of the deal even—there is always some residual effort that didn't quite get
automated and that is now added to their full plates. No human enjoys the
revised situation.

Augmentation, by contrast, spots the human weakness or limitation
and makes up for it—we might say accommodates it—without pain to the
worker. The first major round of grocery checkout automation, the scan-
ner technology introduced in the 1980s, did this for clerks. It made up
for their imperfect memories of prices and sometimes fumbling fingers to
render them more productive. If you are a motivated knowledge worker,
trying to do your best, augmentation has your back.

And even beyond that aim to shore up your weakness, augmentation
spots your relative *strength* and works to amplify it, to build on it, or simply
to allow you to run with it.

Camille Nicita is CEO of Gongos, a metro Detroit company that helps
corporate clients like General Motors and Reebok gain greater insight
into consumer desires and behaviors. That's a line of work that some
would say is under threat as big data reveals all about buying activity.
Nicita concedes that sophisticated decision analytics unleashed on large
data sets will uncover new and important insights that her colleagues
would miss. But, she says, that will give her people the opportunity to
go deeper and offer clients "context, humanization and the 'why' behind
big data." Her shop will increasingly "go beyond analysis and translate

that data in a way that informs business decisions through synthesis and the power of great narrative." This sounds an awful lot like what economists Frank Levy and Richard Murnane refer to as the human strength of complex communication. It also sounds like an ideal partnership of human and machine, in which the value each brings to the arrangement is amplified by the other—in other words, it sounds like augmentation.

The best investments in intelligent machines, Nicita thinks—and this is the core belief of an augmentation strategy—do not usher people out the door, much less relegate them to doing the bidding of robot overlords. They allow people to take on tasks that are superior to—more fulfilling, better suited to our strengths, more value-creating than—anything they have given up.

The technologies, therefore, might be the same—there are not separate categories of automating tools and augmenting tools—but the intents behind the applications of the technologies are 180 degrees apart. Automation starts with a baseline of what people do in a given job and subtracts from that. It deploys computers to chip away at the tasks humans perform as soon as they can be codified. Aiming for only cost savings, it limits managers to thinking within the parameters of work that is being accomplished today.

Augmentation means starting with what minds and machines do individually today and figuring out how that work could be deepened rather than diminished by a collaboration between the two. The intent is never to have less work for those expensive, high-maintenance humans. It is always to allow them to do more valuable work.

Wheels for the Mind

We are not the first to think that machines should be designed and built to make people more capable, not to make them redundant. For example, when he was a young man, Steve Jobs shared some of the philosophy behind his work at Apple, starting with the observation that what "really separates us from the high primates is that we're tool builders." Jobs had seen a study that compared various species in terms of their efficiency of locomotion; it showed, for example, that the condor used the least energy to move a kilometer. Humans, about a third of the way down the ranking, weren't nearly so impressive. "But then somebody at *Scientific American* had the insight to test the efficiency of locomotion of a man on a bicycle," Jobs explained. "And a person on a bicycle blew the condor away—it was completely off the top of the chart. And that is what a computer is to me. It's the most remarkable tool that we have ever come up with. It's the equivalent of a bicycle for our minds."[3]

Jobs was almost assuredly inspired by the late Doug Engelbart in this (who in turn was inspired by MIT computer visionary Vannevar Bush). Engelbart, the inventor of the point-and-click computer user interface, and the mouse to use with it, was perhaps the first to embrace the term augmentation, which in his view involved getting machines to perform the mechanical aspects of thinking and idea sharing. In 1962 he published a widely circulated paper: "Augmenting Human Intellect: A Conceptual Framework."[4] He even founded an Augmentation Research Center, which in 1969, by the way, constituted one end of the first Internet link ever made. (The University of California, Los Angeles, was the other end.) Jobs borrowed not only Engelbart's interface ideas, but also his desire to create "wheels for the mind."

Going back further, Norbert Wiener, the MIT colleague of Vannevar Bush whom we mentioned earlier as the author of *The Human Use of Human Beings*, was expressing his hope already in 1950 that machines would free people from the drudgery of repetitive industrial work so that they could focus on more creative pursuits. Computers (or as he styled them, "computing machines"—the word "computer" referred then, even in an MIT professor's writing, to the humans hired to perform calculations) had only recently proved their value by performing mathematical functions quickly and accurately, but it was easy to speculate that they would in time exceed humans' intellect in other ways. One phrase from Wiener strikes us as especially prescient: "the machine plays no favorites between manual labor and white-collar labor."[5]

So we want to acknowledge a rich history of people thinking in terms of augmentation, while also refining the term a bit further. First, when we talk about augmentation we are talking about a relationship between humans and machines that is mutually empowering—a point on which we will elaborate in a section below. Second, we would define augmentation as only existing when the human worker is able to create more value by virtue of having the machine's help, and to personally reap greater gains by doing so. Deloitte has referred to augmentation of and by smart machines as "amplified intelligence"—a term that captures the same sense, although it doesn't contrast as neatly to "automation."

We also like the concept of augmentation because it goes beyond the economists' favored term of "complementarity." Economists refer to technologies as having either the power to substitute for human labor or to complement it. Since humans don't want to be made redundant, the option they are left with is complementarity, an arrangement in which humans continue to do what they do best, while computers contribute what they do best, and together they produce great value. Complementarity is good as far as it goes: Humans get to keep (at least some of) their jobs, while enjoying their work more because their skills and knowledge are effectively supported and enhanced by technology. But we think the relationship should go further. What if the effect of the pairing were to make humans *more* capable of what they are good at (and likewise, machines even better at what they do)? That would be augmentation. More than a division of labor, it would constitute a multiplication of value.

Forms of Augmentation: Superpowers and Leverage

In the realm of knowledge work, we've seen augmentation by intelligent machines take four forms, and we can further group them into just two categories. The first two we would class as superpowers, and the second two as leverage.

When a machine greatly augments your powers of *information retrieval*, as many information systems do, we would call that gaining a superpower. Indeed, in the Terminator film franchise, out of all the superhuman capabilities Skynet designed into its "cybernetic organisms," the one filmgoers covet most is the instant pop-up retrieval of biographical information on any humans encountered. It was the inspiration, for example, for Google Glass, according to the technical lead on that product, Thad Starner.[6] (And although we had to say *Hasta la vista, baby*, to that particular product, Google assures us it *will be back*.)

When Tom wrote a book about knowledge workers a decade ago, there were already some examples of how empowering such information retrieval can be for them. He wrote in some detail, for example, about the idea of "computer-aided physician order entry," particularly focusing on an example of this type of system at Partners HealthCare, a care network in Boston. When physicians input medical orders (drugs, tests, referrals, etc.) for their patients into the system, it checks to see if the order is consistent with what it thinks is best medical practice. If not, it asks the physician if it should change the order. (It leaves the final decision up to the doctor.) When the system was implemented in two major hospitals at Partners, it led to a 55 percent reduction in serious medication errors. Many hospitals use such systems now, and increasingly they will keep track of costs and patient health behaviors as well. Perhaps at some point they will also assist physicians with diagnosis, though this is a much more difficult problem. In any case, it's a straightforward and successful example of a "superpower" augmentation, and no human clinicians have lost their jobs because of it.

But let's say that these intelligent machines went on to do the *essential decision-making* in a situation, and that the decisions were more informed and rendered more quickly as a result. That is also a superpower—the second type—that can augment a human. Many, many decisions are challenging for humans but not controversial. Would you, for example, want your thermostat to check in with you every time it detected a decline in heat, and let you make the decision to reactivate the furnace? Workplaces have their endless equivalents, and they are not restricted to the world of process control. They relate to many human questions as well. Having smart machines that can process, consider, and act on routine matters in milliseconds, leaving you to deal with thornier issues, constitutes real advantage. This is why the U.S. Department of Defense wants future generations of fighter jets to be equipped with AI. They want to give pilots a cognitive advantage in battle, by allowing them to focus on the tasks that require their human discretion, rather than have their attention consumed by the nontrivial task of flying the plane.

The line between what constitutes augmentation and what constitutes being at the mercy of machines is constantly shifting, and is not always logical, yet somehow has a rightness to it. A great example came with the

Apollo flights to the moon in the late 1960s and early '70s, which involved ongoing battles between the engineers who wanted computers to fly the rocket and capsule, and the astronauts who wanted to retain control. The astronauts were willing to concede that they needed the Apollo Guidance Computer to navigate. As astronaut David Scott later said: "If you have a basketball and a baseball 14 feet apart, where the baseball represents the moon and the basketball represents the Earth, and you take a piece of paper edgeways, the thinness of the piece of paper would be the corridor you would have to hit when you come back."[7] But they wanted to do the work of landing the vehicle on the lunar surface themselves. Why? Maybe it was just a point of pride, because for these trained pilots, landing had always been the hardest part of flying. The engineers maintained that this human seizing of control was unnecessary and that flight computers— although primitive by today's standards—could have managed the landing at least as well. But ultimately the astronauts won out; in all six landings, according to Apollo historian David Mindell, the astronaut took control from the computer and landed the lunar module. They didn't want to be, in the memorable words of test pilot Chuck Yeager, "spam in a can."[8]

If the first two forms of augmentation are about giving you what you wish you could have, the latter two are about taking away what you wish you didn't. Here we're talking not about superpowers but about leverage. Much of your job probably involves mundane tasks you mastered long ago, and only wish you could offload so that you could take on higher-order work. Most of all, you probably wish you could jettison the noncore work—such as filling out your expense report—that isn't even related to the value creation you are paid for.

A self-administered form of this style of augmentation is when we and millions of others use tax preparation software like TurboTax to file tax returns. We supply a knowledge of our tax situations and the sources of data on it, and TurboTax supplies the rules and calculations, points out relevant tax documents throughout the process, evaluates our responses for errors, and tells us how likely we are to be audited by the IRS. We would like to think that we bring something to the party. For example, we humans make the decisions about just how charitable a supposed charitable donation is, and TurboTax dutifully deducts the contribution. We remember that we already paid tax on a consulting fee in Brazil, and TurboTax serves up the foreign tax credit form when requested. But we're also more than relieved to see a level of intelligence in the computer program that saves us from bringing too much to the party.

Likewise, inside law firms, many of the tasks that lawyers perform— deciding what areas of the law to address in a case, reassuring clients, tracking new developments in the world that will raise novel legal issues— require judgment, empathy, and creativity. But other aspects of the job, including document discovery, contract provision extraction, and the generation of standard wills and trusts, are increasingly codified and tedious to perform. It's no surprise that these tasks are rapidly being whittled away by smart machines. There are still 1.3 million lawyers in the United States, and the number grows every year—so we're not yet feeling the need to start a "Save the Lawyers" campaign. No doubt most of these attorneys see their greater salvation in the escape from drudgery.

A last form of augmentation, also a kind of leverage, is the smart machine that helps you become a better version of yourself. Consider the new class of devices that have recently exploded on the consumer market that allow you to set personal goals and capture the progress you are making toward them. As part of what is known as the "quantified self" movement, they create feedback loops to tell you how you are doing on the (often nonwork) objectives that matter to you—whether you're training for a marathon, trying to stay mentally sharp, or doing therapy to recover from some setback. In a way, this kind of leverage works not by erecting supports but by countering some of the regrettable tendencies of your human self, such as a lack of willpower or self-discipline. Increasingly, we think, technology in the workplace will perform this role for ambitious workers with individualized objectives.

This is a good place to restate what we noted earlier: The choice of technology is not what makes a human–machine relationship augmenting rather than automating. Even the most autonomous smart machines can still allow for some human augmentation on the margins. In all four of these categories, it is easy to imagine the technologies one would choose—and all too easy to see how the same technologies could be tools of surveillance and limitation instead of superpower and leverage. Intent is everything. But when the intent is to augment human capabilities, any kind of digital intelligence can be put to the task. Working in partnership with a machine can let you be you, only better. And it can let you keep your job, while making it a better one.

Whatever Happened to the Fifteen-Hour Workweek?

If you were reading this book half a century ago, you might be very surprised to find us referring to augmentation as something that would help you retain your work, not be rid of it. In 1928, John Maynard Keynes penned an essay he titled "Economic Prospects for Our Grandchildren," which argued that decades of productivity and technology improvements would leave those progeny with a new kind of problem: figuring out what to do with their vast leisure time. He wrote: "For the first time since his creation man will be faced with his real, his permanent problem—how to use his freedom from pressing economic cares, how to occupy the leisure, which science and compound interest will have won."[9]

Keynes expected that by now we'd all be working about fifteen hours per week. Obviously that prediction didn't come to pass. But the rise of smart machines suggests anew that substantially increased leisure might be on the horizon. If these machines can automate many of the tasks we perform at work today, will we spend substantially more time at leisure?

Our answer is "probably not," and there are a variety of reasons for this. Some economists argue that we have taken the benefits of our increased productivity in increased consumption—we keep working more in order to buy more. Sociologists argue that busyness has gained status as an end in itself. Psychologists argue that work is more inherently satisfying than we think.

We think that another reason why intelligent machines haven't reduced—and probably won't reduce—labor dramatically is that we are using them at least sometimes with an augmentation mindset. We—both individual workers and the organizations that employ them—do view smart machines as tools for augmenting work rather than automating it. They have been and will be aids not to job replacement, but rather to job expansion.

Think about, for example, the simple spreadsheet. It makes financial budgeting, planning, and report generation much faster and more productive. If organizations had taken an automation perspective on the tasks for which people use spreadsheets, they would have done the same number of budgets, plans, and reports after spreadsheets were invented, and done them with many fewer people at lower cost.

Instead, most organizations and individuals appear to think of spreadsheets as a tool for doing ever more analyses. Few if any financial analysts were replaced by spreadsheets, but substantially more analysis was done. Rather than consuming more of a fixed pie of work, spreadsheets and other productivity technologies expanded the pie.

As newer, more intelligent systems come along, we could imagine that they might eliminate or substantially reduce human performance of tasks. They might finally lead to that fifteen-hour workweek. But our belief is that they will—and should—follow the path blazed by spreadsheets. Instead of replacing knowledge workers, they should give them more to think about. Some decisions and actions may be taken by automated systems, but that should free up knowledge workers to accomplish larger and more important tasks.

Of course, there is a downside to working as much as knowledge workers tend to (particularly in the United States) today. But there is perhaps an even greater downside to not working enough or at all. The price we have to pay for thinking expansively about work is never having enough time to do it all.

The Augmentation Cuts Both Ways

In a recent paper examining the effect of computers on labor, David Autor, an economist at MIT, suggests that very little human toil these days is utterly unaffected by smart machines: "The fact that a task cannot be computerized does not imply that computerization has no effect on that task. On the contrary: tasks that cannot be substituted by computerization are generally complemented by it. This point is as fundamental as it is overlooked."[10]

Autor is pointing here to the idea of augmentation, and we would add that it can go both ways. Humans augment the work of computers and robots, just as computers and robots augment the work of humans. Sometimes most of the intelligence will come from the machines, and sometimes from humans; the decision-making split between them will often be something other than 50/50, and it will rarely stay static over time.

So let's flip the discussion we've been having about augmentation to the other side. If you were a machine, what shortcomings would you readily admit to, and wish to have a human making up for? It's possible to think of several ways in which machines surpass their own serious limitations by working in tight coordination with humans. At a minimum, they rely on people to fill in these key capabilities:

- **Design and create the machine's thinking in the first place**
  For the most part, it is humans who design and write computer programs, analytical algorithms, and so forth—the building blocks of automated decision systems. Despite advances in machine learning, automated programming, and so forth, it would currently—and for the foreseeable future—be very difficult to create such systems without a substantial amount of human labor and guidance. Automated tools will continue to make humans more productive in this role, but we will continue to drive and oversee the creation process.

- **Provide "big-picture" perspective**
  Humans are good at taking a big-picture perspective, which includes such skills as seeing how a particular solution fits into the whole, knowing that the world has changed in significant ways, and comparing multiple approaches to the same problem. We know when to look for new sources of information and where to find them. We know (usually) whether something "makes sense" or not. We know when the boundary conditions for a system have changed. Because this type of thinking is not very structured, computers aren't good at it.

- **Integrate and synthesize across multiple systems and results**
  We humans know that any one system or decision approach is likely not to provide the only possible answer. We're pretty good at assessing which of several sources is most likely to be correct,

or at triangulating across multiple answers. Freestyle chess players choose among several different systems for each move, as we'll discuss below. Analytics experts try a variety of different models, and take the best combination of explanatory power and reasonability. Some users of IBM's Watson have decided to develop alternative systems to see if they can perform particular cognitive tasks better. It is true that some machines are programmed to try out multiple methods and see which works best (often called ensemble methods in machine learning). But humans do it more often.

- **Monitor how well the machine is working**
  Analytical models and cognitive systems are designed for particular contexts. When context changes, they are likely to function less effectively. In most cases, the systems don't know that they aren't working well anymore and, even if they do, they don't retire themselves from the job. It is the role of humans to observe that systems no longer provide high-quality answers and need to be updated or replaced. If they've worked well for a long time, we may be hesitant to fire them, but we have to be sensitive to their useful life span.

- **Know the machine's weaknesses and strengths**
  All cognitive systems, just like humans, have weaknesses. They have algorithms based on poor-quality data, or shortcomings in their decision-making processes. An automated commercial underwriting system in an insurance company, for example, might do a great job on florists but be weak in assessing the risks of beauty salons. It's the job of a human underwriter in this case to realize that the system might recommend a policy that isn't priced correctly.

- **Elicit the information the system needs**
  It's often not that easy to get the information an automated decision system needs to do its work. In automated financial planning, for example, it's relatively easy to figure out the ideal stock and bond portfolio for a wealthy individual. But if you're trying to determine a family's retirement needs, you have to input current spending levels,

risk tolerance, likely retirement dates, and so forth. The client could enter that information him or herself, but it's often difficult to come up with such data. A human financial planner can help to motivate clients and elicit difficult information. There are many other settings in which humans can play the same type of role.

- Persuade humans to take action on automated recommendations

  Computers can make great decisions, but those decisions often require implementation by humans. In the same financial planning scenario mentioned above, a computer could recommend that more savings are needed to meet retirement goals, but it might take a persuasive human to motivate the client to save more. A computer may come up with a medical diagnosis and treatment plan, but compliance probably requires doctors and nurses who understand the plan, can translate it for the patient's consumption, and can motivate the adoption of new health behaviors.

There are undoubtedly other ways in which humans augment computers. Some augmentation opportunities will arise from the specific application domain. We mentioned the automated loan underwriting system that turned down former Federal Reserve chair Ben Bernanke for a mortgage refinancing. In banking, insurance, and other industries with a large number of seemingly routine decisions, there are often people like Bernanke who fall outside the normal categories and rules. If you want your bank to be the one that provides desirable customers like him with services, you need to be able to deal quickly and easily with exceptions— which means having people at the ready to respond to them. Even more problematically, health insurance companies have been known to decline coverage of potentially life-saving treatment. There are certainly opportunities for machines to help with such decisions, but just as certainly, many decisions about human lives are too important to be left to machines. The general point to be made here is that machines need augmenting when *there are important exceptions to rules and structured logic.*

Finally, we'd argue that, if the goal is to provide *truly exceptional or differentiated products and services at scale,* only an augmentation arrangement can accomplish that. We're all familiar with completely automated customer service, and most of us have developed strategies for finding a human to talk to about our problem (you know—pressing zero or saying "agent"). The menu of call center information options often just doesn't cut it. If you want your service to be high quality, or if you want your products to be differentiated from competitors, having computers churn out your processes is unlikely to do the job. When we talk about companies with high reputations in the marketplace, we seldom talk about their automation. Instead it's the creativity of a master designer, or the "human touch" from a customer service agent. We humans are pretty good at detecting machine-generated personalization or any sort of standardized communications. Although the machines will probably get better, our ability to detect machines will, too.

Some of the machine-augmenting roles we have listed may only be temporary windows for human workers, but that may be enough to provide jobs or even careers. In virtually all the augmentation arrangements we've described, the people have had to learn to work differently. If you're a knowledge worker hoping to keep your job (and prosper) in the age of smart machines, you've got to learn a lot, change what you do, and sometimes swallow your pride at the prospect of becoming their helper.

Learning from Freestyle Chess

Several writers who touch on what we are calling mutual augmentation do so with reference to chess. It's definitely a realm in which some humility on the part of humans is called for. In one-on-one matches, we know the best chess players are computers these days. Yet the trouncing isn't so complete as you might have been led to believe. The economist Tyler Cowen (not surprisingly, a chess champion in his youth) and *The Second Machine Age* authors Erik Brynjolfsson and Andrew McAfee use the example of "freestyle chess," in which human chess players are free to use as much help from computers as they wish.[11] The two of us personally don't play chess much (we like to get paid for thinking that hard), but we gather that under these rules, people often manage to beat the best programs. And although freestyle chess is a unique situation, the particulars of why that is true do seem to suggest possibilities for other forms of augmentation:

- Different computer programs are good at different chess situations, so the humans can bring awareness of each program's strengths and how to integrate them. (Computer chess programs aren't very good at noticing that there are better programs than themselves, and recusing themselves in that situation.)
- Humans are better at the contextual knowledge of when a move is easy and when it is hard, so they can urge their computers to make a quick move when it's feasible.
- It appears to be quite possible to excel at computer chess even if you are not an expert chess player—you just have to know a good move when you see it.
- It took humans to decide to build chess programs in the first place, and they continue to improve them.

On that last point, for example, Anson Williams, one of the world's best freestyle chess players, and his team member Nelson Hernandez developed a chess position database with more than three billion moves in it. As Hernandez told us about Williams (whom he has never met face-to-face), "His value-add is that he knows how to create an advanced decision-support system. But where he has a competitive advantage over the field is in his big-picture vision of how that system ought to be structured in contemporary (and ever-evolving) competitive landscapes." That sounds like an exemplary augmentation role to us.

We want to be careful not to rely on chess too heavily as an example of the augmentation approach. Although it has a huge number of permutations (said to be greater than the number of atoms in the universe), chess is certainly more structured than many real-life situations, and it's relatively invariant over time. While that makes it easier to write a chess-playing computer program than one for less structured and fixed domains, it also makes it easier for humans to understand and compare chess programs. And most people don't make their living by playing chess or any other game, so the extensions to keeping or losing employment are limited at best.

Yet we do think that people in many types of jobs can learn some valid lessons by analogy. To keep winning the game you're playing, even against very smart machines, you probably need to work in partnership with some of them. You need to learn what they do well, and not so well. You need to be constantly looking for a computer program that is better than the one you are using. You may need to invest in some data and analytics assets to improve your performance. And if possible, you need to learn enough about the computer programs to be able to improve them yourself. The other safe approach to ensuring your usefulness to the game, of course, is to be an author of the computer programs that play it.

In chess or elsewhere, since it is sometimes difficult to say in an augmentation situation who is augmenting what, or what is augmenting whom, we should be careful about parceling out credit and blame for the result. As a human, don't tell yourself that you are more capable than the computer, or it will probably embarrass you. Fortunately, computers don't have egos, so they are unlikely to lord it over us. They may, like *2001: A Space Odyssey*'s HAL, advise us not to unplug them. But as long as we're working with them, and winning the game we want to play, we won't want to.

The Five Options for Augmentation

For those fixated on the threat of automation, there is essentially one move available (and only to an increasingly small set of people): a step up to cognitively higher ground. Continued employability depends on being able to occupy those rarefied realms of rational decision-making not yet conquered by computers. Reframing the challenge as augmentation opens up a broader range of strategies for individual job holders and seekers. In place of that one possible step, now multiple steps reveal themselves as viable:

- Stepping Up
  Moving up above automated systems to develop more big-picture

insights and decisions that are too unstructured and sweeping for computers or robots to be able to make.

- **Stepping Aside**

  Moving to a type of non-decision-oriented work that computers aren't good at, such as selling, motivating people, or describing in straightforward terms the decisions that computers have made.

- **Stepping In**

  Engaging with the computer system's automated decisions to understand, monitor, and improve them. This is the option at the heart of what we are calling augmentation, although each of these five steps can be described as augmenting.

- **Stepping Narrowly**

  Finding a specialty area within your profession that is so narrow that no one is attempting to automate it—and it might never be economical to do so.

- **Stepping Forward**

  Developing the new systems and technology that support intelligent decisions and actions in a particular domain.

The "stepping" names have been useful to us, but trade off some precision for pithiness—and there may well be more possibilities. Although we've tried with these five categories to be, as consultants like to say, "MECE" (mutually exclusive and collectively exhaustive), by all means let us know if you spot a sixth or seventh option. The point is that there are various ways to make a living alongside smart machines, and they call on different human strengths. In almost every job type we've thought about, we've been able to find different people taking different steps. The remainder of this chapter will show this in a few illustrative professions. First, because it is such a clear example of a job threatened by automation, we'll look at insurance underwriting. Then, for greater context, we'll look briefly at how teachers and financial advisors are stepping up, aside, in, narrowly, and forward.

A Brief but Exciting Tour
of Insurance Underwriting

To hear the people at impertinent website Careersearch.com talk, you'd think pursuing a career as an insurance underwriter was not very exciting. In the page on their site devoted to the occupation, they begin by telling potential job seekers this:

> Pro baseball player, ballerina, astronaut, and insurance under-writer: these are just a few of the occupations people dreamed of having as children. With a little strength of will, spirit and determination, you can live those childhood dreams. Whether it's hitting that 500th homerun or being the first person to fake stepping on Mars, if you can perceive it you can achieve it. Of course, the same holds true for the insurance underwriter. While many might feel that this job is out of their reach, with enough tenacity and dedication it can be done. You can become an insurance underwriter.[12]

Ah, the snark of the Web. But the fact is that more than 100,000 Americans are doing this job and, according to the Bureau of Labor Statistics (BLS), earning an average annual salary $62,870 at it. It's a quintessentially white-collar profession at the heart of an information-based industry.

And as such, it's starting to get a little terrifying. A decade ago, that average annual salary was meaningfully higher in constant dollar terms. And looking to the future, the BLS sees only declines in the number of underwriting jobs. Its projection of a 6 percent drop between 2002 and 2012 is not as precipitous as what it expected for postal service clerks (32 percent), data entry keyers (25 percent), or embalmers (15 percent)—but such a drop will no doubt put more downward pressure on wages. And it has everything to do with the rise of smart machines. As early as 2009, a Deloitte survey found that fully 30 percent of large life insurance firms were using automated underwriting, and another 60 percent had plans to implement it.[13]

What exactly is an underwriter? Technically speaking, it's the enterprise that agrees to take on the risk involved with some asset or venture, for a fee. Why is it called that? Because in the 1600s, parties willing to insure merchant ships embarking on open-sea voyages literally wrote their signatures under posted descriptions of the cargoes. (Many such notices of voyages were posted at Edward Lloyd's coffeehouse in London— the origin of the Lloyd's of London we know today.) But within today's big insurance firms (and banks and real estate companies), underwriter is also the job title given to people entrusted with the core work of evaluating risks and coming up with the fair price an asset owner should pay (usually in the form of an insurance premium) to be insulated against the possibility of loss. It's a job that takes heavy math skills, because it means calculating many factors of different weights to come up with that ideal price that will beat the competition's offer to a customer while yielding a profit for the firm. That's a task, of course, best done by computers these days—and that's why, for anyone attuned to risk, the underwriting profession itself might look exciting. It has all the appearance of a sinking ship.

As we launch into the underwriting world, and introduce the five steps that will become familiar to you in the next several chapters, we should acknowledge our debt to Michael Bernaski. A veteran management consultant focused on financial services, Bernaski has helped to devise and implement automated systems for more than twenty years. He talked to us at length about the role of humans in environments undergoing automation, perhaps because he feels a degree of guilt "about all the insurance underwriters whose careers we disrupted." While he doesn't use exactly our five terms in talking about how human underwriters still provide value, his observations and ideas helped us think of them. And for what it's worth, he doesn't feel that underwriting is a sinking ship, because "all these new tools mean we can truly innovate risk solutions."

The fundamental problem for humans in this context, Bernaski emphasized, is that the traditional core of the job—which is understanding the "microstructure of risk," or how different attributes of businesses affect the likelihood that they will make a claim, and how that likelihood should change the price of insurance—is the kind of task computers are made for. The most sophisticated underwriting systems generate literally millions of different pricing cells and do so easily, because it is only a matter of following logical rules and equations. Computer systems gain an even greater advantage as devices with sensors—cars, trucks, boilers, and other types of equipment—start reporting regularly on their own performance and usage. With such massive amounts of data to consider, humans are truly out of their league. Dealing with the "Internet of things" is something computers are capable of. Humans, not so much.

Yet that doesn't have to be the end of the story. Underwriters who can learn to focus on other strengths they bring to the job can survive this capture of its core, and even come out better for it—perhaps never regretting that forgone career as pro baseball player, ballerina, or astronaut.

The Underwriter Who Steps Up

One way to respond to a computer encroaching on your work is to see it as that extremely competent assistant that allows you to step up—which, in the realm of underwriting, might mean taking responsibility for "portfolio management." That calls for judgments not about the microstructure of risk, but about its "macrostructure"—the threats facing the company, or even its region or the planet, that change the risk profile of whole swaths of business decisions. Is the company's entire portfolio unbalanced in some way, or should it adjust to reflect changes in the broader world? In commercial insurance, for example, stepping up might mean flagging a high reliance on insurance policies on owned farming equipment just as farmers are increasingly making use of equipment services from manufacturers. It might involve noticing, as Bernaski once did, that a company has relatively little business in urban areas in an era of "reurbanization" by both boomers and millennials.

This kind of thinking involves hunches, not codified logic—at least in the early stages of portfolio thinking. It's just not something that computers do well, at least not at this point. There simply isn't data to analyze or clear rules to articulate in the early stages of portfolio management.

The Underwriter Who Steps Aside

A decade ago, Tom happened to visit a company that had largely automated small-business insurance underwriting. A manager there said, "We keep some human underwriters around because somebody has to explain to agents why we have turned down their customer." Communicating negative news turns out to be a task that, whether or not computers are capable of it, agents insist be performed by beings capable of empathy. Even more helpfully, a good underwriter might emphasize the factors a customer could address, such as their driving record, versus harder-to-change elements, such as where they live.

The same kind of fellow-feeling is important when entering relevant data into an automated system—since it usually has to be elicited from a customer or an agent. Michael Bernaski points out that this does not merely involve keyboard accuracy. On the data input side, for example, human underwriters are often good at spotting inconsistencies in inputs. A canny underwriter might realize, for example, that the zip code provided by a customer in a car insurance application is not one served by public transportation—so the customer's report that he takes public transportation to work is likely false. More generally, he notes, "expression of customer preferences for financial products is fluid and qualitative." In other words, it often requires subtlety to understand a customer's information and what types of financial products they want and need. We've heard from other financial advisors, for example, about the challenge of disentangling the sometimes conflicting priorities of husbands and wives. It's unlikely that computers will figure out anytime soon where such differences bespeak deeper issues—and when that day comes, the real threat will be to marriage counselors.

The Underwriter Who Steps In

Underwriters with a special affinity for technology might prefer "stepping in" to the smart systems that are automating decisions and actions, and making them better as a result. Their companies will need experts on how automated underwriting systems work who can modify and improve them when necessary and ensure that they continue to work well over time. Often, consultants like Bernaski play this role, but organizations with the scale to justify it, and that don't want to pay high consulting fees forever, should have such people on staff.

Playing this role requires knowledge of both the profession of underwriting and the art of embedding expertise into rules and algorithms. Stepping-in professionals also have to be able to evaluate the overall success of underwriting in terms of comparing premium income versus claims over time. "There has to be a continuous feedback loop," Bernaski notes, "and expert underwriters are the key to making it work." The best ones are able to identify faulty logic, missing conditions, and other circumstances that would dictate the need for modifications to the systems.

The Underwriter Who Steps Narrowly

In underwriting as in many other professions, it's possible to focus your efforts to such a degree that your own growing knowledge of a narrow specialty remains well ahead of what has so far been automated. Bernaski says, for example, that he sees no automated systems going deep in all types of commercial establishments. A company might insure a lot of small retailers but still find, when a prospect with a chain of dry cleaning shops applies for a policy, that it lacks current understanding of the complicated environmental risks involved.

Keeping such narrow expertise up to date in human specialists is, in general, cheaper than taking the extra step of embedding it into decision-making computers. For an underwriter to take this step, of course, he or she needs to accumulate expertise in a very specific domain and resolve to remain at the leading edge. Undoubtedly that will involve working with computers, but the role of the technology will remain a supporting role.

The Underwriter Who Steps Forward

Stepping forward, in any field, means building the next generation of labor-saving tools—and this is certainly the point of many careers in a field as readily automated as underwriting. Some people will be able to take this step as full-time employees of insurance companies, since many of them build their own systems (and some, like Munich Re and Swiss Re, even sell their solutions to other firms). Other professionals will work for outside vendors, including large systems firms like Accenture and CSC. In fact, most of the people we know who do this sort of work typically go back and forth between employment at consulting firms and insurance companies. But many stepping-forward types are true entrepreneurs, who not only spot the need for new solutions but have the range of skills required to market, sell, and support them.

Before we move on to exploring how the same five steps look in other fields, this is a good moment to stress that while they are "mutually exclusive" in their definitions, they often coincide in individuals' careers. As an example, let us introduce Lisa Tourville, all of whose jobs have managed to combine stepping in and stepping up. She's a health-care actuary by training, and she's spent most of her career studying and acting on how medical risk affects the cost of health care. But most actuaries don't get terribly involved in the computer systems that analyze and automate decision-making about health-care costs and prices. Tourville is a conspicuous exception.

From her first job out of college, Tourville worked not only with actuarial data and analyses, but also with the computer systems that provide automated pricing figures. She did this for employee benefits in general, dental insurance, hurricane catastrophe insurance, and in her most recent jobs, health insurance. For health insurance giant UnitedHealthcare, she began to step up—not just looking at individual insurance policies, but forecasting the impact of new technologies and macroeconomic conditions on health-care costs. At Humana, another large firm (recently acquired by Aetna), Tourville continued her focus on modeling external trends, but she also led the company's focus on analytics and data-driven decision-making. She was responsible there for the Business Intelligence and Informatics Competency Center, and had responsibility for $50 million of analytics-oriented projects and systems.

At her current employer, Anthem—the second-largest company in the U.S. health insurance industry—she's still stepping in and stepping up. She's responsible for the "Commercial Health Care Economics" function, analyzing medical expense trends and understanding their movements, as well as the systems that report on such topics. She also previously led the Medicare Health Care Economics function at Anthem.

As with Tourville's career, for most knowledge workers there are constantly shifting options in terms of job content and role. What a computer does will change over time, and the primarily human domains will probably shrink over time. Work in the age of smart machines means constant change and adaptation.

Two More Fields, Same Five Steps

Now that you've got a clear understanding of the difference in the five ways of stepping, let's think about how they translate to a couple of other realms of knowledge work: teaching and financial advising. As we've already noted, teachers are threatened in their roles as personalized curriculum designers and transmitters of content; technology can do both of these functions quite well. While some rabble-rousers (notably Andy Kessler, a former hedge fund manager) argue that teachers will (and should) disappear with the rise of these technologies, it's more likely that teachers' roles will simply adapt. We're inclined to believe Thomas Arnett, a researcher on innovation in education, who predicts technology will "automate tasks such as taking attendance, handing back assignments, and checking multiple choice or fill-in-the-blank answers on tests and quizzes"—and even that it will "take care of some basic instruction and give [teachers] real-time data for tailoring lessons to student needs"—but that many aspects of teaching will remain too vital and essentially human to be replaced.[14]

Teachers who *step up* in a technology-rich environment will, for example, do the big-picture planning of curriculum units, and the overall questions of what must be taught. They will also determine how technology can most appropriately support those goals. Teachers relieved of the rote aspects of instruction can also join administrators in identifying and addressing systematic problems and trends in education, and responding to patterns in school and student performance data. Some will do this as part-time teachers, consultants, or members of "data teams."

Stepping aside in the teaching context will often mean focusing on facilitation and student relationship skills. Facilitation aims to bring out and encourage the wisdom of a group of students, rather than transmit knowledge to them. It models for students how to help and learn from each other, and fosters a desire to learn more in doing so. Someone stepping aside from the smart machines in the classroom might focus more on setting expectations, monitoring and adjusting student behaviors, and establishing a learning culture within the classroom. These kinds of softer skills may be discounted by some advocates of content-focused teaching and testing, but the truth is that success after leaving school is highly correlated with students' social strengths.

Stepping in involves, again, cozying up to the smart machines entering your field. A stepping-in teacher would, for example, embrace blended learning—calling on educational technology when it's most useful, and reverting to face-to-face education and facilitation as appropriate. They might more broadly serve as a resource for their schools on such mixtures. They might even become online-learning consultants, employed by educational technology vendors. Many teachers find the onslaught of technologies overwhelming and perhaps intimidating. But the stepping-in teacher welcomes the training or learns enough on the job to not only effectively use but find more uses for these tools.

Stepping narrowly in the teaching context might involve working with students who have unusual needs. They might be learning impaired, gifted, or native speakers of other languages. Some schools, for example, hire "onset and rime" specialists to focus on giving students with dyslexia and certain other learning difficulties the benefit of this alternative approach to phonics. Others hire specialists in helping students whose native languages include Hmong and Mam. In each of these specialties, the demand is sufficiently small and the educational approach sufficiently unstructured to make automation-oriented software unlikely.

The people who are *stepping forward* in education are most likely to work in so-called ed tech firms that develop software for schools and districts to adopt. Some of these firms are startups; others are branches of traditional vendors to schools, such as publishers. McGraw-Hill Education (MHE), a spinout of the publishing company, has hired a number of people in new offices of its Digital Products Group in Boston and Seattle who would not typically be found in either publishing or educational settings. They include data scientists, software engineers, and data visualization experts, along with analytically and technically skilled product managers, content developers, and other roles. Senior managers of the group have backgrounds as management consultants, chief information officers, and data scientists—but most also have experience in the education industry, and some were even K–12 teachers.

Teaching is a great profession to think about in terms of our five steps because automation technologies are just beginning to be introduced in it. To a current teacher, it may seem unnecessary to think much at all about who will win or lose in the age of smart machines. Yet the writing is on the chalkboard: These technologies will ultimately have profound impact. As traditional teaching jobs decline in number and value, the steps we describe will become more common.

Steps for Financial Planners and Brokers

The decisions traditionally made by financial planners and brokers—specifying what financial assets a client should invest in—are increasingly being made better by computers. This trend even has a name—the "robo-advisor." But the same steps available to underwriters and teachers can work for this group as well. Start again with *stepping up*, which in financial advising includes determining which types of investments automated systems should even consider in their allocations. As global financial environments (interest rates, economic growth, etc.) change, stepping up means saying how automated advice should change with them. At Betterment, for example, one of the larger and more successful startups in the robo-advisor space, there is a "Behavioral Finance and Investing" department made up of five experts focusing on how to improve their system's investment advice, determining the right asset allocation, changing investment management strategies over time, and "behavioral design"—trying to nudge Betterment customers toward more rational economic behaviors with their investments.

Stepping aside to perform tasks that computers don't do well is a viable prospect for many financial advisors. Grant Easterbrook, who covered financial technology firms as an industry analyst (he's now moved to a financial technology startup) told us that, while creating an investment portfolio is relatively easy to automate, it still requires a human touch to provide complex financial planning for individuals with substantial assets. Such broad planning includes tax planning, estate planning, life insurance, and other decisions that not only require nuanced information gathering but are also interrelated. Human advisors can "motivate the client to gather all of that information," says Easterbrook, and correct for the fact that clients "are often overly optimistic about their finances and undisciplined about following up." David Port, who has written on the rise of robo-advisors, also emphasizes the value of advisors who care about their clients' goals. Port notes, "The heart of the value proposition for flesh-and-blood advisors is the ability to be a trusted resource to clients, not only in the various areas of planning, but as a source of objective information and advice, delivered with a personal touch."[15]

Planners and brokers who *step in* take full advantage of robo-advisors as supersmart colleagues. Once their firm adopts a particular tool, they are quick to familiarize themselves with the logic it relies on to make its decisions and are not shy about telling the technologists in their firm and external vendors to modify and improve it. If the advisor is independent, he or she advises clients on which technology is best suited to provide guidance on a given question.

There is a long and lucrative history in *stepping narrowly* in financial advice—accumulating expertise on a narrow investing topic and making that your specialty. That might mean becoming expert on a single type of investment—single-premium annuities, for example, or convertible bonds—or a particular type of client. The financial services company USAA, for example, which specializes in insurance and investments for current and former members of the military, has a group of financial advisors who specialize in the needs of just that type of client. USAA does have an automated advice system, but it doesn't focus specifically on the needs of service members and veterans.

Finally, there seem to be endless opportunities for *stepping forward* by building new investment technology applications. As with education, many of these entrepreneurial types work in startups; indeed, in his analyst role, Easterbrook kept tabs on more than one hundred startups in the "robo-advisor" category alone. But large financial advisors, such as Charles Schwab, also develop their own automated financial advice systems. (We describe Vanguard Group's augmentation approach in detail in Chapter 10.)

In this chapter we've provided an overview of the idea of augmentation and the five "steps" we see people taking to leverage and be leveraged by smart machines. We've looked briefly at these options in a few different industries—insurance underwriters, teachers, and financial advisors. Now it's time to go deep on each way of stepping. In the five chapters that follow, we'll provide more examples and plenty of guidance on how you might proceed if you're inclined toward a particular kind of step. All of them involve reconsidering your relationship to the smart machines increasingly entering your workplace. But none of them feels like capitulation. Any of them can take you in a direction where you'll be happier in your work—and more valuable to your employer or customer—than you've ever been before.

4

Stepping Up

Ron Cathcart was not happy about his move to Seattle. The city itself was fine—much warmer than Toronto, where he'd spent most of his career as a banker—but his new job was somewhat problematic. He'd taken the role as chief risk officer at Washington Mutual (WaMu), a large (in fact the largest in the United States) savings and loan company.

Shortly after taking the job in December 2005, Cathcart realized that the promises made to him of a substantially enhanced enterprise risk management function were rather hollow. Risk was "isolated from the rest of the business and struggling to be effective," he noted later in testimony to Congress.[1] Cathcart also learned that the year before he came, the bank had adopted a "Higher Risk Lending Strategy" aimed at marketing adjustable-rate mortgages (ARMs) and home equity loans to subprime borrowers. As was common at the time, the goal was to sell the loans to Wall Street in a securitization process.

While the organizational context seemed less than fully supportive, Cathcart embarked upon a program of action to improve the monitoring of risk at WaMu and eventually to reduce such risk. He placed risk managers in each of four business units. He began a review of credit policies and limits. He hired additional credit risk modelers, and encouraged them to build a variety of quantitative models to identify any problems with the bank's loan portfolios and credit processes. This work required a broad range of sophisticated models including "neural network" models; some were vendor supplied; some were custom-built .

Cathcart, who was an English major at Dartmouth College but also learned the BASIC computer language there from its creator, John Kemeny, knew his way around computer systems and statistical models. Most important, he knew when to trust them and when not to.

The models and analyses began to exhibit significant problems. No matter how automated and sophisticated the models were, Cathcart realized that they were becoming less valid over time with changes in the economy and banking climate. Many of the mortgage models, for example, were based on five years of historical data. But as the economy became worse by the day in 2007, those five-year models became dramatically overoptimistic. Cathcart was asked by the bank's chairman not to disclose these painful facts.

You probably know that things only went downhill from there. Despite his efforts, Cathcart observed numerous problems in the data on which the company's risk models were based. As his company's mortgage bank and others in the United States adopted "no documentation" loans, he realized that you could no longer trust a borrower's income data. Cathcart and his army of PhD analysts also noticed—after considerable detective work—that second home ownership, once a sign of wealth, had become an indicator of high likelihood of mortgage default. Cathcart tried to change and tighten credit and underwriting standards, but he lacked control over the problem at the bank's mortgage subsidiaries.

The more Cathcart sounded alarm bells about the level of risk at WaMu, the more he was shunned by the senior management team. Executives canceled meetings with him, and he was excluded from presenting to the board of directors. By early 2008, Cathcart felt obligated to notify the board and the U.S. Office of Thrift Supervision that risk levels had become dangerously high. Shortly after doing so, he was fired by Kerry Killinger, the CEO and chairman. Killinger himself would be fired a few months later, but WaMu was placed in receivership by the Federal Deposit Insurance Corporation (FDIC) in September 2008. It was the largest bank failure in U.S. history.

Cathcart was unable to save the company, but he did save his career. He testified before a U.S. Senate subcommittee on some of the issues we've described at WaMu. He's now the head of Enterprise Risk Supervision at the New York Federal Reserve Bank, helping to design "stress tests" for banks in the United States and representing the country at global financial conferences on capital requirements and risk. There are presumably few bankers anywhere who would have a better sense of enterprise risk than he after what he's been through.

While he might wish he had done so at a more successful institution (and before coming to WaMu, he did), Ron Cathcart stepped up into automated systems. He recognized the need for greater insight on risk, so he sponsored the creation of automated and semiautomated analytical models. He realized that they were lacking in some respects, so he had them modified. He figured out when you could trust the models, and when you couldn't. "Math only goes so far," he noted. He used the analyses and results they provided, along with other inputs, to make important decisions and take actions. He took a big-picture perspective on risk and the need for change in his institution.

What Stepping Up Means

Stepping up with cognitive technologies means to move up a level from working directly with a particular smart system. It involves making high-level decisions about augmentation and the relevant technologies—where to use these types of systems, how things are going with systems already in place, and how each new system fits into the overall context of the business or organizational process. It often involves less direct contact with a particular automated system itself and more evaluation of the decisions that a variety of automated systems are making. If automated systems make small, repetitive decisions, those who step up make larger, more sweeping ones.

The step-up role may not preserve a large number of jobs as automation advances—most organizations have only a few people in such roles—but it is important out of proportion to the numbers. It's at the top of the augmentation pyramid. In fact, it is usually those who occupy this role who make the high-level decisions affecting other human roles relative to automated systems. They're deciding what smart people do, what smart machines do, and how they work together.

Like Ron Cathcart, many of the step-up incumbents are senior executives. It's not surprising that the people who make decisions about what automation to use under what circumstances would be pretty high in the organizational hierarchy. In most cases, this won't be a CEO-level decision, but it will be someone who controls some resources and people, and who has responsibility for an organizational outcome—improving performance, cutting cost, or making better use of human employees.

It may be useful to describe the step-up role in a variety of different contexts. As we discussed in the previous chapter, in an insurance company or bank that uses automated policy or loan underwriting, a step-up role might involve setting the overall risk or credit portfolio parameters to guide such automated decisions. Because many day-to-day decisions about risk and credit acceptance have been automated in these industries, many of the remaining jobs are referred to as "portfolio management," which constitutes a step up from individual decision automation. Someone in this role attempts to optimize performance of the entire set of automation systems, trading off growth, profitability, and the total exposure to risk.

Investing also involves portfolio management, of course, and the step-up role is highly relevant there as well. Detailed decisions at investment banks and hedge funds about which stock or bond to buy are frequently made by computers now. But the step-up investors furnish the criteria by which computers make their decisions. At Bridgewater Associates, which runs the world's largest (and one of the most successful) hedge funds, computers make a lot of the day-to-day decisions to tune the investment portfolio. The company is committed to artificial-intelligence-based investing and even hired David Ferrucci, who led the IBM team that developed Watson, to help build new AI-based models.

But Ray Dalio, who founded the firm and is now its co–chief investment officer, is noted for his big-picture view of the world. When asked what the essence of his investment approach is, he says things like "I understand how the economic machine works" and that he succeeds by "stepping back to see things at a higher level." An article about Dalio described it this way: "Many hedge-fund managers stay pinned to their computer screens day and night monitoring movements in the markets. Dalio is different. He spends most of his time trying to figure out how economic and financial events fit together in a coherent framework."[2]

Bridgewater holds a weekly meeting to discuss "what's going on in the world," the insights from which are used to modify portfolios and models. It's likely that Dalio hired Ferrucci to put that big picture into a structured system. A statement from Bridgewater about Ferrucci's team's work suggests such a focus and that it will be a process involving augmentation more than automation: "Ever since 1983 Bridgewater Associates has been creating systematic decision-making processes that are computerized. We believe that the same things happen over and over again because of logical cause/effect relationships, and that by writing one's principles down and then computerizing them one can have the computer make high-quality decisions in much the same way a GPS can be an effective guide to decision making. Like using a GPS, one can choose to follow the guidance or not follow it depending on how it reconciles."[3]

In marketing, a step-up job might involve coordination and pursuit of the many opportunities for automating marketing decisions. A LinkedIn job description featured such a role for a "Sales/Marketing Automation Specialist," who would "manage and execute marketing campaigns utilizing integrated automation and CRM [customer relationship management] platforms." The automation specialist would also be expected to "work closely with various groups including strategy, sales, product development and account management to build, automate and monitor successful demand generation campaigns."

Lots of corporate and marketing jargon there, but you get the idea. It's collaborative across the organization, it involves working with multiple automated systems, and it means manipulating those systems to achieve better marketing results.

In the legal profession, stepping up might mean overseeing all automation initiatives, including e-discovery, although we have not encountered this as formal role in law firms. Most likely, it is the province of heads of technology or knowledge management.

What Those Who Step Up Decide

There are three basic types of automation decisions made by people who step up. One is the identification and evaluation of automation opportunities. What key functions involve codified knowledge within an organization? What software already exists to do similar things? Where is there economic opportunity from automation? Those who step up set the agenda for automation. The decision to embrace automation technologies is not binary; since automation systems typically support particular narrow tasks and decisions, there are many decisions to make about implementing it within an organization.

A second key decision type involves high-level work design. Once an investment in smart machinery has been made, how should the process of getting work done be altered? Which tasks will be done by computer, and which by humans? Do we rely on humans for the most difficult and complex cases? Do they handle only the exceptions that the system kicks out? How and when are computer-made decisions reviewed? Finally, what happens to the people who are no longer needed by this process? These work design issues are obviously important and play out over years; they need considerable thought and planning.

One early adopter of automation on a broad scale for insurance underwriting was Allstate. As described by former consultants to the company, this adoption took place in the mid-1990s, and the head of the "personal lines" business (providing property and casualty insurance to individuals, typically for cars and homes) played the step-up role in work design. After the decision was made to adopt automated underwriting, some people were able to move upstream to portfolio management and enterprise risk management. But the business leader realized that not everybody in the underwriting organization would "make the cut" to move up to portfolio management. Some underwriters were really good at communicating and working with agents, so a new role specializing in that function was created. The business leader started to prepare people to move in one direction or the other. About a thousand people were involved in the transformation. Ultimately about a third of them went into portfolio and market management, a third went into agent relationships, and a third didn't have the skills for either of these, so they lost their jobs.

The third type of decision someone makes in a stepping-up role results from monitoring the results of the revised work arrangement over time and noticing that the world has changed, but the systems haven't. How is the investment portfolio performing? What is the aggregated risk exposure for our company? How is our brand being represented by the programmatic digital ad buys on various publishers' websites?

This was the type of thinking that Ron Cathcart used when he was working at Washington Mutual. As the overall credit environment for mortgages deteriorated, he realized he needed more analytical models to understand the extent of the problem. He also realized that the models his group used were "black boxes" to managers in the business; data went into them and risk warnings came out, but there was no visibility into the logic involved. If his group hoped to persuade managers to take on less risk as housing prices fell, their tools should be far more transparent.

All models and decision rules are based on particular business and economic contexts and sets of underlying assumptions. Sometimes those assumptions are clearly articulated; more frequently they are not. A good step-up manager is constantly asking whether the world has changed in such a way that would make the decision rules and algorithms less relevant.

This can be an everyday role, or a quite exalted one. Tom once asked Larry Summers, the former president of Harvard and top-level economic advisor to President Barack Obama, what he did in his hedge fund job at quant firm D. E. Shaw. He responded that, primarily, he went around to the quants who built automated trading models and asked them what the assumptions were behind those models, and how the world would have to change for those models to become invalid. For this he was paid $5.2 million a year for working a day per week. Nice work if you can step up to it.

A Step-Up Example in Automated Journalism

The people who decide that smart machines are appropriate for their organizations, and then lead the implementation of them, are perhaps typical of technology innovators in general. Whatever the technology, stepping up with regard to it starts with understanding the potential value of a tool, and can extend all the way through identifying vendors, financing the deal, designing new work arrangements, changing culture and behaviors, and modifying surrounding infrastructure. Perhaps the best way to illustrate the attributes of those who step up in their work is to provide a detailed example.

Today, Lou Ferrara is the chief content officer at Bankrate.com, a publisher of financial research and information which is exploring how the generation of some of its content could be automated. But he first introduced automation into content production in 2014 and 2015, when he was a vice president and managing editor for Entertainment, Sports, and Business News at the Associated Press (AP), which provides news content to broadcasters, newspapers, and websites around the world. Ferrara also oversaw the newsroom's delivery of "digital products." He led the development of several technology-based innovation projects (including user-generated content, advertising tweets, and social media), but we'll focus here on his leadership of the automation of business and sports news for AP.

AP is now using an automated story-writing tool called Wordsmith, from Automated Insights. The tool generates prose accounts of corporate earnings and sports events. The project started in 2014 and has been expanded since then; when we checked in 2015 the system was cranking out 3,000 earnings reports per quarter (versus 300 per quarter by human journalists in the recent past), with plans to get to 4,700 per quarter by the end of the year. In sports, the plan is for the system to begin generating stories soon about Division I college baseball, and Division 2 and 3 basketball and football, which will add thousands of stories a year for fans of those teams.

Our conversations with Ferrara about his background have helped confirm our belief that technology innovators are made, not born. And they can be made in midcareer. Ferrara spent the early part of his career as a newspaper reporter and editor and worked for twelve years in Sarasota, Florida. The Sarasota newspaper launched a twenty-four-hour news TV station around the time it launched its Web operations in the early years of the dot-com boom, in the 1990s. By the time Ferrara left Sarasota, he was overseeing the TV and Web operations and innovating through multiformat reporting and publishing. He was building all-digital, nontape video systems before they became the norm. His team began using emailed photos from hurricanes, perhaps before the term "user-generated content" was coined, and certainly before Twitter existed. In other words, he stepped up with other technologies well before automated content came along. That's probably typical of step-up folks.

Along the way, Ferrara acquired an important attribute of those who step up: He sees the bigger picture. When he looked at AP's situation, he saw several factors that suggested the potential for automation, including scarce resources, pressure on margins, and a need despite these limitations for more content. AP's customers may be constrained for newsprint space, but there are few if any constraints on online content volume. As Robbie Allen, the CEO of the automation software vendor Automated Insights, put it, "The sign of a true innovator is someone that can look into the future and map a course from how to get from here to there. Lou understands the pressure on the publishing industry. . . . While the publishing industry isn't known for being the most forward-looking from a technology perspective, Lou has been a shining example of how to use new technologies to help the Associated Press adapt and gain new ground in the digital world."

The testimony from Allen suggests another hallmark of step-up types: They build an ecosystem of partners that collectively makes progress, and profits from it. In fact, AP invested in Automated Insights and gained a substantial return on its investment when the vendor was acquired in 2015. And this wasn't the only partnership that Ferrara nurtured; he also worked, for example, with Stats Inc. to automate publishing of sports statistics, and with SNTV, a sports news agency, both of which AP also invested in.

Ferrara displays another attribute of step-up innovators: He gets out a lot. He participates in conferences, including the most recent South by Southwest. He meets with venture capital investors and firms, as well as leaders of tech companies. He's not a self-promoter, preferring to be quiet about it, but manages to trade ideas with all kinds of people. You can't grasp the world of automation and other emerging technologies by sitting at your desk.

Ferrara was somewhat cautious in redesigning work to accommodate more automation, as would seem advisable for anyone stepping up. Why alienate your knowledge workers by seeming quick to devalue their contributions? The initial focus was on earnings reports for companies that were too small to receive attention from human reporters. Likewise, in its sports coverage, AP focused on college divisions and event categories that had been previously neglected. Ferrara was widely quoted as saying—and he repeated it internally—that human reporters would not lose their jobs because of the automated reporting. "The type of work we want to automate is not at the core of what we do," he noted. "We're automating elements that require a lot of data processing work—this is labor that is done well by machines. Beat reporting, source development, obtaining documents, investing in relationships, and talking to company leaders—you need humans to do that, and you need a lot of them to do it really well."

Ferrara assigned a small team to test the system, work out the bugs, and make sure the stories were written correctly. The system is already generating substantially fewer errors than human journalists. Great attention was paid to writing quality. Despite high initial skepticism about the system, he said, many reporters eventually were impressed. And indeed, none lost their jobs as a result of its implementation. None seem disappointed, either, to give up earnings reports, which were never the most scintillating business journalism.

Summing up, Ferrara's mindset at AP was not to automate human work, but to augment it. Before he left AP in October 2015 he built an infrastructure of capabilities so his team and colleagues could continue along those lines. In March 2015, for example, AP established what is probably the world's first "Automation Editor" role, one function of which is to look for more automation opportunities at AP. We'll return to that position, and its first occupant Justin Myers, in our Chapter 6 discussion of stepping in.

It should be clear that organizations wanting to employ cognitive technologies need internal change leaders like Lou Ferrara as much as they need external innovations from technology vendors. The journey of taking an augmentation project from the external market to a successful internal project is full of roadblocks and potholes. Successful implementation of these technologies and human roles doesn't just happen; it has to be driven by people with vision and managerial skill.

Seeing the Big Picture

As we've said, computers are not very good at seeing the big picture and noticing that it has changed in some fundamental way. Step-up folks, if they're good at their jobs, *are* good at this. They need broad perspective and penetrating vision to spot the augmentation possibilities appropriate for their organizations, sort out which tasks should migrate from people to machines, and recognize when an augmentation approach their organization previously implemented no longer makes sense.

People who can see the big picture can answer—often easily and creatively—the following types of questions:

How does your company make money (or how does your nonprofit organization succeed)?

What's happening with your customers, and what do they think about your company?

How is the economy changing?

What's happening in the broader society, politics, and demographics?

What are regulators likely to insist upon?

What initiatives that other companies are pursuing now will likely come to your company soon?

These kinds of issues and trends can't always be captured in data. By the time there is systematic and reliable data on a topic, the world may have already changed. It's certainly good for those who step up to consult data and analytics, but they also have to read and converse widely, and try to make sense of it all.

Another phrase for seeing the big picture is having "situational awareness." This term is often used in the military and by pilots to mean a complete perception of what is going on around oneself. In order to get it, a pilot, for example, needs to consult instruments, computers, and navigational aids inside the cockpit (and computers often use this data to fly the plane in "automatic pilot" mode), as well as look out the window now and then. Anyone stepping up in a work setting should be doing the equivalent.

Yet another phrase for this capability is "systems intelligence"— knowing how all of the pieces of a system work together. A "Systems Intelligence Self-Evaluation" website asks such questions as "I quickly get a sense of what matters," "I view things from many different perspectives," and "I perceive connections between seemingly unrelated things."[4]

Whatever you call it, if you see the big picture you can begin to see how smart machines can figure into it. Those who have stepped up in the financial investments industry perhaps noticed, for example, that members of the millennial generation are, as investors, very comfortable with technology and rather uncomfortable with coming into an office and discussing their financial situations. At the same time, someone taking a broad view of the investment landscape might have noticed the shift away from stock and bond picking by experts, to index funds that invest in major segments of markets. From such observations, the idea might occur quite readily to create a "robo-advisor" capable of proposing portfolios of these types of investments.

For that matter, the rise of cognitive technologies is a big-picture idea in itself. It's not surprising that these types of systems would take off, given macro trends relating to the power of computers, the intensity of global competition, and the shift from goods to services by mature economies. These all drive many companies to seek new ways to increase the productivity of knowledge workers, and smart machines have come along as excellent and powerful means to do that.

Building an Ecosystem

Have you ever seen a LUMAscape? If not, do a quick online search for one. If you don't have an Internet connection as you read this, we're referring to a series of infographics put together by Luma Partners, an investment banking firm that does deals in the marketing technology space. Different LUMAscapes focus on different categories of tools—one is devoted to the technology behind display ads, another is all mobile, and another all social—but they all have something in common—their almost comical squeezing of hundreds of vendor logos into a page-wide space. We are guessing that there is more change—more new vendors, more new products, more companies entering and leaving the space—in this area than any other technology category on planet Earth.

Andrew Daley has to live the LUMAscapes every day. He's the vice president of member acquisition at Zipcar, the pioneering car-sharing service acquired by the Avis Budget group in 2013. Member acquisition means finding new customers and the primary approach to that is digital marketing—much of which is automated.

Daley has been in digital marketing since 1999, but he's not sure that anyone is an expert on programmatic buying (automated purchase of digital ads) and marketing automation. But, he admits, he works with them every day, so he might qualify as much as anyone.

Until a couple of years ago, Daley says, Zipcar wasn't that sophisticated in digital marketing. It turned over almost every decision about software platforms and automation approaches to a single digital ad agency, and it didn't study the results in much detail. Then Daley and Executive Vice President and Chief Marketing Officer Brian Harrington decided that they could get better outcomes if they took more control over the process.

They still felt a need to work with an ecosystem, because—as we suggested in describing the LUMAscape—the amount of new technology is "overwhelmingly complex," as both Daley and Harrington described it, and a smaller company like Zipcar still needs external expertise. But they decided to rely on focused external expertise, and found agency partners who employ automated tools within each marketing channel. Zipcar uses the partners to actually "turn the dials" on the automated systems, and Daley and his colleagues monitor the results. It's clearly an augmentation situation rather than pure automation.

To show how specialized this expertise has become, Zipcar works with one company on the programmatic buying of digital display ads, another one on automated search engine optimization, another on YouTube video advertising, another for automated Facebook ad buys, and so forth. Across all these channels they are "almost 100% programmatic," according to Harrington, and Daley notes that in each of them they strive to be scientific about evaluating results and optimizing positive outcomes. It's Daley's job to manage the overall ecosystem for new member acquisition, and he manages a lean team that looks over all the channels for twenty-six different geographical markets. Daley says there is no way so few people could manage all the channels without both automation and external partners.

The "programmatic" systems don't run on automatic pilot. Daley says that Zipcar's goal in digital marketing is to observe who signs up as a member, and then to find other people like them. The automated marketing systems let them study all the people who convert with them, and create look-alike profiles. Regardless of where they are on the Internet, Daley and his team try to find them.

There is also a complicated internal Zipcar budgeting structure that Daley and Harrington have to work with. Each of the twenty-six geographic regions has a budget for marketing. For a particular campaign, Providence, Rhode Island, might have X dollars to spend, whereas New York might have Y. Daley and his colleagues pool advertising dollars from each market and put them to work on their behalf. At the end of the month he has to go to each market and tell them what they have achieved. Programmatic buying is helpful in this regard, because it's easy to turn ad buys on and off as budget limits are reached. Now the corporate marketing organization can avoid over- and underspending much more easily in order to achieve its acquisition objectives.

Stay Close, but Move On

Like Lou Ferrara at the Associated Press, those who step up need to stay somewhat involved with the projects they initiate, but because they look over a collection of such efforts, they must also be able to extricate themselves from the day-to-day activity. When a system is up and running, they need to monitor its performance but also move on to new possibilities for applying cognitive technologies.

In Chapter 6 we describe Mike Krans, who as an Accenture consultant was one of the first people we observed really "stepping in" to automation. Now, however, Krans makes his living in a stepping-up role. He's the chief information officer for personal lines (individual insurance) at Hanover Insurance. In his new job he needs to identify new opportunities for automated systems as well as monitoring the performance of already-implemented ones.

Krans, in any of his managerial roles, felt the need to stay close to the automation projects he oversaw. He commented in an interview, "As my career has progressed, I have had to move up in terms of my closeness to the work. You get further from the floor and other people are doing the day-to-day implementation. But I still try to stay connected to the work and to the people doing the work. I don't want to be perceived as just a manager who doesn't understand the technology or the details of the project."

The right amount of attention for him to pay to projects, however, changes over time. At this point, having overseen so many rules-based automated underwriting projects, he recognizes that these systems have become something of a commodity in insurance—and even that "they are becoming passé." His attention is better spent figuring out how to harness new sources of data (such as geospatial data from satellites, which can reveal hazards in a business's environs that should be factored into its insurance costs) and how to employ more advanced predictive and text-based analytics.

It's sometimes a challenge to stay close enough to an automated system to monitor its effectiveness while still shifting your attention elsewhere. Those who step up may need to set up regular review intervals to assess whether a system is still doing its job or not. We humans have a tendency to let such systems and operations hum along until a disaster happens, and that tendency needs to be fought.

Careful Work Design for Automated Business Functions

At the heart of augmentation is careful design of the work to maximize the strengths—and minimize the shortcomings—of both humans and machines. It is the step-up managers who will lead the work design process, as Lou Ferrara did at AP.

In some cases, step-up role incumbents may not have the luxury that Ferrara has in promising that humans won't be laid off because of automated systems. If one of the goals is headcount reduction, it will be their responsibility to think carefully about all the work humans currently perform, identify the tasks that can be done by machines, determine which will still be done by people, and manage the transition.

As we've noted, the right level to think about work design is the task, not the entire job. People in jobs typically perform a variety of tasks, and some of those are more automatable than others. In the insurance underwriting example at Allstate we described earlier, the work design process identified three key tasks—individual underwriting decisions, aggregated risk portfolio management, and agent communications. The computer did most of the individual underwriting, but humans were necessary for the other two, and to oversee and maintain the underwriting.

In other cases much of the work that automated systems do will be incremental—not replacing human tasks—as at the Associated Press. That's largely the situation in the field of digital marketing, where humans never really did a lot of decision-making about what ad to place where, what search term yields the highest click-through rates, and so forth. That work required computers from the beginning.

In such situations, the key is to preserve important human attributes along with the computer-oriented ones. That's the focus, for example, of Adele Sweetwood, who leads global marketing for the analytics software company SAS. As we will learn from Shane Herrell in Chapter 6, a "step-in" guy in digital marketing at SAS, many of the online marketing activities at the company are automated. It's Sweetwood's role to ensure that the automated tasks are consistent with the company's brand image and creative content. She notes, "We use a lot of automation, in our own SAS software and in digital ads, which isn't the focus of our software. The key is for the automation to be consistent with how you set up campaigns, how they drive to channels, and so forth. We need people who can relate the data and analytics and automation components to the business." Sweetwood believes the key skills are a combination of creative orientation and technology focus. She adds, "People are bringing creative messages to marketing in a technology-intensive way, and you have to be aware of both."

In this type of environment, the work design for marketing activities needs to ensure that the creative messages enter at the beginning of the process, and that they fit well with the automated tasks that distribute them across channels. It would be all too easy to let automated systems make decisions that drive marketing content in the wrong direction. Sweetwood monitors not only the automated decision outputs, but also the work of her human marketers like Herrell, to make sure that the intersection of creativity, imagination, and automated execution is a felicitous one.

Creating a Balance

If an augmentation effort is going to succeed, it's incumbent upon the step-up executive to create a balance between computer-based and human skills. Computers can analyze data and make consistent, accurate decisions. Humans supply the content and process and relationships that other humans (customers and other employees) find interesting and gratifying. This balance is necessary in every field in which automated solutions are possible.

In insurance underwriting, for example, automated systems will probably make the most accurate and consistent decisions about whether to accept an insurance risk and what price to charge for it. But they can't break the news to an agent that while this particular policy is being turned down, we still want her customer's business and a few minor changes in the application might yield a different outcome. The step-up executive will ensure that both tasks are performed well.

In financial advice, it's likely that a robo-advisor will create the best mix of risk and return for an individual client. But can an automated system determine the optimal risk level for a household when a husband and wife are miles apart in their tolerances? Can it persuade a client not to buy high and sell low, and to remain calm when everyone else is panicking? It's that mix of codified investment knowledge and investor psychology that makes for a loyal, long-term client.

In marketing, which has long been the province of creative types, how do you balance that with data, analytics, and automated algorithms? As Mike Linton, chief marketing officer of Farmers Insurance, put it in an interview: "Can everything in marketing be analytical and automated? I don't think so. How to motivate customers is still something that requires a substantial creative element. You can use analytics and automation to be smarter about moving around the more creative spaces." Linton says that marketers still need unaided creative ideas, but with new analytical tools you can test them after they are created.

Those who step in need to be fully devoted to making automated systems work on a daily basis. Those who step forward need to build them. Those who step aside and those who step narrowly are trying to flee from automation—or at most using it to support their own jobs—and so they can't be counted upon to consider its potential for an organization. Only the step-up people have the knowledge and objectivity to consider what should be automated and what shouldn't, and how to combine these capabilities in a way that is both efficient and still pleasing to customers and other stakeholders.

What Those Who Step Up Look Like

You're a candidate for stepping up if . . .

- You are in a position to have some oversight over automated systems and how they are implemented within your organization;
- You are interested in technology and how it can improve your business processes;
- You're comfortable leading change initiatives and have done so successfully in the past;
- You are a "big picture" person—you see the forest more than individual trees;
- You are quantitatively oriented enough to assess performance and outputs of an automated system and process;
- You're not a programmer by any means, but you're not intimidated by computer systems and are comfortable with their application;
- You don't hesitate to intervene when something isn't working well anymore;
- Your predominant goal is not to put all humans out of work.

You can build your skills for stepping up by . . .

- Talking with vendors and users of automated systems to understand their potential;
- Consulting with others in your industry on how automated systems should perform;
- Reading widely about industry trends and developments;

- Stepping back and thinking about where your business is going;
- Developing relationships with "step in" and "step forward" practitioners;
- Getting experience with other types of technologies by championing their use in your organization.

You're likely to be found in . . .

- A senior management position within your organization;
- Organizations that take risk or invest on a broad scale;
- Information-intensive businesses and functions;
- Organizations that are progressive in the use of technology;
- Businesses or professions that are undergoing a lot of change;
- Settings where leaders and colleagues appreciate new ideas and skills.

Chapter 5

Stepping Aside

We mentioned earlier that our "step" names are great for helping us sort out the possibilities for working with machines, but they give up some descriptive perfection for the sake of parallelism. *Stepping aside* is the name we worry about most. It sounds defeatist. Stepping aside is what politicians do when they lose the nomination. It's what discredited CEOs do when their successors take charge. It's the polite, face-saving term for being tossed out.

That's an unfortunate connotation, especially for a step that is in reality centered on humanity's greatest triumphs.

When *we* talk about stepping aside, we mean letting the machines in your field take over the tasks they do best—and simultaneously choosing to base your own livelihood on forms of value that machines just cannot deliver. So stepping aside is also what a creative writer like Malcolm Gladwell is doing when he pens his bestselling books. He often describes data-rich research but he leaves the doing of it to social scientists and their computer-filled labs, allowing him to focus solely on the art of storytelling. It's what an empathic actor like Robert Downey Jr. is doing when he leaves the distracting administration of his movie-star schedule to devices in the hands of, as *Rolling Stone* magazine reports, "10 or so casually dressed young folk who are so generationally at ease" with them.[1] It's what master politician Bill Clinton is doing when he manages to rise, in the boom years of the Internet, to become leader of the free world without touching a keyboard. Charisma just doesn't come through as an email attachment.

The case we will make here is that there are enough capabilities and traits that humans still have a near-monopoly on that we don't all have to beat machines at their own game. Instead we can choose to work in domains that computers aren't particularly good at now, and are unlikely to be good at any time soon.

Many jobs already rely more on nonprogrammable skills than others—and these are the fields where many experts say the employment prospects will be brightest in the future. Our argument pushes further to say that not only will today's occupations centered on nonprogrammable strengths be the last to go, but also, many other occupations will be transformed to rely more on such strengths and will turn into happy job-hunting grounds for humans, as well. Indeed, as computers perform the parts of these jobs that are computationally difficult, different kinds of people than have traditionally held them will be able to move in and bring whole new dimensions to the quality of the work.

The Right Stuff for Humans

Most people who work in offices would rank Ricky Gervais high among the comic geniuses of our time. The creator of the original, British version of the TV series *The Office* has a sharp eye for the dynamics between coworkers and an uncanny ability to tune his portrayal of a white-collar boss to its optimal cringe-inducing frequency. Take the scene where his character, David Brent, interviews a young woman applying to be his secretary. "Tell me about yourself," he starts. But as she begins with the degrees she's completed, he interrupts: "Too boring—tell me about *yourself*." It's an awkward moment. But Gervais doubles the awkwardness by adding an oddly precise gesture as he says the word *yourself*—using his two index fingers to draw some kind of shape of the self in the air. After still worse attempts to seem the hip boss, he announces: "You've charmed me. Yeah? You've got the job. Quick decisions. [He points to his head as though these are his specialty.] I'll make it. Good. We'll cut your notice with the place you are right now. And we'll put you on a month's probation, just to see if we . . . [another inexplicable finger-pointing gesture completes, at least for him, the thought]. Yeah? Good. Good."

If it is possible to go into a cringe cramp, Gervais is the man to put you there. And this is just one pitch-perfect scene. Or maybe it doesn't come across that way to you, because you really have to see the performance to appreciate it. Either way, our point is made. It's hard to imagine a computer taking over any part of what Gervais does to earn his pay.

This is what stepping aside is: pegging your earning power to forms of value machines can't deliver, and probably never will. Note that this poses a very different question than *what work can I do without a computer?* That question was answered recently by *Off the Grid News* (which we felt a little sheepish reading online). Without claiming to be exhaustive, it listed eleven ways to make money without tapping into shared utility infrastructures like the Web[2]:

- carpentry
- painting
- remodeling
- artwork (especially high-quality artisanal work)
- beekeeping
- herbs and traditional medicines
- housecleaning
- home delivery service or driving service
- pet sitting
- babysitting
- animal care

There are a lot of interesting jobs there, but to surface even more (and more high-paying) possibilities, we're suggesting that the question be asked differently. Instead of *what work can I do without a computer?* let's ask: *What work can't be done by a computer, without me?*

Any job requiring empathy would fit that bill. Consider a recent essay by Heather Plett, an executive coach and teamwork facilitator. Plett's own work requires high empathy, so when her mother was succumbing to cancer and required a palliative care provider, she was appreciative of that nurse's skill. Reflecting on it later in an essay, she said the provider's care went beyond direct service to the patient and could be "defined by a term that's become common in some of the circles in which I work. She was holding space for us." She goes on to explain that phrase: "What does it mean to *hold space* for someone else? It means that we are willing to walk alongside another person in whatever journey they're on without judging them, making them feel inadequate, trying to fix them, or trying to impact the outcome. When we hold space for other people, we open our hearts, offer unconditional support, and let go of judgment and control."[3]

Three things stand out for us in her essay. First, the extremely valuable service Plett describes is so essentially human that it is impossible to imagine it being delivered by a machine. Second, let's admit that since none of what she is talking about can be codified, it also won't be gained by four additional years of STEM (science, technology, engineering, and math) education. Third, we're impressed that a notion like holding space is "commonly discussed" in any professional circle. We admit that coaching and facilitation, and of course hospice care, are extreme examples of situations requiring the human touch. But it is also true that empathy is valuable in any kind of work setting where one's clients, coworkers, and other stakeholders are humans. Now try to think of another kind.

Humor and empathy are just two "right brain" human capacities we would be awfully surprised to see computers excel at. As a fuller list, in the nonexhaustive spirit of *Off the Grid's*, many stepping-aside jobs will also center on knowledge work that requires creativity, courage, and conviction. Ethics, emotions, and integrity. Taste, vision, and the ability to inspire.

If anything proves that taste belongs on that list, it's the empire of domestic goddess Martha Stewart. Does she use a computer? Of course—she even built a digital media company. But no matter how helpful it might be in housing databases of recipes and gardening advice, it hardly encroaches on the strength Stewart is known for, the art of gracious entertaining. No computer can say better than she whether the hedge fund manager should be seated next to the vintner or the astronaut, and whether the menu should feature Brussels sprouts or kale. On a more modest scale, taste is the stock in trade of personal shoppers and interior designers—both rapidly growing occupations. Personal shoppers, who help people too busy or fashion-challenged to pull together their own outfits, can earn upwards of $300,000 a year. Meanwhile, employment of interior designers is projected (by the U.S. Bureau of Labor Statistics) to expand by 19 percent from 2008 to 2018, faster than most other jobs.

Before we leave the subject of taste, we shouldn't neglect to mention Steve Jobs again. It might strike you as odd that, in a book about the encroachment of computers into knowledge work, the name of Apple's iconic founder would come up in the chapter devoted to stepping aside. But note that whenever Jobs's genius is mentioned, the emphasis is on his sensibilities—his taste. No one denies he had strong technical knowledge, but according to his cofounder, Steve Wozniak, "Steve didn't ever code. He wasn't an engineer and he didn't do any original design, but he was technical enough to alter and change and add to other designs."[4] As an undergrad at Reed College, Jobs studied physics, but also literature, poetry, and calligraphy.

Jobs's genius was the judicious tweak, and his extreme success comes down to the fact that he focused his time on those points where a tweak he could make would make all the difference. We'd say this is one case example of a much broader truth: When someone is called a genius, it's rarely due to their mastery of subject matter knowledge alone. Something else is in the mix that's harder to pin down. They have some noncognitive strength going for them, and they are in a position to apply it to their work in pivotal ways.

People Draw on Multiple Intelligences

People have long thought of abstract reasoning power as defining humankind. It's what separates us from lower animals. It's the essence of our phylum's dominion over the earth.

This capacity for rational thought, so unlike lowly beasts and so seemingly godlike, has always been our pride as a species, and the aspect of our achievement we have worked hardest to hone and advance. Some psychological research has suggested that our "humaniqueness" comes down to four mental strengths that lower orders do not share: generative computation, promiscuous combination of ideas, the use of mental symbols, and abstract thought.

But we humans, in our godlike way, are now managing to create machines in that image, after our likeness. We've endowed them with tremendous power to perform difficult computations and arrive at logical answers to the most complicated questions. Now we're having to admit that they are better at that than we are.

The important thing to understand, however, is that all along we've also been relying on other mental strengths, even if we didn't respect them. As much as we like to give ourselves credit for rationality, research shows our decisions are still overwhelmingly driven by irrationality. Dan Ariely, author of *Predictably Irrational*, puts the proportion at 90 percent.[5] Some of this irrationality hurts us, and Ariely would like to save us from it by making us more aware of our human folly. But much of it is wisdom that allows us to proceed in situations where logical computation can't provide optimized answers. What if we learned to regard human irrationality not as a bug but as a feature?

There is growing evidence that humans succeed by dint of multiple intelligences. For a hundred years, since the first standardized intelligence tests were developed, our sense of mental capacity has centered on IQ. More than centered—fixated. But with Howard Gardner's publication in 1983 of *Frames of Mind: The Theory of Multiple Intelligences*, we should have all gotten the memo. The strengths measured by IQ testing are only a fraction of the intelligence humans draw on, and in which they differ. Gardner named eight forms altogether.[6] Since you may be curious, here they are:

- Linguistic intelligence (which makes some people more "word smart" than others)
- Logical-mathematical intelligence ("number/reasoning smart")
- Spatial intelligence ("picture smart")
- Bodily-kinesthetic intelligence ("body smart")
- Musical intelligence ("music smart")
- Interpersonal intelligence ("people smart")
- Intrapersonal intelligence ("self smart")
- Naturalist intelligence ("nature smart")

It probably goes without saying that these are not the kinds of smarts we typically associate with computers. Later, in the 1990s, Peter Salovey and John Mayer added nuance to Gardner's "personal" intelligences by identifying emotional intelligence, or "EQ."[7] It speaks to the strengths people have—some more than others—in perceiving emotions, under-standing them, regulating their own emotions, and generating emotional responses in others. This is soft stuff, for sure, but don't think for a second it doesn't make major calls on the human brain. Mayer explains it this way: "Our ability to engage in the highest levels of thought . . . includes rea-soning and abstracting about feelings. And that means that among those people that we refer to as warm-hearted or romantic or fuzzy—or what-ever sometimes-demeaning expressions we use—there are some who are engaging in very, very sophisticated information processing."

Stepping aside offers a strategy for more of us than stepping up does, because it allows us to fall back on strengths that are common in humans—so common that, until now, we haven't thought of them as strengths. Sometimes this will just mean doing the kind of practiced tinkering that computers lack the digital dexterity for. As Bran Ferren, former head of R&D for Disney, told the *New York Times*, "People are pretty good at figuring out, how do I wiggle the radiator in or slip the hose on? And these things are still hard for robots to do."[8] More often, the "aside" work is just as "mental" but calls on other intelligences. The financial advisor we mentioned in the first chapter who said he's becoming more of a psychiatrist than finance expert is providing real value to his clients and his employer. But his real problem is that neither he nor his company's executives have yet learned to see the value of the "psychiatry" he's providing—because it's not the form of intelligence he invested in a degree to acquire, it wasn't part of the job description, and it's a relatively unstructured activity.

For some people—and perhaps for most who excelled at the math and investment theory required to get a financial advisory license and the MBA our advisor received—these other forms of intelligence don't come naturally. And even for those who do have multiple intelligence strengths to build on, the bar will rise as these strengths more clearly become the basis of competition for good jobs. Our advisor's company doesn't train him on "behavioral finance" yet, but the good news is that at least it has hired a few experts in that domain.

Can You Really Learn "Noncognitive" Skills?

The stress we're laying here on the value of other intelligences raises an important question: Can these skills be cultivated in the same way that subject expertise can be? If we're going to hang our hats on these skills, we had better figure out how to keep honing them.

And perhaps we should first figure out why we're losing them. On a number of fronts, people seem to be slipping in the soft skills department. At the University of Michigan's Institute for Social Research, scientists study people's empathy levels on a longitudinal basis. Here's what they've found by administering standard personality tests over the decades: College kids today are about 40 percent lower in empathy than their counterparts of twenty or thirty years ago.[9] (And they're more narcissistic, as tracked by the Narcissistic Personality Inventory over the same time frame.[10]) Other social scientists worry about ethics, or the "moral sense" that Charles Darwin thought was unique to humans. It is unlikely there will ever be a rigorous longitudinal study of this, and yet the perception is widespread that many parts of the world are experiencing declines.

And then there is creativity. If you're a fan of TED Talks, perhaps you saw the one that became the most viewed of the entire TED library: Sir Ken Robinson's "How Schools Kill Creativity." In it, Robinson argues that "[w]e don't grow into creativity, we grow out of it. Or rather, we are educated out of it." Children are naturally creative, he claims, but as they grow up, "we start to educate them progressively from the waist up and then we focus on their heads, and slightly to one side." Across generations, that may be having a progressively deteriorative effect. Children are routinely assessed using the Torrance Tests of Creative Thinking—for instance, they are asked to complete partially drawn pictures and to think up alternative uses for objects such as books and tin cans. Kyung-Hee Kim, an associate professor at the College of William & Mary, has analyzed these scores over time and finds that American scores have been declining since 1990—even as its IQ scores have risen.[11]

If these studies are all capturing real phenomena, and the next generation of knowledge workers is truly less empathetic, ethical, and creative, that's a very bad thing. We're entering an era when these soft skills will be more important than ever, and for many people they will be the best hope of gaining and maintaining employment. Not only do individuals need to become convinced of this, but they also have to persuade employers and educational institutions that these types of skills are critical.

The good news is that social and emotional skills can in fact be honed. At the Yale Center for Emotional Intelligence, where Salovey and Mayer's EQ work is continued, researchers work with schools to teach students emotional intelligence and then look at outcomes in their performance and experience. Schools that adopt their RULER curriculum (explained below), they find, have students who are less anxious and depressed; manage their emotions more effectively; are better problem solvers; are rated as having greater social and leadership skills; experience fewer attention, learning, and conduct problems; and perform better academically (by 12 percent in the first year).[12]

The conviction that grown-ups, too, can be taught new tricks shows up in the training budgets of large employers. Corporate America spends an enormous amount on employee learning and leadership development— one study put it at $164.2 billion in 2012.[13] Surveys by the Association for Talent Development reveal that more than a quarter (27.6 percent in 2010) of the learning content corporations used these funds to deliver is soft skills training.

Let's assume, then, that you are going to be stepping aside in your own work—letting computers take over easily codified work and doubling down on your noncognitive strengths. First: Avail yourself of whatever training in this realm your company offers—and take the learning process seriously. Beyond that, how will you build such skills for yourself? Mainly in two ways: by learning from mentors, and by engaging in self-reflective, deliberate practice.

Ryan McDonough is, today, the general manager of the NBA's Phoenix Suns (although he's more familiar to us from the decade he spent in the Boston Celtics organization). Basketball, it might surprise you to learn, is one of the hottest areas right now for applying analytics and McDonough is known as an analytics-oriented guy. "It's changed how we scout players in the NBA," he told a reporter, "changed how we look at guys for the draft." But succeeding in his job is still very much dependent on soft skills, and McDonough picked up some of his from a legend—the late Red

Auerbach, the longtime coach and president of the Celtics, and the winningest figure in the history of U.S. professional sports. "After I got hired, I would call Red and talk basketball and pick his brain," said McDonough. "I'd get out a pen and some Celtics stationery and write it all down and try to absorb as much as I could. I was twenty-three and Red was in his mid-eighties."[14]

What was he absorbing? Scouting advice like "Look for players who're instigators, not retaliators." McDonough says Auerbach "liked guys who initiated physical play, who created an advantage physically, kind of brought the fight to the other team and lifted your team's energy and effort." And he taught McDonough to pay attention to the player's relationship with his coach. Summing it up: "Look for high-character, unselfish guys who are tough, physical, and play the right way, who care more about winning than paychecks and stats." It's interesting to note here that these keys to success are themselves traits that wouldn't show up in a player's stats—and would therefore be invisible to the analytics.

In McDonough's appreciation of the tacit knowledge he gained from mentors—he also says "working under (Celtics president of basketball operations and former player) Danny Ainge was the best thing that happened in my career"—is a lesson for anyone who wants to win by stepping aside. It also didn't hurt that his dad was sports reporter Will McDonough, whom Dan Shaughnessy of the *Boston Globe* (no slouch himself) describes as "the toughest, most street-smart and knowledgeable of all-time."[15] The first way to soak up deeply human strengths is to spend time with the humans who already have them.

But there is a second way, too, to develop soft skills like creativity, empathy, humor, and taste—and even character traits like integrity, ethics, and courage. It's deliberate, reflective practice, using some consistent framework.

We mentioned that, at the Yale Center for Emotional Intelligence, the framework is captured in the acronym RULER: They teach people to *recognize* the emotions they are feeling, and then to *understand*, *label*, *express*, and *regulate* them. This isn't the only possibility for structuring the process of honing soft skills. Another one comes from Eugene Sadler-Smith of the University of Surrey, in his research report "Using the Head and Heart at Work." He outlines five elements involved in developing soft skills: exposure, practice, feedback, reflection, and personal experience. The important thing, for the individual learner, is to adopt some framework like this that can bring discipline to the task of focusing on a strength and building it.[16]

Part of any conscious attempt to build a strength should be a defensible way of measuring progress. We suspect that one reason why "left brain" skills so dominate discussions of human intelligence is simply that they are so easily assessed and compared. The yardsticks we use to measure human achievement—our "performance metrics," to use business parlance—always push us back to believing that more hard skills training is the answer. Yet that belief constrains us to a narrow track, and the same track we have designed computers to dominate. We are limiting ourselves to running a race we have already determined we cannot win.

It might even be that our attempts to have humans keep pace with machines militate against the development of other human strengths. Psychologist David Weikart's famous longitudinal studies of early childhood education found that preschoolers in a low-income neighborhood who were subjected to direct instruction in skills like reading and arithmetic later displayed deficits in social and emotional development vis-à-vis their counterparts in the studies whose preschool education was "play based." Those schooled by direct instruction were, at age twenty-three, found to have more instances of friction with other people, and more evidence of emotional impairment. They were less likely to be married or living with their spouse, and they were far more likely to have committed a crime: 39 percent of them had already been arrested on felony charges (versus 13.5 percent of the "play" group) and 19 percent (versus 0 percent) had been cited for assault with a dangerous weapon.[17]

Why would this be the case? Developmental psychologist Peter Gray speculates: "Those in classrooms that emphasized academic performance may have developed lifelong patterns aimed at achievement, and getting ahead, which—especially in the context of poverty—could lead to friction with others and even to crime (as a misguided means of getting ahead)."[18]

As William Zinsser observed when he named "humanity and warmth" as two of the most important qualities of writing well: "Can such principles be taught? Maybe not. But most of them can be learned."[19]

The Artisanal Jobs Add Up

We've implied that this "stepping aside" category will offer a lot of jobs—but so far, we've shown you the likes of comedians and lifestyle gurus, bestselling authors and leaders of the free world. You might also have pictured the off-the-grid types like artisanal cheese makers and antique furniture restorers. And you might be wondering: How could this possibly add up to large-scale employment? We have two things to say in response.

First, you might think the work for artists and artisans is limited but in fact it is unlimited. Look at the growth of Etsy, the online marketplace for all things hand-made. As of March 2015, it had nearly 20 million active buyers considering the wares of 1.4 million sellers. On the services side, more people than at any time in history are making their living as sommeliers, magicians, and wedding planners—and as therapists, life coaches, and bereavement coordinators. The pay for these non-STEM jobs seems to be getting better, not worse. A 2011 study by the National Endowment for the Arts looked at the 2.1 million artists who make up 1.4 percent of the total U.S. workforce (eleven distinct occupations were covered: actors, announcers, architects, dancers and choreographers, designers, fine artists, art directors and animators, musicians, other entertainers, photographers, producers and directors, and writers and authors). Looking at the data from 2005 to 2009, NEA found the median salary for artists to be $43,000, higher than the $39,000 earned by the average U.S. full-time worker.[20]

Second, we're seeing a lot of jobs that have been focused on fact recall, logic, and computation and that have centered on the use of computers now moving into new territory. Much of the job content in organizations will become more EQ oriented. We expect, for example, to see a large-scale shift in this direction in teaching. Stepping aside, in other words, need not mean joining some artists' colony. It can mean bringing more art to your work.

On some level, we all recognize that teaching is as much about soft skills as formal knowledge of either subject matter or pedagogy. It's like the observation we made about geniuses: Ask anyone about their greatest teacher ever and you won't hear about the ones who knew Emily Dickinson's oeuvre by heart or could do algebra problems fastest. Teachers have most impact when they motivate and inspire, when they make learning relevant to our lives and instill in us a love of learning. (We've always loved the great teaching advice offered by Carl Buehner: "They may forget what you said—but they will never forget how you made them feel.") Now imagine that the ability to make this human connection became the first hurdle for teaching-job candidates to clear, rather than the third or fourth. It can become that, to the extent that computer augmentation helps with the direct instruction. Our broader point is that lots of jobs have required both kinds of intelligence, and unfortunately the gating factor has been the computerlike end of the spectrum. Now there will be more jobs that lay the emphasis on skills at the humanlike end, and employers will hire more for them.

Business journalist George Anders recently wrote an essay arguing that empathy would emerge as a "must have" skill by 2020; he cited its role in the work of sports coaches, nurses, and other jobs we might loosely categorize as among the "caring professions." Then, surprised by the uptake of the piece among his largely corporate readership, Anders decided to do a little research into their realm. He used a job search site called indeed. com to "go hunting for a six-figure job" and specifically queried the site for listings that paid that much while calling for qualifications such as "empathy," "good listener," "emotional intelligence," or "rapport." That small-scale search on a single day revealed more than a thousand high-paying jobs available only to high-EQ types. But it was the variety of the jobs that really surprised Anders: "Employers prizing empathy in these high-paying jobs stretch far beyond the predictable 'compassion sector' organizations such as hospitals, clinics and foundations. They also include global heavyweights in the fiercely competitive worlds of tech, finance, consulting, aerospace and pharmaceuticals." Anders goes on to cite some of the world's best-known companies in those fields.[21]

And empathy is just one noncognitive, noncodifiable skill. Knowledge workers will also be increasingly sought and rewarded for their imaginations and ability to think outside the box—their "design thinking" skills, to use the current buzz phrase. They'll be valued for their skills in storytelling, for the personal stamp they put on their product, and for their embrace of the art of their work. It must be starting to sound like we think a majority of knowledge worker "suits" can transform themselves into "creatives."

That's exactly what we do think.

Augmentation in This Step Mainly Frees People Up

David Atlas is the chief marketing officer at a startup called Persado, which is in the business of "persuasive language." The company makes software that generates marketing messages, and counts among its customers Verizon, Vodafone, American Express, Citigroup, Norwegian Cruise Lines, and Expedia. Yes, this means that email pitches, display ads, and tweets are being sent out—and are convincing people to part with their hard-earned money—without the benefit of human brainpower. Scarier still, Atlas claims he's seen the machine-made prose result in an 80 percent order-rate improvement. But he insists "it doesn't really put copywriters out of business." He says the product is "less a robot replacement and more a bionic man"—an "algorithmic prosthesis."[22]

And we're with him on this. The direct-mail-style missives Persado sends out are the equivalent of AP's college basketball recaps—the most codifiable kind of prose marketers churn out. It's easy to imagine, given the finite components involved—headlines, promotional offers, product descriptions—and the finite number of synonyms for any word, that some optimal combination could be found that would make the highest number of consumers say "yes." But copywriters "at best might write two, three, four versions and compare," Atlas points out, while Persado can test millions. So here is the question we will put to you, if you're a marketer: Do you wish you had Persado's job?

If you're the kind of person who in the past had the brains and education to compose and refine effective direct-mail pitches, you are more likely today to be involved in "content marketing"—producing blogs and op eds, commissioning proprietary research, and planning events with "thought leaders" in your sector. Or you might be penning sustainability reports, or expressing your brand's solidarity with worthy causes, or engaging various stakeholders. If software can hold down the fort on direct mail and allow you to take on these more nuanced and fulfilling assignments, we say more power to it.

This is going to be the main way that machines augment the knowledge worker who steps aside—taking away tasks that sit alongside the engaging ones—and most often it will be purely administrative chores that they remove. Artificial intelligence won't help much with the essentially human strength a person brings to his or her work, but neither will computers claim it for their own. British game developer Ed Key recently mused along these lines about how artificial intelligence might be useful to him. Bemoaning the fact that he quit a corporate job in order to work full-time on his game Proteus, only to find that "80 percent of my time was spent doing business stuff" that had nothing to do with game design, he said: "Things like creating trailers and contacting the press, tweeting the screenshots—maybe an AI agent could be helpful for that. Self-promotion is something you might delegate to a robot who is your biggest fan."[23]

But in some cases, augmentation actually will amplify some high-value, noncognitive strength—and we might say, help the human bring *more* humanity to the work. Using machines will deepen the empathy, or heighten the creativity, or refine the taste that people bring to the table.

A good example is the new capability of IBM's Watson to find novel combinations of food ingredients that add up to palatable dishes. Chefs, of course, are very creative people—and computers don't even eat. But gastronomy is also, on one level, just chemistry. Lav Varshney, a computer scientist at IBM, explains that Watson entered the world of haute cuisine when a database of already highly rated recipes was fed into it. The next step was, akin to the marketing-message software, to "remix them, substitute things, do all kinds of other modifications and generate millions of new ideas for recipes."[24] But it wouldn't be feasible to prepare all of those and foist the results onto courageous taste testers. To predict which will be the best ones, Watson tests its recipes against other criteria drawn from chemistry and psychology research into how humans respond to different flavor compounds.

So, imagine you are the hot molecular gastronomist Ferran Adrià, or some other chef whose clientele is always hungry for novelty. Are you about to be chopped? Probably not. But are you poring over Watson's output for surprisingly palatable combinations you had never thought to try? You probably should be. If nothing else, it will reinspire you with the knowledge that, despite your three stars, you haven't seen everything yet.

Truly creative types are receptive to such stimulus wherever it can be found—and increasingly it can be found in software. Renowned choreographer Merce Cunningham was an early convert. He began as early as 1989 using computer software to compose dances, and a major part of its appeal to him was the revelation of the possible. Using animated figures programmed to reflect the (sometimes stretched) physical limits of dancers, he was able to experiment with ideas liberally. In an interview with the *Los Angeles Times*, he explained: "The computer allows you to make phrases of movements, and then you can look at them and repeat them, over and over, in a way that you can't ask dancers to do because they get tired."[25] The same computer animation skills have augmented the work of movie animators at Disney/Pixar and DreamWorks, but creative and talented animators still have jobs.

Perhaps more surprisingly, artificial intelligence can also stretch the social skills humans bring to their work. In a corporate setting, customer relationship management systems are an example. By keeping a well-organized record of prior contacts and reinforcing good discipline on the selling process, these systems help free up salespeople to focus on the schmoozing that is their strong suit. But they also augment those interpersonal connection skills by compiling, over time, a larger social memory than even the greatest salesperson has. Prospects' former jobs, mutual friends, kids' activities, food allergies? They're all in there. The human salespeople can focus on how to use them artfully in conversation.

Social memory is a great realm for augmentation because it's one of those traits we value very much in humans—but that, frankly, many humans aren't that great at. Into that same category we'd put patience. If you're the most patient person in the world, we have an occupation to suggest: become a speech therapist to autistic children. The work is vital—only persistent therapy can keep autism from closing a person off to the world—but it requires the forbearance of a saint.

Or, some clinics are discovering, of a robot. David Hanson, a former Disney imagineer and now CEO of Hanson Robot, had the idea to build a cute one named Zeno, with help from Dan Popa at the University of Texas at Arlington, the Autism Treatment Center in Dallas, Texas Instruments, and National Instruments. Therapists operating Zeno from out of view use it to invite interaction in a way that does not overwhelm the child's limited social processing circuitry. Zeno can serve up the same conversational gambit in exactly the same way in each session, till it becomes understandable and nonthreatening. It never (at least in a psychological sense) burns out, or even so much as sighs in frustration. Already, this machine-augmented approach is succeeding. Children who have never spoken to their human therapists have spoken to robots.[26]

Are Deeply Human Strengths Really Unassailable by AI?

This a good point for us to pause and ask the existential question. If machines are already capable of augmenting our noncognitive strengths, are they knocking on the door of having them? And will they then surpass our abilities on these dimensions just as they have in computation? How are we so sure that humans will continue to have work to step aside to? Is life even worth living? Let's start with humor.

People love to laugh, as attested to by the enormous canon of humor and joke books. Glancing at our own bookshelves, one immediately catches the eye: *Jokes Every Man Should Know*. (It's Julia's.) It's a slim volume, because the compiler, Dan Steinberg, is being superselective, promising to dig through the pile of available material and give us only the pony. (You'll get the reference.) Setting the bar high, he leads with this:

> Two hunters are in the woods when one of them collapses. He doesn't seem to be breathing. His eyes are glazed.
> The other guy takes out his cell phone and frantically calls 911. He gasps: "My friend is dead! What can I do?"
> The operator says: "Calm down, I can help. First, let's make sure he's dead."
> There is a silence, then a gunshot is heard. Back on the phone, the guy says: "OK, now what?"

But an even slimmer volume would be the Compendium of Computer Jokes. Here, the classic entry might be this:

What's the difference between leaves and a car?
One you brush and rake, the other you rush and brake.

That one came straight from software, wholly unaided by human wit, via a branch of computer science known as computational creativity. Don't forget to tip your Wi-Fi. The source is a program created in the 1990s by the University of Aberdeen's Graeme Ritchie and Kim Binsted, called the Joke Analysis and Production Engine, or JAPE. And while you might not have gotten a belly laugh out of it, it might also set you to wondering. With Moore's law behind it, how long till it's headlining at Caesars Palace?

The incursion of machines into what has been strictly human territory is a theme that science fiction authors and filmmakers love to play with. In the 2014 film *Interstellar*, for example, the running joke of the film has the Matthew McConaughey character, an astronaut named Cooper, repeatedly adjusting the onboard robot's humor setting. TARS is capable of quips as dark as the ones Cooper favors, but in some fraught moments they aren't welcome. At one point Cooper dials the setting down to a very low level. The next utterance from TARS is, you guessed it, a pun. Other films take the notion of computers moving into emotional territory more seriously. In Steven Spielberg's *AI*, the focus is on love, and we're left with a provocative paradox. The only being capable of endless devotion is the programmed one. In *Surrogates*, humans no longer have a lock on physical beauty. To put one's best face forward is to send a robot out on one's behalf.

In real life, computational creativity really is trying to encroach on realms we might consider sacred to humans, and work we could never imagine to be soulless. Take art. In the case of the Painting Fool, created by computer scientist Simon Colton, the machine not only generates portraits but does so according to its self-assigned mood—and later reflects on whether it has produced something that conveys that mood. On the receiving end, the successful commercial software Flickr has for some time used machine learning to identify and serve up images it finds on the Web. At a recent conference, Flickr developer Simon Osindero said the technology is now moving beyond simply identifying that an image fits a user's search term and is capable of subjective judgment. It allows the company, he said, "to build a model that estimates the perceived beauty of an image."[27]

Computers also generate original music. Our favorite example might be the procedural music generator created by two graduate students that uses PDFs of academic papers as inputs and, based on their text, creates not only lyrics but also a melody well matched to their tone. It's called the Scientific Music Generator, or SMUG.

Or take creative writing. Prose-generating software may be, for now, very limited. Beyond the "persuasive language" of marketing, it is being used to churn out simple news stories, as we've discussed. In 2014 the Associated Press announced that "the majority of U.S. corporate earnings stories for our business news report will eventually be produced using automation technology."[28] But computer scientists are working to make machines into better writers, even capable of good fiction.

Mark Riedl, an associate professor at the Georgia Institute of Technology, has led the development of Scheherazade, a program that generates short stories by drawing on previous accounts written by people about real-life situations. Meanwhile, the premise of a story can be generated by something called the What-If Machine, or WHIM. (We get the sense people in the AI community are all aware of the system recently invented by two Italian AI scholars to produce humorous acronyms.) WHIM analyzes vast quantities of prose to be able to posit the unlikely. "What if there was a little whale who forgot how to swim?" is one thought-starter it came up with. We've heard worse ideas for a children's book.

Tony Veale, one of the pioneers in computational creativity, likes to distinguish between strong and weak forms of it. Weak computational creativity systems, he says, produce outputs that they themselves cannot appreciate as creative. The human user must filter and classify the system's outputs for it. Strong systems not only produce novel and useful outputs, but critique, rank, and filter their own outputs to select only the very best. Computational creativity is a young field, but already its strong forms are developing, and the writing is on the wall. Output from machines will be increasingly indistinguishable from human output. But that's a long way off—and even then, it may not mean we will pay anything for machine-painted pictures, or want to curl up with machine-written stories, or laugh at machine-told jokes. As Geoff Colvin argues in his book *Humans Are Underrated*, we may well value human-generated content simply because it is human.[29]

When Value Depends on Human Involvement

In an article called "The Prose of the Machines," *Slate*'s senior tech writer Will Oremus tries to provide some reassurance by pointing to what good human writers do so well. "We're good at telling stories. We're good at picking out interesting anecdotes and drawing analogies and connections. We're good at framing information: We can squint at the amorphous cloud of information that surrounds a news event and discern a familiar form. And we have an intuitive sense of what our fellow humans will find relevant and interesting." But the next paragraph gives the lie to his confidence. "In theory," he admits, "well-designed software programs could acquire such soft skills with enough data, development, training, and processing power."[30]

A better question to ask than *what goes into the making of good prose?* might be, *what do readers get out of it?*

We mentioned that filmmakers like to explore these ideas. Alex Garland's original script for *Ex Machina*, one of the more recent entries (at this writing) in the robot-run-amok film category, puts a question on the table about art. The reclusive AI scientist who sets its plot in motion reveals in one scene that he owns a Jackson Pollock painting—or maybe he doesn't. He programmed a painting robot to replicate exactly the Pollock he had purchased and then, with the two indistinguishable, randomly chose one and had it destroyed.

The horror of that moment—you mean you might have destroyed the real Pollock?—is the key to the point we think Garland wanted to make. There is somehow a difference in how we feel looking at the work the artist actually touched versus a reproduction of it, no matter how faithful. It matters to us that it came from a human hand and is an authentic product of the human condition. If you've ever visited Lascaux II in south-western France—the scale reproduction of the cave complex where the world's most famous cave art was discovered—you know this. No question, the copy is impressive as a technical feat, and is a brilliant solution for saving the real site from further destruction. Yet to stand in it is to profoundly miss the sense of wonder that comes with standing where ancients also did.

This is why computational creativity shouldn't scare us, even when things reach the point—as they have—that machines are mounting their own gallery shows. Christie's and Sotheby's have little to fear.

It isn't only in the arts that people will continue to put a premium on work that is done conscientiously—that is to say, with a consciousness. That's the truth behind most of those hand-made soap sales transacted on Etsy. It's the reason fly fishermen will pay thousands for a bamboo rod crafted by Glenn Brackett or one of his "boo boy" colleagues at Sweetgrass Rods. It's the reason that, no matter how good Watson gets in the kitchen, we'll still prefer dishes served up by chefs who can savor the food themselves, and who take joy in seeing that we do.

Augmentation Will Boost These Strengths More than Automation Has

Before we move on to our next possible move, "stepping in," we want to make a particular point about automation versus augmentation in the stepping aside realm. Automation has always taken what it could off people's plates. The point has not been to make you, the worker, more capable but to need less of you. The prevailing mind-set of automation says we should look at what humans do today that computers could do more cheaply, better, more quickly.

Because computers have just one kind of intelligence, this has meant that they have been introduced into processes that are all about applying that kind of intelligence. As George Mason University professor Phil Auerswald observes, "The fact that digital computers are able to outperform humans in performing mental tasks thus should come as no surprise: they were designed to do just that."[31] Thus we see rampant computerization in the workplaces of actuaries and digital marketers. Walk into some other workplaces, however, and there is scarcely a computer to be found. Workers who rely on human strengths beyond computation have been left to scrape by with their Bronze Age tools.

As the world shifts to an augmentation mind-set, however, we'll see machine developers deliberately looking for ways to help humans perform their most human and most valuable work better. The academic work we've been describing in this chapter, designed to apply AI to creative endeavors, will be matched by growing interest and investment on the commercial side. Those of us who want our human strengths—our creativity, empathy, humor, and curiosity—to take us further and faster will get our own wheels for the mind.

What Those Who Step Aside Look Like

You're a candidate for stepping aside if . . .

- You have some prominent noncognitive, noncomputational strengths—empathy, humor, creativity, etc.;
- You are either extremely good at working with people, or very creative and productive when working alone;
- You are already making a good living at your profession or job;
- You've never felt that your job would soon be taken over by a computer or robot;
- You have never read that key tasks in your job have been outsourced or computerized;
- You can say with honesty that you rarely do the same thing every day;
- You would have difficulty even writing down or describing for someone else how you do your job.

You can build your skills for stepping aside by . . .

- Choosing a college major or courses that don't involve programmable skills;

- Learning new artisanal skills to add to your portfolio;
- Cultivating a unique, idiosyncratic perspective on what you do for a living;
- Adding human-derived and interesting content to everything you do;
- Thinking carefully about how technology can support (but not automate) your unique skills;
- Abandoning aspects of your job that can be done by a computer;
- Leaving your boring, repetitive job and going out on your own.

You're likely to be found in . . .

- A sole proprietor (you) or small business, or small niche within a large organization;
- A human services organization;
- Organizations that are not aggressive users of technology;
- Businesses or professions that are doing the same thing they have done for decades;
- Settings where adoption of technology is slow—for a good reason.

6

Stepping In

Have you ever aspired to be a "purple person"? That's how one insurance organization, XL Catlin, describes those who step in at the intersection of business and automated decision technologies. Jim Wilson, the lead data engineer at the company, was chatting with his boss, Kimberly Holmes, about the people issues the company's "Strategic Analytics" group faced every day. Holmes describes the situation: "The business people, the actuaries, know what data they need and can define requirements, but don't have the skill set to design a data architecture that gives them the data they need. Technology people don't understand the business requirements, but they can design the data architectures." Wilson used a colorful analogy to describe this particular problem: "It's like the people in IT speak blue, the people in business speak red, but we need people who speak purple."

The name stuck at XL, so Holmes seeks "purple people" to translate the needs of the business for analytical and automated systems into the high-level designs for those systems. Other people may actually develop the models and write the code, but the systems couldn't exist without those who speak purple.

In this book we'll refer to them as people who "step in" and help to create, monitor, and modify automated systems within organizations. They're at the core of the augmentation idea and bridge the business and organizational requirements for automated systems with the capabilities of technology. They're not intimidated by automated systems and are willing to jump into the "belly of the beast" and do whatever is necessary to make them work. They're capable in technology, but in most cases their focus is on making it useful in a business or organizational context.

In this chapter we'll explore a variety of issues involved in stepping in. We'll argue that although it sounds like a new idea, it's actually been going on with previous generations of technology. We'll explore a couple of different types of people who step in, and then describe what all of them seem to have in common. We'll conclude with some of the attributes that help people succeed in the step-in role. Along the way we'll introduce you to some good examples of people who have successfully stepped into automated systems in their work, including:

- Shane Herrell, digital marketer at SAS Institute;
- Mike Krans, an expert in insurance underwriting automation;
- Andy Zimmermann, a teacher in the New York City schools;
- Alex Hafez and Ralph Losey, who have stepped into legal automation in a couple of different ways;
- Dr. Doris Day, an example of stepping in with regard to health-care (dermatology) automation;
- Edward Nadel, who monitors risk for Internet startup Circle;
- Travis Torrence, an intermodal dispatch analyst at the trucking firm Schneider National.

Stepping In Has Taken Place Before

There have probably always been people who bridged technical and business environments. As long as there have been complex technologies, there have been people who "stepped in" to understand them and to help apply them to solving business and organizational problems. In the industrial revolution, mechanics and technicians invented or improved industrial machinery to make textile mills more effective.

For example, Paul Moody, a weaver and mechanic who worked in the Massachusetts textile industry in the early nineteenth century, had no compunctions about stepping into that form of technology. He co-invented the power loom, invented the filling frame, improved the "double speeder," and improved upon the mechanism for powering the machinery.

Instead of having his weaving skills be automated by these machines, he invented and optimized new technical capabilities. His industrialist boss, Francis Cabot Lowell, got most of the credit (and had a mill town in Massachusetts named after him), but it was Paul Moody who made these new approaches to work successful.[1]

Professor James Bessen of Boston University notes in his book *Learning by Doing* that progress in the textile industry of the time—the Silicon Valley of its day—was not just a function of new, more automated textile technologies. To make those technologies hum, a cadre of experienced people had to emerge. These people—of which Paul Moody was certainly one—made the technologies work in context.[2]

Bessen cites an account by Henry Lyman, a successful cotton manufacturer from Rhode Island, of the early use of the power loom and other textile machinery in New England. An unnamed weaver steps in and saves the day: "[T]he company had no one, at first, to start the machinery; they began to grow discouraged. The warper worked badly, the dresser worse, and the loom would not run at all. In this dilemma an intelligent though intemperate Englishman, by trade a hand weaver, came to see the machinery. After observing the miserable operation, he said the fault was not in the machinery, and he thought he could make it work; he was employed. Discouragement ceased; it was an experiment no longer. Manufacturers from all directions came to see the wonder."[3]

It is certainly true that similar step-in roles were necessary with other new technologies. When we studied the difficult and expensive implementations of large, complex enterprise systems (from vendors like SAP and Oracle), many organizations sang the praises of "power users" who could connect business requirements and technological capabilities.[4] They were the "purple people" of their generation, and companies of all stripes tried to "see the wonder" by employing such individuals.

Today, those who step in work not with textile machinery, but with systems and analytics that make automated decisions. In order to do that, they still have to function at the intersection of the technology and the business needs that the technology addresses. Stepping in means that these people must understand not only the technology, but also the business process into which the technology fits. Like their predecessors, these people have to be "purple," speaking the language of both business and technology, and serving as a translator between those worlds. Also like their predecessors, they'll be in great demand, and everyone will want to "see the wonder" of their works.

Stepping Into Automation Technologies

Even with automated systems, stepping in has been going on for a while. We (Tom, to be specific) encountered our first step-in person for automation technologies about a decade ago. Mike Krans was then working for Accenture and had the job of helping insurance companies implement automated underwriting systems. This was one of the first areas of broad automation in business. By the time we encountered him, Krans had already been working with such systems for a decade, and had helped install them across many of the largest insurers in the United States.

While working for Accenture, Krans fell between the "step in" and "step forward" categories. He had a computer science and artificial intelligence background in college, and he actually wrote some rule-based programs for underwriting and claims. But his primary focus has been not on writing automation programs but on tailoring them to fit the needs of particular companies. After doing this at Accenture for many years, he shifted to "step up" managerial roles (for which we briefly mentioned him in Chapter 5) at insurance companies like Travelers and Hanover. He's currently the chief information officer for personal lines insurance at Hanover.

Krans's primary focus in working with these systems has been, in a sense, to broaden the community of step-in people. The goal of his automated system implementations was to bring light into the "black box" of artificial intelligence—to make the decision rules transparent and interpretable enough so that business users could monitor and update them. Some of the systems he worked with could end up having a couple of thousand rules, but his goal was always to make them as easily understood as possible.

Krans also worked with underwriters and actuaries to help them find out which rules were working and which ones needed to be modified. After the rules were put into the system, he would help them create and analyze a series of reports generated off a data warehouse. They showed the profitability of the business unit over time, and how it varied based on the specific rules "fired" in a particular case. They could even tie specific rules eventually to the insurance claims paid in that case and the premiums charged. There was a complex division of labor here: Software vendors supplied the rules engines, underwriters supplied the rules, and Krans and his colleagues mediated between them to implement and optimize the entire system. He said that there were not only rules to address and modify, but also aspects of the business process by which the underwriting or claims processes were accomplished.

As Krans reflects on his work today, he says there are several factors that made him successful. One is an insatiable desire to learn. He didn't know much about the technologies he had to work with in insurance automation when he began his career, and he did everything possible to learn about them. After he more or less mastered the technology, he began to master the business side of underwriting. Working with companies on inputting thousands of rules about the field does tend to make you an expert. Krans figures that he probably could have been an underwriter after seeing all these rules.

Another factor is being at the intersection of business and technology. He is the prototypical purple person in that regard. He has always used technology and business in his roles. His last job at Travelers was on the business side, and now he's back in a technology position at Hanover as a CIO.

Krans also mentioned other factors, such as a personal fascination with technology (other people buy personal computers—he builds them), the ability to work closely with vendors, and keeping up with technology and how it's used in insurance even as he moved up the managerial ladder. "I always wanted to be able to add value and insight to the projects I oversaw," he said.

What Those Who Step In Are and Are Not

People who step into automated decision-making are, we suppose, the closest that humans get to smart machines. They may not have created them, but they understand, work with, and collaborate with them. They may have previously done a similar knowledge work job to the smart machine and have been "promoted" to work with it. In that sense, they both augment and are augmented by smart machines. Augmentation has made them and their organizations much more productive. Their role involves both identifying situations for which the machine isn't well suited, and helping it to deliver even greater productivity advances over time.

In fact, the most common automation scenario we've seen is that those who step in are among those left standing when many jobs were being replaced by technology. Let's look back at insurance underwriting for just a moment (we promise this is one of the last times). Perhaps, for example, there were once one hundred people doing underwriting. Ten of those underwriters are identified as experts. An automated system is implemented and the ten experts are retained in underwriting. Their role is to step in with the automated system. This might mean:

- Supplying their knowledge of underwriting situations to the machine;
- Dealing with the toughest, most important underwriting cases—those over a certain dollar amount, or those for which key information is missing;
- Monitoring the performance of the underwriting system;
- Knowing when the system needs to be updated or revised, and supplying expertise for that as well.

How do these ten feel about the change? Well, we suspect that they may miss some of their colleagues. And some may feel that the computer doesn't make decisions as well as they did (but they are probably wrong about that—humans are known for their overconfidence in decision-making). But the automation of the process also has considerable benefits for them. First, their status as experts is recognized. Second, they get to work on the cases that really require their expertise, rather than the typical, boring policy applications that once took a lot of their time. They get exposed to the leading edge of technology and insurance. And perhaps most important, they still have jobs.

But like anyone else, those who step in have no guarantee of continued employment. The fact that computer "clones" have taken over the routine aspects of their jobs frees them to do more interesting work, but it also obligates them to work hard to find new sources of their own value. One key source is to help the computers get better at their roles. Those who step in should use every available brain cell to move the augmented process forward—to make it faster, cheaper, and more accurate in its decision-making. This is the key responsibility of the step-in role.

We've defined what those who step in do. What do they not do, and how does this role relate to the other ones we describe in this book?

- They are not the bosses who decide what should be automated and what shouldn't. That's a "step-up" role for the most part. Those who step in are doers. Instead of managing other people who do the work, they can be viewed as doing their jobs while managing the computers that do the work.
- They are not the programmers who develop the systems—that's a "step-forward" role. The step-in role incumbents may well help to configure and tune the system, but they don't spend the bulk of their days writing code.
- They are not the researchers who decide whether the systems can be built successfully or not. The step-in role is a practitioner role. It involves using automated systems in day-to-day work.

Of course, there is often some overlap between the step-in role and others we discuss in different chapters (as we saw with Lisa Tourville in Chapter 2). Some managers may combine step-up and step-in responsibilities. Some may be capable of building systems, and do so occasionally. And some may also do a bit of research on automated systems. In health care, for example, we've found that the doctors most likely to step in are based in academic medical centers. They have often conducted clinical trials using automated systems before using them routinely in their practices.

Dr. Doris Day (not the actress but actually a dermatologist in New York City) is a good example of this phenomenon. She was one of the earliest in her field to adopt Melafind, an automated tool for looking at skin lesions and determining their likelihood of being cancerous. The device projects several different wavelengths of light into the skin, allowing a look below the surface. The diagnostic tool gives her comfort in assessing lesions that are not clearly cancerous, and not clearly benign, either—those that she has some level of suspicion about. As a result far fewer biopsies are necessary. A classification of low likelihood of cancer is also comforting to patients. Dr. Day uses the tool in her daily practice with patients, but also conducted a clinical trial of the device in her work with NYU Langone Medical Center.[5]

What Value Do Step-In People Provide?

At the simplest level, people who step in make automated systems work. They may help to configure a system during initial implementation. They will observe its initial decisions and see if they are good ones. They will develop ways to measure the ongoing performance of the system to see if it continues to decide wisely and well. And when the system needs to be changed, they will modify it. They may or may not have other jobs than watching over these systems (many also handle cases or decisions that are too big or complex for the automated system), but they more than likely once made the decisions that the computer makes today.

They may do their work in a variety of different contexts. Some, like Mike Krans, consult within or to organizations on how automated systems should be implemented and tailored. Such systems are rarely ready to use "out of the box" from a vendor. Since every organization makes decisions differently, the specific rules or algorithms that the organization wants to use need to be put into the system.

And those decision criteria—particularly if this is the first use of an automated system—are unlikely to be sitting there handy on a piece of paper in a file drawer. Instead they're in the minds of experts. Extracting and formalizing them is no easy task. People who did this work in the early days of expert systems were called "knowledge engineers," and it's still an important component of the step-in role. They may be the experts themselves, or they may facilitate the process by which expertise is sucked out (delicately and diplomatically, we hope) of human brains and put into machines. Only people who understand something of the domain to be automated, as well as how the automation software works, are likely to be able to perform it.

Since those who step in are the liaisons between the system and the business, they may also teach the people who work with the system how it works and when interventions may be necessary. One of the step-in exemplars we interviewed was Andy Zimmermann, who teaches math and science in a public middle school in Brooklyn. He told us, "You get the feeling that much of the educational software wasn't designed by teachers," so someone who understands the software will probably need to do some instruction of those who don't. It's not just a matter of communicating technical detail, but also inspiring enthusiasm for software that can make a knowledge worker's job easier. Of course, communicating enthusiasm for software that replaces knowledge workers is somewhat more difficult and touchy.

Step-in practitioners are often the public face of automated systems. Most systems don't explain or interpret their decisions very clearly, so that often falls to humans. In insurance underwriting, for example, the underwriters who step in often take on the responsibility of communicating with insurance agents—or at least communicating with the communicators—about the technical reasons why a policy was accepted or turned down (mostly the latter—apparently when people get what they want, they don't want explanations as often).

Kevin Kelley, who heads the Predictive Analytics department for a large specialty property and casualty insurer, told us that it's important to tell a story that agents can understand, even though the model that made the decision may be very complex. He notes, "Our company's underwriters are professionals, and they need to have more information so they can effectively communicate decisions with the production team. The reasons provided need to be such that they can explain their position, especially if the message is negative. They cannot just reference a 'black box.'" Kelley said that his employer's agents are independent, and can take their business to a variety of companies. So he said that underwriters communicate with agents directly about the results of an underwriting decision and will try to put a more positive spin on it. Kelley notes, "If they have to turn down a policy application, they can say, 'You'll be most successful if you bring us this kind of business.' Or they might say, 'We turned down this business, but overall we accept eighty-five percent of the applications you bring us.'"

While Kelley's company's models are increasingly automated, no current automation approach can identify all the positive aspects and success patterns in an agent relationship. It's only the human underwriters who can play that role. Kelley notes, "It's not just the best math in the model, but how do you get the information out there to those who are affected by it."

Some of those who step in may also prevent problems of various types—poor system design, a malfunction, or malicious hacking of a system. To know when a system is working well is also to know when it's not working well. An accomplished tender of an automated system can see when results are not within expected limits.

Stepper-inners may also work closely with vendors as part of their jobs. Several we interviewed said they spent a good part of their time in that role. Shane Herrell, the Global Search Program manager at the software company SAS, works with (using them, not developing them) digital marketing automation programs extensively in his job. He said that he spends a lot of time working with automation software vendors. He described the challenge of working with the mind-boggling number of marketing and "ad tech" vendors: "I try to review a lot of their capabilities, but when I think they have some promising capabilities, the evaluation really begins. I 'open up the hood' of their software and try to figure out what functionality they have and how it can align to our marketing and technology goals. Sometimes it takes up to six months to fully evaluate new software. I also participate on the customer advisory boards of some vendors. . . . If I find out something useful I can spread the word globally to all SAS marketers. At the end of the day, it's my job to figure out how the technology can help us be better marketers and improve the customer experience."

Andy Zimmermann, the New York City schoolteacher, said he also spends a lot of time with vendors. "A lot of the software is pretty new," he says, "and the vendors haven't tested it with students much. I tell them what it's like when their software is being used by a roomful of seventh graders." That's a sobering thought for any provider.

An obvious career alternative for these people who have stepped into automation technology is to go to work for the vendors of such technology. Those who actually build new software would generally fall into the "step-forward" category (see Chapter 9), but there are opportunities for consulting to and supporting customers that step-in types would probably excel at. Zimmermann said that he'd consider working for a vendor at some point; he noted that having a former teacher who has used software extensively would probably be a good thing for many vendors.

Shane Herrell at SAS said he's considered going to work for a vendor, but he likes being able to work with a variety of different vendors' tools now, as opposed to only one if he were employed by a vendor. He's been complimented by several vendors on his well-thought-out feedback on features and usability that ultimately leads to an improvement to the vendor's platform. Indeed, giving a lot of feedback on how software actually works within an organization is extremely important for a vendor.

Finally, those who step in are also integrators of various types of automation technology. Given that artificial intelligence is inherently narrow today—each program does only a single decision or automation task—these automation experts will have to work across a variety of tools and content sources.

Zimmermann provides an example of using a broad tool kit. His Brooklyn school is one of the early adopters of "School of One," an automated "adaptive learning" tool. It determines what students know on a particular topic, offers them relevant educational content, and assesses whether they have learned it. It's an amazing tool that treats every student individually. However, it's not necessarily enough in itself to meet some of the more nuanced and complex needs of the classroom teacher. Zimmermann works with his colleagues (he teaches in a group of six) to evaluate and adopt new technologies for specific purposes. They include an alternative adaptive learning platform from Khan Academy (Khan content is also included on the School of One platform), Class Dojo for student behavior management, Google Classroom for student collaboration tools, Socrative for rapid student polling, and Plickers for rapid student assessment without tablets or PCs.

Shane Herrell, the digital marketer at SAS, also plays the integration role across multiple automation tools. He works across a variety of digital channels—display ads, video, search, social media, etc. Herrell finds it stimulating to work across channels, but each channel has its own automation approach and tool set. Display ads use "programmatic buying." For video ads, Herrell uses Google's YouTube advertising platform. He uses another platform for automation tracking and reporting of search engine optimization (SEO). He uses another set of tools for search ads that work across Google, Bing, and Yahoo. In addition to these channel-specific automation tools, he also uses a cross-channel platform that supports "report automation, automated URL handling, bulk editing, day parting, scheduled actions and bidding capabilities" (according to the vendor's website). In short, integration might as well be Herrell's middle name.

Were You Born to Step In?

Some people seem born to step in; others have to make a conscious change in career direction. If you were born to the role, you've probably been working with some form of IT for a long time. You may have been interested in technology while in school, and perhaps gravitated toward a career of working with it. When automation technologies came along, you were already there, ready to step in and help your organization deal with it.

Ralph Losey is one of those people. He's a senior partner at Jackson Lewis P.C., a large national labor and employment law firm. Losey became a lawyer in 1980, when computerized legal research was just beginning. He immediately gravitated toward it—he'd been a computer hobbyist and gamer for several years before he completed law school—and could help his case teams find any law or document it needed. He became a commercial litigator, but he always dabbled in computerized legal research.

The automation technology "e-discovery"—remember, it automatically sorts through millions of documents to determine which ones are relevant to a legal case—came along at about the turn of the twenty-first century. Losey was ready, of course. He began to specialize in it, and eventually abandoned commercial litigation for a full-time e-discovery focus as a senior litigator. He helps both clients and other lawyers plan and interpret results from e-discovery projects, which are primarily used to determine what documents should be read or turned over to the other side in a case. He goes well beyond that, however, developing case strategies based on e-discovery outcomes. In addition to serving clients and his firm on these topics, he also writes a blog,[6] has taught e-discovery at a law school (where such courses are still relatively rare), and is widely viewed as a leader in the e-discovery field. We're sure that whatever other automation technologies come along in the legal field, Losey will be on top of them at an early stage.

The other alternative—a career transformation toward automation technologies—is represented in the same e-discovery field by Alex Hafez. Hafez is still early in his career, but he's become well ensconced as an e-discovery senior practitioner. Hafez told us that he was also always a bit of a "gadget-head" and employed a lot of technology in his personal life. But he didn't apply technology to his legal career early on. He attended what he calls a "second tier" law school, and didn't study e-discovery there. But he quickly got a job as an intellectual property lawyer at a mainstream firm on the highly paid partnership track. Unfortunately his career in "big law" was derailed by the financial crisis, and he was laid off from the law firm.

What to do next? Hafez took a commonly used legal career strategy, going into "contract document review." This is when humans look through lots of documents (emails, memos, and so forth), most of them scanned into computers, to determine whether they are relevant to a case. It's labor intensive, but since it pays $30 an hour versus the $300 an hour charged by large law firms, it's a relative bargain for commercial litigation firms.

Hafez worked his tail off as a contract document reviewer and made a pretty good living at it. But he had two problems with the job. One, it was pretty mind-numbing; his brain was only saved by the audiobook novels he listened to while at work. Two, he questioned whether contract document review had much of a future. He'd heard about e-discovery software and wondered if it might eventually put him out of a job.

So Hafez decided to take action before the machines fully took over. He set out to remake himself as an e-discovery expert, undertaking a series of educational activities:

- He gave up audiobook novels and started listening to podcasts about e-discovery at work;
- He read *eDiscovery for Dummies* (yes, there is such a tome);
- He forked over $3,000 to attend the weeklong "Georgetown eDiscovery Training Academy" (while also giving up $2,000 in weekly earnings);
- He took a two-day program to qualify as an administrator of an e-discovery software vendor's program, which he found "boring" but "incredibly informative";
- He hired a resume consultant to spiff up his on-paper credentials, and signed on with an e-discovery recruiting service.

This story does have a happy ending. Hafez got a permanent job as Senior eDiscovery Project Manager for a large vendor in the field. He steps into large e-discovery projects, adjusting and configuring the system to find the right mix of documents. He can string together complex Boolean search strings, and can recommend more sophisticated analytics and "predictive coding" software for a higher level of automation. Like many of the others who step in, he tries out and integrates a variety of different software tools, and works closely with vendors.

Alex Hafez's story suggests that augmentation is a viable prospect for anyone willing to put in the time and effort to master a new, automation-driven field. The needed knowledge is out there; it just takes considerable initiative to master it.

It's also important to point out that Hafez didn't have to take a couple of years to go back to school. He was able to add to his existing law school background with a specialized course or two and some autodidactic reading. He also got a lot of learning on the job. Rather than a massive retraining program to create more people who can step into augmentation roles, we think this sort of "educational bricolage" ("construction or creation from a diverse range of available things") will be the most common approach.

In addition to this organic-versus-transformed distinction, there are some other ways in which those who step in differ from each other. Some are more technical in their backgrounds, others more business focused. Some work from inside a company, others work from consulting firms or vendors. Some actually do the work of monitoring and overseeing automated systems, while others manage people who perform that work. Since "stepping into automated systems" is not a recognized job category in most organizations, it's not surprising that there would be some variation in the kinds of people performing the role.

What Those Who Step In Have in Common

Despite some differences in these step-in people, they have several key attributes in common. First of all, most of their work is driven not by formal job assignments, but by passion and commitment. Again, since the role of stepping in doesn't exist on an organization chart yet, those who play it usually have other formal responsibilities. Their jobs are to teach, to see and treat patients, or to serve clients. There are some exceptions—Ralph Losey's work with his law firm evolved to focus almost exclusively on working with e-discovery tools and strategies—but even he worked for many years on the basis of his passion.

So we hope it's clear that those who step in have passion and commitment, but about what, specifically? One attribute they share is a passion for learning, and the willingness and ability to seek the learning out. Since most established educational programs in schools and colleges don't really address automated solutions yet, these people have been largely self-directed educationally. They have a strong motivation to learn, but they don't expect the learning to be spoon-fed. There is no master's in automated solutions yet, no law degree with an e-discovery concentration. It's hard at most universities to find a single course on such topics. As Alex Hafez's career transformation suggests, it is certainly possible to find educational resources to prepare for jobs and careers involving stepping in, but they are not neatly packaged at this point. Those who step in will have to configure and piece together the knowledge and training that they need to do their jobs. And as we pointed out in the last section, much of their learning will be on the job itself.

One focus is information technology. Everyone we interviewed had a clear passion for learning about new technologies and applying them to their jobs and organizations. In many cases, they were also passionate about using technology in their day-to-day lives. E-discovery attorney Ralph Losey is an ardent player (and even creator) of video games. Alex Hafez calls himself a "gadgethead." Shane Herrell, the digital marketer at SAS, said, "At heart I am a technology geek." Fortunately, at this particular point in history there are many people who exhibit this level of passion for technology, so we should have many future candidates for stepping in.

It's also important not to be intimidated by automation or analytics. Those who step in don't typically build entire systems, but they need to be conversant with how they work, and they may sometimes modify the systems they use. This doesn't require a degree in physics or math—only a desire to get to the bottom of things. Edward Nadel, for example, is a recent college graduate who works as a risk lead for the Internet startup Circle, which lets consumers easily transfer money to each other (he previously had a similar job at another Internet startup, Square—and looks forward to a job at Triangle). His job is to monitor the recommendations of automated risk management systems and decide whether a suspicious transfer should be approved or not. Nadel didn't build the automated systems that Circle uses to monitor risk, but he knows the factors they use in scoring a transaction. If he thinks he sees a pattern of false negative or positive scores, he'll do some quick analysis (typically using the query language SQL) of the data to determine what's going on. Then he'll discuss it with the company's data science team, which builds and modifies the systems. To do that he's had to learn the language with which the team and the company describes risk data and risk management systems.

Nadel is not a math or statistics geek; he majored in history and legal studies in college. But he feels the desire he had to get to the truth of an historical event drives his desire to understand what's going on with a risk transaction. It's an important role, because—like many other step-in practitioners—he's the interface between the automated systems and customers. No customer likes to have a transaction denied, so Nadel is diligent in trying to get to the right answer, and skeptical that the computer is always right. If he were intimidated by technology or automated answers, he wouldn't be successful in his role.

A related technology-oriented passion, however, is for application of systems in a business or organizational context. These people don't just geek out—they spend their time and energy thinking about how to use technology to educate kids, solve clients' legal problems, or get more potential customers to see digital ads. Remember, "purple people" are purple because of their mixture of blue (technology) and red (business) interests. Or maybe the colors are the other way around, but in any case it's a mixture.

A good example of this combination can be found at Schneider National, one of North America's largest truckload, logistics, and intermodal services providers. It's a complex business, moving close to 18,000 daily loads, utilizing more than 13,000 drivers and 50,000 trailers/containers. To manage and optimize this complexity, Schneider has been implementing various forms of analytical decision-making for a couple of decades. The analytics are increasingly automated as well, from guiding order-acceptance decisions to recommending optimal appointment times to automatically matching loads with drivers. Each hour, Schneider's planning systems evaluate millions of potential driver tours over a multiday horizon.

One person who has stepped into such systems at Schneider is Travis Torrence. He's an Atlanta-based "Intermodal Dispatch Analyst" at Schneider and has had the job for a couple of years. During his time, Schneider introduced a new version of its dispatch optimization system, Short Haul Optimizer (SHO), which matches container loads to available drivers. It's Torrence's job to work with the SHO system to dispatch the markets he manages. He is also required to monitor its capabilities and encouraged to recommend ideas to the operations research group that works on improving the SHO algorithms. Stepping in like this is well within his capabilities, however; he has a degree in business with a focus on logistics and information systems.

So does Torrence just sit back and watch the machine work? Hardly. While it has definitely made him more productive in his job—he can dispatch about seventy-five drivers a day using the systems, which is about double what he could do previously—there are numerous tasks that still require a smart human.

One of the biggest issues is ensuring data quality for the information in the system. The optimization system usually comes up with great results, but it requires correct data about when drivers are actually available, how much time they have to drive, when trains are actually arriving, ramp congestion, and so forth. There are systems for all of these bits of information, but reality is sometimes different from what the system says it is.

On a typical day, for example, Torrence might start by taking a look at what the SHO system is recommending for the day. He would then check the quality and currency of the data, particularly with regard to the drivers. He might contact some drivers to nudge them into adjusting their available times in order to make for a better fit with available loads. He might contact customer service to see if there is any customer flexibility on delivery windows. He might monitor traffic information and weather to see if driving times are reasonable. He might examine the total set of loads going out to see if congestion at the ramp will be a problem.

Travis Torrence had his job before the new SHO system was put in place and it's been a dramatic change in his role. Even though some key decisions—at least the initial cuts at them—are made by the system, he says the job is definitely more interesting than it was before SHO was implemented. "You're not bogged down in covering one load," he commented. "It gives me an opportunity to explore other areas of the process, and to learn more about how the data is coming in and make it more accurate. Since I'm not looking at every single load anymore, I can focus on the bigger picture now."

As with Torrence's job at Schneider, even though automated systems are automated—supposedly working without human intervention—humans are still involved in almost every case of such systems. Automated radiology systems exist, but so do radiologists. Legal automation is progressing apace, but there are still (perhaps too many) lawyers. So anyone who steps into automated systems will have to step into the work attitudes, behaviors, prejudices, and perceptions of human beings.

One key part of dealing with those humans is explaining how automated decision systems make their decisions. As the primary interface between the organization and the system, those who step in need to provide description and reassurance that the decisions are rational and effective. Many automated systems have aspects of a "black box," in that the rules and algorithms are either too complex or too inaccessible to nontechnical users.

Those who step in must also have a passion for improvement. This typically means that they focus on a defined work process with a beginning, an ending, and a series of steps. It means they should be oriented to measurement—measuring how decisions are made and their impact before the automation intervention, and then after. Because it is usually those who step in who need to determine whether a system is working effectively or not, they have to be constantly measuring its results.

In fact, one might even go so far as to say that those who step in must be analytical and measurement focused. The purpose of automation is, in most cases anyway, to improve performance. Vendors of automation systems have told us that one cannot underestimate the demands for reporting on performance by customers, and that different customers want different types of analyses and reports. It is normally the step-in employees who are generating the reports and making them available to the various stakeholders in the process.

Finally, those who step in must have a passion for change—keeping up with it, creating it, adapting to it, and helping others adapt to it. The technology that they work with is changing all the time, so they have to be attuned to those changes and their implications. As we have noted throughout this book, the automation of knowledge and decision-oriented jobs could be one of the most important and sweeping changes in history. It won't happen successfully without a lot of change-oriented effort of various types—evangelizing, hand-holding, iterating, replacing, and many other gerund forms. The step-in job of today probably won't even be very much like the one of tomorrow.

The Future of Stepping In Is Bright

We think that anyone who's capable of stepping into automated decision systems should do so. In general, the future for this group is very bright. It's as if we're in the early days of the industrial revolution, and there are very few mechanics for the power looms and spinning jennies that inventors have come up with. Those who know how to set up, get running, and maintain these new machines are going to be in huge demand. We certainly haven't found any people with this focus and set of capabilities that are out of a job today.

Perhaps we should include here the obligatory complaint that there aren't enough STEM graduates, at least in the United States, to fill out the ranks of the stepping-in role in the future. Maybe the existence and awareness of jobs like these will attract more students to these fields. You don't necessarily have to get a degree in a STEM field to do well in one of these jobs, but you can't be totally STEM-phobic—some courses in those fields are at least necessary.

We do have one concern about the step-in group of the future, which we hinted at when we discussed insurance underwriting. Many of those in the step-in role were chosen because they were experts in the jobs that were automated. They were experienced and knowledgeable underwriters, marketers, or accountants. They put in their time making nonautomated decisions, and because they did that often and well, they were judged qualified to step in.

But we often hear that because of automated systems, companies don't need to hire many entry-level workers anymore. The computers make the entry-level decisions, and senior people step in to work with the smart machines. But where will the step-in workers of the future come from if they can't start at the entry level?

This issue may be somewhat responsible for a general dearth of entry-level positions these days. Lesley Mitler, head of a firm that coaches people to get hired for entry-level jobs, notes in a blog post that entry-level jobs are no longer entry-level: "Take a look at the qualifications section of any entry-level job posting. Employers all say they want at least one or more years of experience. At least one year of experience required for a job that is supposed to be for someone right out of college?!"[7]

We seem to have automated away the first few rungs of the traditional career ladder. In automating the routinized work that people used to cut their teeth on, they have also eliminated the means to pick up essential "soft skills" to be effective with customers and within a large organization. Employers may no longer be willing to pay a human to do work that can easily be codified, and which they want to have performed at a routinely high quality and quickly.

Thus older people in the job look back at the ladders they climbed to their current job—a job in which they are expected to apply judgment and think strategically—and they see the first few rungs missing. The museum curator sees museum docents replaced by robots and kiosks and headset tours. The United Nations interpreter sees the translators wiped out by Google Translate. The architects see the junior architects replaced by CAD software. The lawyers see the junior lawyers replaced by e-discovery software. When young people ask them for advice on how to get a start in the field, they can't point to the first foothold.

This problem also applies to some of the other augmentation roles we've described, but it falls most heavily on the step-in role. And it's hard to see how educational institutions could provide the specialized knowledge firms need in the step-in jobs. This is particularly true when most universities are lagging behind in being able to teach students about contemporary automation technologies. Faculty weren't trained in them, and so they can't really teach students about them. This is a huge issue right now in digital marketing and automated marketing technology. There is a great demand for knowledge in the area, but few schools have anyone who can teach it. There is also the issue that some schools—prestigious law schools, for example—consider automation technologies insufficiently academic to be worthy of study.

In order to enter step-in roles at early levels in their careers, students will need to acquire as much knowledge as they possibly can while in school, and as much on-the-job training as possible in internships. Or perhaps smart employers will create training programs for selected new hires with the specific objective of helping them step in. Time will tell, but this is a problem that's going to bite a lot of organizations in the rear if they don't take action soon.

What Those Who Step In Look Like

You're a candidate for stepping in if . . .

- You are a business or professional person first and an automation/technology expert second;
- You could be described as a "purple person"—bridging the gap between business or organizational need and technology capability;
- You're good at interfacing with both silicon- and carbon-based lifeforms;

- You're not a full-time technologist, but you follow developments in IT and are not at all intimidated by it;
- You are willing to learn a lot about the logic of how an automated system works and a little about how it is programmed;
- You are willing to translate for other humans the specific decisions that an automated system makes;
- You are not now, nor have you ever been, a robot, android, automaton, avatar, or cyborg.

You can build your skills for stepping in by . . .

- Taking computer science classes in college;
- Studying machine learning and AI in online courses;
- Taking courses, listening to webinars, reading white papers from cognitive technology vendors who sell into your industry;
- Talking with developers of cognitive technology about their systems;
- Interviewing experts about the key business processes in your organization;
- Studying the output of an automated decision and practice explaining it.

You're likely to be found in . . .

- Industries and businesses where automation is taking hold;
- Information-intensive businesses and functions;
- Organizations that are progressive in the use of technology;
- Businesses or professions that are undergoing a lot of change;
- Settings where leaders and colleagues appreciate new ideas and skills.

7

Stepping Narrowly

It is one of the more bizarre quirks of nature that, like clockwork, every forty-eight years, a horde of black rats is brought forth seemingly from nowhere to devastate the crops of northeastern India. In the remote villages of Mizoram, where most farmers grow barely enough to sustain their families until the next harvest, the economic effects of the rats descending from nearby hills, tens of millions strong, are severe. (We can only speculate about the psychological ones.) But while it has long been noted that this rat population explosion, and subsequent collapse to prior levels, coincides with the flowering of the surrounding bamboo forests, those forty-eight-year intervals have made it hard to gain an understanding of just what is going on.

And that is why Ken Aplin came to town. Aplin is a zoologist with a particular focus on rodents, and within that genus, a particular focus on rats. When he learned about the *mautam* (which means "bamboo death" —the rats eat so much of it) and the fact it would occur again in 2006, he realized he had to go—and by the time the date rolled around, National Geographic was funding his research and sending a film crew. The resulting documentary treats us to scenes of Aplin in the dead of night, his flashlight's beam catching the reflections of little eyes in its sweep, his sensors capturing the evidence of movement underfoot.[1]

Aplin is someone whom we would describe as stepping narrowly—and we're not just referring to rat avoidance. He now knows more than anyone on a topic about which most of us know basically nothing. For whatever work arises that requires thorough understanding of the *mautam*, he's the man. And while he may be an extreme example, the path he has chosen is one we think many could learn from.

In an age of relentlessly encroaching automation, some human work will be granted a dispensation not because it is fundamentally emotional or otherwise unsuited to computerization by the nature of the tasks. Instead, this work will resist automation because no one can make a strong economic case for automating it. Vital as it may be in particular situations or at certain moments, its extremely specialized nature means that a very small number of people are able to handle the world's demand for it.

Remember, it takes resources to design and build an automated solution, and even as those costs steadily fall, they have not become utterly trivial. Even more important, once an automated approach is devised, resources are required to maintain it, especially by updating it with new discoveries or improved protocols. As we saw in Chapter 6's discussion of "Stepping In," only people with sufficient knowledge of a field can make these updates. But in narrowly specialized fields, where those people by themselves can cover the demand for the work, it isn't likely they will allocate much time to building and updating systems that no one else needs to use.

It isn't random that we would begin this chapter with a scientist—it's often the case that quests for new scientific discovery take people into niches where their expertise is unrivaled. At the same time, stepping narrowly isn't *only* for scientists. We would put investment banker Greg Carey in the same category; he's the expert you want if you're trying to finance a new stadium. And Claire Bustarret: Her deep familiarity with paper-making techniques through the ages makes her invaluable if you suspect a forgery. And Kelly Falls, general manager of Hyperco, who has forgotten more than you'll ever know about the right springs to install on your race cars.

These people are the opposites of jacks-of-all-trades. Not one of them is a one-man band. They love their work, and they do it well. And computers are leaving them to it.

Machine-Unfriendly Economics

Earlier we wrote about the advantage enjoyed by the "stepping-up" worker—the kind of person who strives to see the big picture and make expansive connections across disciplines, while leaving detailed work to computers. The kind of person we're describing in this chapter is essentially the opposite of that. So how can this also be safe ground for human employment?

To be sure, the encyclopedic knowledge these professionals take pride in accumulating is just the kind of data that is easily plugged into databases. Their rich social networks could be replicated on the Internet. The decisions they make are often very rule based, and follow very structured processes. In many cases these decisions could be made faster and better by computers than by human minds—assuming the effort had already been made up front to render those routines and data into software. But there's the rub. That effort rarely is made, because the returns on the investment are so unattractive. It requires too much to equip machines for which there will just never be many buyers.

Here's a great example of how much it costs currently to build an AI solution to make good decisions in a relatively narrow realm. In 2012, the MD Anderson Cancer Center, part of the University of Texas system, started a project to apply IBM's Watson technology to the question of how to treat individual patients' leukemia therapies. With access to the full medical literature archives and to details about a specific case, the machine would be able to draw up the same kind of treatment plan a particularly well-informed oncologist would. The *Wall Street Journal* reported in 2014 that the project, the largest at that point for Watson, amounted to a nearly $15 million deal—and two years in, the system was still at least a year from generating its first usable treatment plan. Executives at MD Anderson reportedly raised $50 million to support the broader transformation goals around the project. Overall, IBM hopes to generate $10 billion a year in Watson revenues. Numbers like these make it clear why IBM, when it chose targets for Watson's first commercial applications, zeroed in the health-care sector. Both the amount we spend on health care— approaching 20 percent of gross domestic product in the United States—

and the incidence of its problems is so large that there is clear potential to make huge efficiency and service quality gains. And the initial cost hurdle, which would be an awfully big pill to swallow in most other sectors, is manageable in an industry that has historically passed costs on to insurers and employers.

The same cannot be said for the business of specifying race car springs, or attesting to the age of old manuscripts, or even structuring the finances of new stadium construction—as big as the investments are in that realm and as comfortable as Greg Carey's employer, Goldman Sachs, is with applying computers to financial decision-making. And yet, as we'll discuss below, these narrow realms of knowledge work are still plenty big enough to provide livelihoods for the few people sufficiently interested to find their way to them.

We don't mean to be blithe about the march of technology, and the tendency for jobs that have been uneconomical to automate to suddenly become economical. It is probable that many people who today hold tiny monopolies on specialized tasks they have mastered will see computers come to threaten them. Indeed, we were reminded of this in a recent conversation with Alastair Bathgate, founder of Blue Prism, the company we mentioned in Chapter 2. He sells "robotic" process automation to businesses that enables them to automate routine back-office process tasks, even where the numbers of knowledge workers performing them are not vast. We put quotes around the word "robotic" there because in fact this is software; the human's replacement in the process has no physical embodiment. But the word still seems apt, because what is going on here is that a flexible computer program is being instructed on how to interact with the major information technology backbone systems of the business in just the same way a human worker would.

An example is the use of Blue Prism software by Britain's Co-operative Bank. Traditionally, its employees have followed a typical process when a customer has called to report a lost or stolen credit card. Having gleaned the relevant information from the customer in a conversation lasting perhaps five minutes, the call center agent would spend twenty-five minutes interacting with a variety of different internal systems to cancel the existing card, enter notes on the account, provide for delivery of a new card, and so forth. By programming software to perform these rather mundane and repetitive tasks (investing in, as Bathgate calls it, robotic process automation), Co-operative Bank has enabled agents who were dealing with two lost-card incidents per hour to deal with perhaps a dozen.

This is classic automation stuff, but the difference we want to underscore—which is the basis of Blue Prism's growing business—is that this provides a way for an individual department in an organization to automate a process without asking for new functionality in the underlying systems of the enterprise, or even for any help from the IT department. As Bathgate explains, this opens up a whole new realm of work for automation that wasn't economical to automate before. "We discovered there was a long tail of automation that hadn't even started to be addressed," he says. While robotics had been applied heavily to repetitive work in manufacturing, "the *clerical* factory had been left largely untouched."

"Long tail" is a key phrase here, because it is the modish way of referring to the realm of specialization (and again, we're not just talking about rats). If you're trying to remain employable by stepping narrowly, then you are moving into the far right of the normal distribution curve of your trade, where the total numbers of transactions get smaller and smaller. And, as with so many aspects of computer encroachment, you will need to keep stepping further than the advancing lines of automation.

For another example of this ongoing march of specialization, take the various fields of medicine that are facing increased degrees of automation. Over the past couple of decades, MD graduates who wanted to be in demand (and who didn't want to be on call during nights and weekends) chose medical specialties like radiology and pathology. If you didn't want to actually see sick people face-to-face, these were your chosen fields.

Now, however, automation threatens the more routine and lucrative aspects of these jobs, like mammogram interpretations for breast cancer (20 million a year in the United States) and Pap smear readings for cervical cancer (33 million a year). The smart doctors are moving to subspecialty fields that are less easily automated—interventional radiology, for example, which combines radiology and surgery, or fine-needle aspiration (FNA) biopsies in pathology. These too may be automated in future years, but there will surely be sub-subspecialties by that point.

So we're convinced that people who carve out specialized niches for themselves in the economy can continue to occupy them profitably for the foreseeable future. That's partly because they are doing work so little called for that they can become monopoly suppliers of it, while enjoying that work so much that they aren't inclined to charge extortionist rates. And it's partly for another reason: As the leading practitioners of their trade, they are driven to, and given every opportunity to, keep getting better at it. Machines, at best, play catch-up.

How Do You Get to Be So Narrow?

We've already taken some shots at the people who advocate putting young people through more and more years of formal education (especially STEM education) so they can remain employable in an age of machines. So why not take another? As infamous as academe is for splintering its disciplines and pushing students into intellectual tributaries (as the old joke goes, "learning more and more about less and less until eventually you know everything about nothing"), the way it goes narrow is not the answer, even for those who choose to step narrowly.

The value of a foundational education is clear—one that establishes some grounding in a field. That's where the narrow-stepper discovers a topic of interest in the first place and gains the credential to get a first foothold in an occupation. But beyond that discovery, school often doesn't agree with developing specialists, precisely because the curriculum can never be as focused as they want on their particular passion. For this reason, people who step narrowly sometimes don't excel in school. They just don't see the point of mastering all those other subjects that count as "distribution requirements" for their degree (and factor into their GPA). Those subjects are not their destiny. This is why we hear surprisingly often that one of the "greats" in some field is a college dropout. When Bill Gates and Steve Jobs went to college, computer science was just one class out of several they took in a semester, but it was where they wanted to spend all their time. Even by the time Mark Zuckerberg arrived at Harvard, and computer science had become a popular major, the school couldn't offer him enough coding coursework to keep him interested.

Assertions like this should come with the obligatory warning label: Don't assume that because Steve Jobs didn't need a college degree, you don't, either. Most of us are well served by having some sheepskin among our credentials; U.S. Census data show the mean income of college graduates to be $58,613, versus $31,283 for high school graduates, and occupations that typically require postsecondary education are projected to grow at a faster rate than occupations that don't. But we won't go so far as to claim that Jobs succeeded *despite* his dropping out. He was right to drop out—because he already knew where his strengths and passion lay, and was clear-eyed about the fact that college wasn't going to accelerate his progress along those lines.

For many people, their destiny is less apparent, and what counts as foundational is not always obvious, either. Since we're on the topic of people who carve out niches, we can't resist bringing in David Esterly, the world's foremost practitioner of the work formerly done by Grinling Gibbons (1648–1721). Perhaps you are familiar with Gibbons? If not, best to think of him as Esterly sums him up: Britain's unofficial woodcarver laureate. He was renowned in his lifetime for the high-relief intricacy and naturalistic beauty of his work, and kept busy with commissions to adorn churches and royal residences. When Esterly, who carries on that tradition, was in his late twenties, he had no inkling that he would turn his hand to carving, much less to the very particular style of it practiced by one man. Esterly's education at that point consisted of a BA in English from Harvard and a PhD from Cambridge, where he wrote his doctoral dissertation on Yeats and Plotinus. Once he discovered the work of Gibbons and became entranced with it, he began working in the same style, experimenting with techniques to achieve Gibbons's effects, and immersing himself in the history of the man and his times.[2] But who is to say that his prior, formal education was off course (although a PhD might be a bit far along the route)? A grounding in the humanities can serve a craftsman in many ways.

Often the most valuable niches to step into professionally exist at the intersections of two broader areas of knowledge not normally studied together. In a recent article posted on the New York City Bar website, we are introduced to four lawyers with, as the piece is titled, "Unusual and Highly Specialized Practice Areas."[3] Abram Bohrer, of Bohrer & Lukeman, grew up in a family with freight-forwarding business and is an expert on aviation law. John Fabiani, of Fabiani Cohen & Hall, knows a great deal about equine law, which "involves everything from insurance issues to partnership disputes, misrepresentation, and syndication of interests in valuable racehorses." No surprise: he owns several himself. Staci Jennifer Riordan, of Fox Rothschild, spent years working in the fashion business and now specializes in fashion law. M. Dru Levasseur, whose own female-to-male transition opened his eyes to discrimination based on gender identity, is today's best-known practitioner of transgender law.

Thus, finding a narrow specialization is largely a matter of following your passion, which has always been an important factor in career choice. But some passions are more likely to succeed than others, so some rational analysis about your narrow field of choice is also a good idea. What you need to examine is whether, in that famous cliché from Wayne Gretzky, you are skating where the puck is going to be. There should be strong indicators that there will be a market for your services, that there won't be too many other people in it, and that the field isn't likely to be automated. Each of these is a guess, but they can be educated guesses.

To predict whether there will be a market for your narrow specialty, you might want to consider macroeconomic and demographic trends, for example. If you decide that you want to work with old folks' needs for relocation assistance, for example, you might want to make sure you live in a country with a rapidly aging population (Japan would perhaps be best for this, but the United States isn't a bad bet, either). If you are thinking of joining David Esterly in creating woodcarvings to be used in Western European churches, you might consider that more churches are being converted into condominiums in Europe today than are investing in expensive new decorations.

Then there is the issue of just how crowded your field will be. Does the U.S. Bureau of Labor Statistics (or a similar organization in another country) already recognize your intended job category? Is there a Wikipedia entry for it? Lots of Google hits when you search for information about it? All are bad signs for having the domain to yourself. Finding out that several universities are offering courses—or God forbid, majors—in your specialization is not a good sign, either. If your parents seem extremely puzzled when you explain your choice of career, that may be a very good sign.

Finally, you need to think about whether the field is likely to be automated. We've provided plenty of clues in this book, but here are a few others to think about. If your job could be outsourced to India, it could probably be automated. If you don't need to see humans to do it, it might well be automatable. If you can write down the knowledge and decision rules you need to conduct this profession, somebody might well turn it into software. Finally, if someone has already created even an experimental project to automate your target job or key tasks within it, you might want to go back to the drawing board and choose another.

Building on Your Narrowness

The magic of successful specialization comes when, having targeted a niche (again, often at the intersection of an area of formal study and an area of particular passion or experience), the practitioner then digs deeper. But this also creates a special challenge for those who step narrowly: continuing to be "findable" even as one's contribution to the overall economy becomes more obscure. Publishing in industry "trade rags" and presenting at conferences are time-honored ways of doing this—although keynote speeches may not be in the cards. (If you're asked to give one, it may be a sign that your field is becoming too popular.)

The Internet, however, has revolutionized the process of publicizing and finding deep expertise. If you're a jack-of-one-trade, Internet connectivity and usage not only helps you deepen your expertise; it also connects you to customers and markets for it. Websites, blogging, and YouTube videos have become popular ways to help people find experts with obscure specializations. Ebay, Etsy, and Amazon make it easier for people to sell formerly obscure products. And Google search is, of course, God's gift to the narrow-stepper.

Social media and other communications technologies help the narrow specialist keep learning more. Once you make clear to your network that you are interested in equine law, friends start passing along anything they spot pertaining to that. You in turn publish your "take" on the item. Meanwhile, you yourself are doing the same, referring items to the small network of other people in your field and becoming known to them as a serious participant in their conversation. Thus you activate a kind of virtuous cycle. You become more expert because you are perceived to be an expert. Soon, when someone searches for "equine law" you come up first (as did "Equine Legal Solutions: Legal Counsel with Horse Sense"), and you begin getting more cases. You start a blog about your cases on equine law, creatively titled "Equine Law Blog," with posts such as "LAWN MOWER SPOOKS HORSE—GEORGIA COURT DISMISSES INJURED RID-ER'S LAWSUIT." You're off and running in this career.

This is why the machine-unfriendly economics of specialization can turn out to be so human-friendly. Even avocations can turn to vocations when artisans can connect with enough interested buyers. The new employment marketplaces that match workers to tasks, or solvers to seekers, might be bad news for undistinguished talent. But they greatly reward the hyperspecialists.

How far can this take people into the long tail? We think it is fair to say: infinitely far. A young friend is a novice filmmaker, hoping to shoot a scene in New York. Finding the right location might be hard, but finding the guy who can find it turns out to be easy. Nick Carr specializes in film location scouting in New York City, and has for the past decade. Another friend is an octogenarian who wants to avoid a move to an assisted living facility. An Internet search allows him to find a certified "aging in place" specialist who can help codger-proof his home. Rebecca Scott is a typical one; she spent years as an interior designer before turning her space-planning expertise to this more particular set of questions. A third friend recently rescued a young fox that had been injured. The question arose: Could it possibly be tamed? Lo and behold, the *Siberian Times* reports that "Irina Mukhamedshina, 24, a professional dog handler, is perhaps the world's leading expert in training foxes as pets." That's a bit further than this friend wanted to go for lessons—but we're willing to bet that, closer to her neck of the woods, Ms. Mukhamedshina has the fox-training market cornered.

The Pursuit of Narrow Expertise

We've been talking about some of the network dynamics that help specialists deepen their expertise by continually putting them in the way of new developments and interesting problems in their field. But of course there is a cognitive element to specialization, too, which calls upon internal resources more than external ones. Having decided to focus on a narrow and challenging subject, how exactly does one achieve mastery?

Browsing on Amazon, we found a guy selling a brief treatise called *How to Become an Expert in Any Field.* (We promise it wasn't because we were buying his previous work, *How to Write a Book in 30 Days or Less.*) His opening advice goes like this:

> First off, no matter what anyone tells you, it may take a "while" for you to be perceived as THE expert in your field. You can certainly get the ball rolling IMMEDIATELY, but it will take a while to establish you as THE expert in your field.
> How long exactly? I'll give you the answer you don't want to hear, but it's 100% accurate: It depends!

Okay, this is not helpful. We really are now taking *How to Write a Book* out of our shopping cart. Luckily, however, there are better sources of insight on the topic. Indeed, the gaining of expertise has become such a hot (albeit itself narrow) subject in recent decades that a fair number of people have become true experts in it. And interestingly, according to two of them—Robert Glaser and Michelene Chi, editors of *The Nature of Expertise*—the main reason that their field took off when it did, in the mid to late 1960s, was the advances that were just then starting to be made in artificial intelligence. If science were going to make computers supersmart, it would help to know what made some humans supersmart first.

To sum up a tremendous body of work in a few sentences, the emerging practical message of this line of work is that, when we look upon a master in some field, we are not seeing someone of ineffable, innate genius. Rather, we are seeing someone who began with a clear sense of direction and proceeded down that path with extraordinary commitment. Their success is the product of relevant training, deliberate practice, and motivational drive. This was the conclusion of Michael Howe, a cognitive psychologist who devoted his career to the study of exceptional intelligence.[4] And it resonates with the famous estimate by Herbert Simon that, on the way to becoming an expert in a substantial topic, a learner engages with roughly 50,000 chunks of information related to it—a mountain of data typically requiring ten years to climb.

If that "ten years to become an expert" rule of thumb sounds familiar, it is probably thanks to the continued efforts of K. Anders Ericsson. His quest for a universal theory of expertise spans, as his faculty page at Florida State University notes, domains as varied as "music, science, golf, and darts." For him a decade is more or less required not because of the number of information chunks one must encounter but because it takes that long for a motivated learner to log 10,000 hours of "deliberate practice." In his most cited paper, he and his colleagues sum up the results of their careful analysis: "Individual differences, even among elite performers, are closely related to assessed amounts of deliberate practice. Many characteristics once believed to reflect innate talent are actually the result of intense practice extended for a minimum of 10 years."[5]

Are there any shortcuts? A famous quote from computer scientist Alan Kay—"The best way to predict the future is to invent it"—suggests there might be at least one: You could pioneer a new field. Few are more expert than Deepika Kurup, for example, at solar-powered water purification using photocatalytic composites, even though she has been at it for only a few years. Her invention of such a system won her an award in 2012— and by the way, she is still a teenager, so she has plenty of time and energy to keep getting smarter about the subject. If this seems like too much to ask of many people, we could rattle off many more new disciplines that have been hatched in very recent years. Among the innovators we might mention would be Kirk Goldsberry, part of the vanguard in the visual analytics of sports; Herve This, the father of molecular gastronomy (the new science of cooking); Lewis D'Vorkin, simultaneously hailed and reviled by his magazine publishing peers as the pioneer of "native advertising" (advertising that looks like editorial content). All managed to break new ground that they could then occupy as leading experts.

But here we'll drop another big name in the field of cognitive studies: Mihaly Csikszentmihalyi. As part of his extensive work to understand the conditions that give rise to creativity, he has found that important breakthroughs tend to come from people who previously gained mastery of an underlying domain—partly because that gives them the grounding to imagine new possibilities, and partly because a novel creation is more readily embraced when others already perceive the creator as someone to be reckoned with.[6] Within most realms, gaining that mastery of a source discipline takes serious time. So, we're back to ten years.

But if there are really no learning shortcuts in stepping narrowly, at least there is the reassurance that machine learning isn't nipping too closely at your heels. To understand why, consider how computers use techniques such as deep learning and neural networks to gain their intelligence. As described by the consulting firm McKinsey, "These techniques give computers the ability to draw conclusions from patterns they discern within massive data sets (anything from all legal cases of the past 20 years to data concerning the way in which molecular compounds react with one another)."[7]

For humans, advancing learning down a narrow path of specialization isn't usually an exercise in gaining a broad enough perspective thanks to the accumulation of "big data" to spot patterns others have not seen. That much data in a narrow field simply doesn't exist in most cases. The approach is more akin to Isaac Newton's method of standing on the shoulders of giants, squinting in one direction, and trying to see just that little bit farther than others. You want to choose an area in which there isn't a lot of data and in which there won't be a lot for a while. Stepping narrowly means pushing ever deeper into a subject, with all the force of past achievement helping you, and learning the next thing about it through the kind of focused consideration and experimentation machines can't manage.

Fortunately, the Internet and the tools for searching it have changed the feasibility of this learning. It makes it possible for an individual with an interest, no matter how distant from the real action in a field, to become knowledgeable about it at the rate they choose. Especially when a young person is able to come up to speed quickly on what is already known, they have the opportunity to take their pursuit of the subject further.

Expect, in the coming decades, to see many more breakthroughs from autodidacts. Even before the Web, it was possible to be self-taught and go far. Take James Cameron, the celebrated director of *Titanic* and *Avatar*. When he decided to get into the filmmaking business, he wasn't enrolled in a film school. "I'd go down to the USC library and pull any theses that graduate students had written about optical printing, or front screen projection, or dye transfers, anything that related to film technology," he later recalled. "If they'd let me photocopy it, I would. If not, I'd make notes."[8] Clearly, Cameron was tremendously motivated to learn. But think how many more people with similar drive can learn today, with a library that is at their fingertips, open all night, and a thousand times more vast.

Augmenting the Narrow with Technology

Anytime you fall in love with a technology, it's a sure sign that you are being augmented by it, not threatened. The valentine we just wrote to the World Wide Web speaks to the question we turn to next: If you choose to step narrowly through the new, AI-filled workplace, how can you hope to be augmented? Our mission in this book is not just to protect your job from machines. We want them working for your benefit.

In that spirit, then, and going beyond the Web's role in delivering content knowledge and connections to your customers, we'll offer three forms that augmentation by machines will take:

- Helping your learning go further, faster;
- Doing ancillary tasks to allow you to stay focused on going ever deeper; and
- Facilitating the connections of your work into larger projects.

First, smart machines will be able to accelerate your mastery of your field not only with content but with better teaching tools. The "expertise expert" Anders Ericsson offers an example (although it happens to be a door on which automation is knocking quite audibly): "Statistics show that radiologists correctly diagnose breast cancer from X-rays about 70% of the time. . . . Imagine how much better radiology might get if radiologists practiced instead by making diagnostic judgments using X-rays in a library of old verified cases, where they could immediately determine their accuracy. . . . There is an emerging market in elaborate simulations that can give professionals, especially in medicine and aviation, a safe way to deliberately practice with appropriate feedback."

Second, you will be augmented by machines capable of performing ancillary tasks in your workplace, allowing you to stay focused on delivering that special value that you are especially capable of delivering, and on pushing your specialized knowledge to new levels. As we write this, Amazon has just launched its product Echo, which joins the growing crowd of "intelligent personal assistants" that already includes Apple's Siri, Microsoft's Cortana, and more. (Remember "Amy" the meeting scheduler, from the Introduction.) These tools will continue to grow more capable and take more of the administrivia out of knowledge workers' days.

Increasing reliance on machines to perform tasks that administrative assistants used to do is hardly a new phenomenon. Travel arrangements are now made through websites and those sites get increasingly good at storing preferences and suggesting options. Voice mail takes messages and now converts them to text. Presentations are made easy to assemble by PowerPoint templates. No one in a big company still fills out expense reports manually. The problem is that the companies have not chosen for the most part to use these useful tools to leverage the assistants' time and allow them to take on higher-level tasks. Instead they have simply removed the administrative assistants and shoved whatever residual tasks remained onto the to-do lists of the people they used to support—effectively deleveraging their most expensive talent. And therefore, no professional we know feels particularly augmented by any of it. Instead, they are acutely aware of the portion of their time for which they are being paid high salaries to put in barely competent performance on tasks normally associated with lower salaries. They are spending less of their day on the work they do particularly well—on the activities that are so valuable to the company's success that they deserved high pay to do them. Neither they nor their companies are better off.

But consider how things will change going forward. Now, with the administrative assistants long gone, any further enhancements to the administrative support tool kit can pay actual benefits in personal productivity. Time saved by an automated expense-report system is time *you* were going to have to spend.

Third, and perhaps most important, smart machines will do a better job in the future of facilitating the connections of your work to others, and synchronizing everyone's efforts to the critical paths of larger projects. At the extreme of this, we now have the software development firm TopCoder, which serves its clients by chopping their IT projects into bite-size chunks to be coded by a worldwide community of developers. (To motivate high-quality work, those far-flung developers are assessed on their contributions and have the chance to visibly climb the scoreboard of the company's "top coders.") Or, if it's a fast turnaround on a transcription that is needed, a company called CastingWords has a solution. It divides the audio file into short segments and sends each piece to multiple remote workers. Any discrepancies indicate someone made a mistake, and the consensus version of each phrase goes into the final transcript. Many hands make fast work. Similarly, the nonprofit organization Samasource sends data-entry work to marginalized individuals in the developing world, where tiny jobs lasting just minutes and paying just pennies give workers an economic boost while containing the damage if some individual worker proves not quite up to the job.

While most of the work that these coordination mechanisms are combining is of a commodity nature—capable of being performed by many people with minimal depth in their field—the same kind of structure also allows for narrow-steppers to plug their specialized talents into larger endeavors without the high "transaction costs" that usually go with outside contracting. Meanwhile, even for those who perform the outsourced tasks that require minimal training, these mechanisms make it increasingly possible to concentrate on a certain type of work, develop real strength at it, and become known for mastery of some very specialized work—thus, to excel by stepping narrowly—because demand for it can be aggregated from all around the world.

In short, it's possible to think of narrow-stepping as taking the filet of work—it's the satisfying stuff situated in the middle, with boring project management process above it and boring paperwork and other ancillary tasks below it. Richard Feynman, in his time one of the world's best-known physicists, was capable of slicing out this filet back in his days at MIT. He simply refused to participate in all the usual housekeeping of a university academic department—the committee memberships, the candidate interviewing, the grant application writing, and so forth. He got away with it because he had a Nobel Prize—no one would dare say any of these activities was the best use of his time. Today it's getting hard to say it about anyone else, either. Many millennial-generation workers, for example, are now saying that they don't want to work in big companies. As they choose freelance solo work they are often choosing narrow work. Part of this is their perception that, the more people doing a job in a big company, the more likely it is that someone is figuring out how to replace them all with a machine. Another part is their realization that they don't have to put up with trivia to ply their trade.

A Matter of Motivation—or Maybe Even Obsession

We think many more people are capable of and interested in stepping narrowly than do so today, and the enablers and economics we've been describing will serve as catalysts. But if we thought those would determine everything about career choices in the future, we wouldn't have written four other chapters of this book about alternative paths to augmentation. There is another big ingredient that goes into the decision to step narrowly: individual psychology. Some people are, and some people just aren't, cut out to hoe a narrow row.

More than anything, stepping narrowly is associated with high levels of intrinsic motivation. Let's face it: Knowing more than anyone else does about rat population dynamics in the *mautam* might score you a National Geographic video but it won't get you your own reality TV series. Much more likely than through any pursuit of fame, you're doing the work for the sheer satisfaction of doing it. You probably have the kind of motivation that Daniel Pink researched heavily for his bestselling book *Drive*, which he boils down to valuing three things: autonomy, purpose, and mastery. People who are really into their work, he observes, get to determine for themselves the direction and pace of their effort. They are fueled by a conviction that accomplishments on their part will matter in the bigger scheme of things. And they delight in solving the hardest puzzles, and attaining the top ranks of performance, in their chosen fields.

You may choose to step narrowly if you dream of that special joy of knowing, however briefly, something that no one else knows or has ever known. Science writer Edward Dolnick, in *The Clockwork Universe*, re-

counts an anecdote about the scientist Fritz Houtermans, who wrote a
pioneering paper in 1929 on how the sun's energy was produced by fusion:
"The night he finished the work, he and his girlfriend went for a stroll. She
commented on how beautiful the stars were. Houtermans puffed out his
chest. 'I've known since yesterday why it is that they shine.'"[9]

The story hints that those who step narrowly are not immune to
pride—but on the other hand, you probably were not familiar until just
now with the name Fritz Houtermans. People like him don't care about
you; it's sufficient to be highly regarded by the people who really understand their work. If it turns out that, due to some rare alignment of the
planets, it is suddenly of broad interest and they are thrust into the public
spotlight, they rise to the occasion. They get the fifteen minutes of fame
that Andy Warhol promised us all. But if those fifteen minutes never
come, they don't feel cheated.

If you think about it, a person like Houtermans is a curious amalgam of
traits. Clearly, he had the self-confidence to set a mission for himself—at
least in an intellectual sense, to boldly go where no man had gone before.
Yet he chose an introvert's profession—one that had him tunneling into
something called the tunnel effect and doing the close calculations that
would illuminate the astrophysics of main-sequence stars. An ungenerous
way to describe this personality type might be to call him an arrogant
introvert.

But the more generous term would be "nonconformist." These are
the kinds of people that filmmaker Errol Morris loves. In one of his best-
known documentaries, *Fast, Cheap, and Out of Control*, he offers up a
character study of four people doing jobs that, at least in 1997, seemed
eccentric in their obscurity: a topiary gardener named George Men-
donca; a lion tamer named Dave Hoover; the world's leading authority
on the colony behavior of naked mole rats, Ray Mendez; and (this is the
one that seems far less obscure today) Rodney Brooks, inventor of autonomous robots. Morris saw a connection, and a romanticism, in their various
versions of control of nature. Undoubtedly he also found infectious their
sheer enthusiasm for their craft.

Bob Sutton of Stanford University takes a more academic interest
in such people, since he studies creativity and innovation in organizations. He calls them "slow learners" of the organization's code—which

he quickly points out is a compliment, because they are somehow more impervious than their peers to "those overarching 'shalts' and 'shalt nots' which govern the actions, imply the sanctions, and in time permeate the souls of organization members." This allows them to keep seeing problems and opportunities in new ways. Reflecting on findings in personality psychology, he reports that three basic traits are key. Original thinkers are "low self-monitors," so they don't pick up on social cues dictating how they should act. Second, they avoid contact with coworkers. (Richard Feynman is a favorite example of Sutton's.) And third, they have very high self-esteem.

We suspect most people who choose to step narrowly today would match these criteria pretty closely. And while the technology and communications enablers we've described will swell their ranks and include many more people, probably those people will have more than just a touch of these tendencies, as well. They will be different than their peers in terms of their motivational psychology—and also in terms of their cognitive styles.

On that point, and in a chapter that has already taken us from rats to mole rats, we shouldn't neglect to sing the praises of hedgehogs. We're referring to Isaiah Berlin's famous classification of thinkers into two types, which was inspired by a line from the Greek poet Archilochus: "The fox knows many things, but the hedgehog knows one big thing." The hedgehog thinker, Berlin explained, sees and interprets the world through the lens of a single defining idea. The fox thinker refuses to invest so heavily in one idea and allows experience to keep suggesting new ones. To step narrowly is to be a hedgehog. And in a world of smart machines, that can be a great strategy for remaining gainfully employed. You can focus on knowing one thing, and make it big.

Niche Businesses Are Built on Niche People

The life of the narrow-stepping expert might seem like a lonely one, given over to freelancers and independent contractors. It isn't necessarily. Firms will create the apparatus—in today's parlance, the platforms—to make these people productive.

In the acclaimed television series *Breaking Bad*, the character Walter White recognizes at one point that he needn't fear any head count reduction, because his exceptional chemistry skills are crucial to his employer's methamphetamine business. Another chemist, asked to evaluate White's work relative to his own, gives him his due: "I can guarantee you a purity of ninety-six percent. I'm proud of that figure. It's a hard-earned figure, ninety-six. However, this other product is ninety-nine . . . that last three percent, it may not sound like a lot but it is. It's a tremendous gulf." In a later scene, when a young guard who has watched White every day claims that he can do the job just as well, White lets loose with an epic rant, letting their mutual boss know how far from mastery the kid is. In the end, it's the guard's head that is cut (this being *Breaking Bad*, quite literally).

Specialized talent hasn't always called the shots as effectively as Walter White, but in knowledge-based businesses, it has always been recognized as central to competitiveness. This will only become more the case as automation of knowledge work continues and many basic thinking tasks are turned into commodities. In order for firms to be distinguished in the marketplace from their competitors, they will have to be able to point to some secret sauce. And as with Walter White, they will have very great incentives to keep them cooking—performing the intellectual feats they are singularly qualified to perform.

A great example is Goldman Sachs, which holds a major advantage in winning any deal involving stadium financing: Greg Carey. "What sets him apart," *BloombergBusinessWeek* learned from interviewing both clients and critics, "is his ability to steer projects through conflicting interests of teams and local government officials. He often does so by using obscure tools available in public finance to help owners get low-interest loans, avoid taxes or tap subsidies." This might sound like the kind of job that a computer, with its encyclopedic awareness of such factors, could do better. It isn't, because as Carey himself says, "every one of these deals is different."

Carey is a great case study in stepping narrowly, and you might even say the journey began with his first steps: His own father was a municipal bond attorney. As a college student he majored in economics, then went to work for Smith Barney, later merged into Citigroup. At Citi, he co-led a group focused on infrastructure—and in 1991, owner Robert Kraft of the New England Patriots came to him for help financing a replacement for Foxboro Stadium. That deal, recalls *BloombergBusinessWeek*, "upended the conventional view of financing for professional sports stadiums . . . [and] established financing techniques that would become Carey's hallmarks."[10] (Maybe there is something to what Csikszentmihalyi tells us about creativity springing from hard-earned domain knowledge.)

But notice what happened next: Carey got scooped up by Goldman Sachs. Traditionally, when professionals have gained such renown in their narrow fields, they have been inclined to quit the less focused firms that were their training grounds and set up their own, niche consultancies. No doubt it occurred to Carey to hang out his own shingle. And no doubt Goldman made it worth his while to abandon that thought.

Goldman is not alone in realizing that the economics of knowledge-based businesses have shifted, and that specialized services that once would have been more valuable as independent, niche businesses should now be even more highly valued by large parent firms. Firms need these pockets of specialized expertise just as individuals now need them. If a firm's capabilities are based on intellectual strengths that machines can replicate, its days are numbered.

Set Your Narrow Course

To sum up this chapter, stepping narrowly is something we'll see more broadly. If left to follow their own idiosyncratic interests, more people would always have been inclined to do so. It has been the lack of educational resources and market efficiency that has forced them to succeed as generalists. But today, and going forward, the economics of specialization work better for people. This would be true whether or not they were looking over their shoulders in a race against machines. Stepping narrowly, however, also has the benefit of keeping them one step ahead in that race.

You may have gotten the impression—at least before this chapter— that the people who choose to step narrowly are those who avoid computers. In fact, they're only avoiding automation technology. From an augmentation perspective, they might enjoy the best working relationships with computers of anyone. Their possibilities for augmentation are highly complementary and tremendously appealing. Like a great lab assistant, the machine does the housekeeping and performs the rote measurements and calculations the scientist has long ago mastered, and this leaves the chief scientist to make a next level of discovery—and experience that very human joy of being the one person who knows about it.

People who step narrowly don't tend to rest on their laurels. Their high levels of intrinsic motivation keep them moving forward in their fields. In the age of smart machines, this will be more important than ever. You may need to be more deliberate about your approaches to practicing and learning, to publishing and otherwise making yourself known as an expert, and to spending as few hours as possible doing work that isn't in your sweet spot. More than anything, you'll need to commit to a line of work that can captivate you for many years, because that's what you'll need to become great at it—and you'll have to be great to succeed.

What Those Who Step Narrowly Look Like

You're a candidate for stepping narrowly if . . .

- You are passionate about a topic that others find esoteric or puzzling;
- You have been pursuing this topic ardently for many years (10,000 hours?);
- You've been able to establish your expertise externally through various means;
- You know of no computer system that has taken over significant components of what you do, or the noncomputerized components are not very codifiable;
- You developed this expertise largely on your own; no educational institutions offer it;
- There isn't much data about what you do;
- You have found a way to monetize your expertise in some sort of job.

You can build your skills for stepping narrowly by . . .

- Getting some basic educational credentials, and then branching out considerably from them;
- Never stopping your pursuit of the field about which you are passionate;
- Seeking out opportunities to deepen your expertise through practice and new situations;
- Pursuing opportunities to use technology to augment your capabilities;
- Constantly monitoring how many other people have adopted your same specialty, and being willing to specialize further.

You're likely to be found in . . .

- The Internet;
- A small business or sole proprietorship;
- A narrow but lucrative area of a larger business;
- . . . if you can be found at all!

8

Stepping Forward

Stepping forward is about creating new cognitive technology solutions for the rest of the world to use. While it's not a huge category of employment today, we suspect it will become one. The category encompasses software vendors as well as companies that are developing their own systems. We think that virtually every software company—and a variety of robot manufacturers and companies in general—will want to hire people who can help them step forward in the automation/ augmentation marketplace. In short, our prediction is that no one will ever go broke automating the intelligence of the American (or German or Brazilian or Chinese, for that matter) knowledge worker.

The rapid hiring of people by smart machines vendors alone would suggest a bright employment future. IBM, for example, has near-term plans to employ about 2,000 people to help develop Watson, 2,000 more just for Watson Health, and an additional 2,000 in the consulting business to implement and support Watson. In how many businesses do people get hired by the ton these days? The company also has and seeks more partnerships with a number of other firms and their employees in its Watson "ecosystem." As we write, open Watson-oriented jobs at IBM alone include such roles as:

Product manager;
Delivery project manager;
Application and platform test specialist;
Mobile application and platform specialist;

Software designer;

Quality engineer;

"Senior medical annotator" (someone who records text attributes);

Security and network specialist;

Cloud deployment and support specialist;

Ecosystem technical manager;

Compliance leader;

Performance engineer;

"Content ingestion" developer (presumably sucking content into Watson);

. . . and many more. If you've got these types of skills, it will be relatively easy to find jobs in this space.

Note that the skills don't necessarily involve "cognitive technology," "artificial intelligence," or "business analytics" skills. Before you stop reading because you don't have a PhD in experimental physics or a specialty in nonlinear stochastic models, be aware that there are many jobs in software vendors of all types—including cognitive software—that don't involve knowing how to code or create new algorithms. Obviously it helps to market or sell software if you can understand how it works, but you often don't need to know in detail.

In this chapter we'll describe some of the jobs involved in creating new (or modified) cognitive technology systems, and what the people who occupy them are like. In the second section of the chapter we'll describe at a high level some of what they are up to—the capabilities and attributes they are trying to put into automated systems to make them a better fit with the needs of humans—in other words, to augment them.

Stepping Forward, Job by Job

In order to create a new type of information system that is used by a variety of people, a lot of different roles are necessary. The IBM Watson list we gave above describes some of them, but they also include a variety of nontechnical roles. We'll describe both the technical and nontechnical roles, and will give a living, breathing example of several of them.

Programmers and Other IT Professionals

—If you're going to be involved in the creation of new software, it helps a lot to know how to program. In the old days, an "artificial intelligence" programmer needed to know how to program in AI-oriented languages like LISP and Prolog. More recently, programming in business rule engines (IBM's ILOG and Fair Isaac's Blaze, for example) was a common approach to automated systems development.

While such jobs still exist, they are not the preferred tools in which most software development in the automation space is done. Most development is done in general-purpose programming languages (Java is the most popular of these by far) and in scripting languages that automate the processing of tasks with a script (Python and Ruby are popular scripting languages). These types of programmers should also be familiar with the tools to store and process big data, including the open-source tools Hadoop and Map/Reduce, Storm, Cassandra, Hive, and Mahout. Finally, people who are interested in programming in this context should be interested in and knowledgeable about some aspect of this field's key movements: artificial intelligence, natural language processing (NLP), machine learning, deep-learning neural networks, statistical analysis and data mining, and so forth.

If you have a basic grounding in computer science and programming, it is possible to develop a sufficient understanding of these automation-oriented tools well into your career. Today there are many online courses related to this field. Stanford professors, for example, have created online courses with companies like Coursera and Udacity in such highly relevant fields as machine learning, natural language processing, algorithms, and robotics. You have to be pretty motivated to finish such courses, but it can be done.

And as the Watson jobs we list above suggest, there are also plenty of IT-oriented jobs that don't just involve programming. Automated/cognitive systems are, among other things, big computer programs. So they need to be project managed, tested, hosted, maintained, and otherwise facilitated like any other program. If you have a background in one of these (slightly) ancillary aspects of software, you can probably find the same kind of job related to automated software.

Data Scientists

—A couple of years ago, Tom and D. J. Patil, now chief data scientist of the White House Office of Science and Technology Policy, wrote (with Julia's editing help) an article suggesting that data scientists held the "sexiest job of the 21st century."[1] It's not that the people themselves were necessarily sexy, but that the jobs were difficult and hard to fill. They still are, though the shortage may be easing a bit, with the introduction of a number of new master's programs in data science at U.S. universities.

Data scientists are likely to be highly valued when the data used by cognitive systems are highly unstructured (voice or text or human genome records, as opposed to rows and columns of numbers) or difficult to extract from its source. They, like some programmers, are likely to be familiar with open-source big data tools like Hadoop. And they also are likely to have either quantitative modeling skills or natural language processing skills.

What do data scientists do day to day in the development of automated decision systems? Automated systems typically use a lot of data, so the data scientist might be scouting around to figure out the next great external data source. After a promising source is identified, he or she might be determining how to get the data into the right format, or how to combine it with the data that the organization already has. The data scientist might also be working on an algorithm to extract insights from the data. Or, since data scientists tend to be good at computational skills, too, they might be architecting or helping to develop the new or modified system.

Sandro Catanzaro, a native of Peru, is the cofounder and senior vice president of analytics and innovation at DataXu, a Boston-based marketing automation software company. In that job he does data science himself as well as managing that activity for the company (though he does more of the latter now). DataXu focuses particularly on the automation of digital marketing decisions—determining the most effective and efficient place to publish ads, placing them on publishers' websites, and determining how effective they are. The company typically has well under a second to make its decisions, and all of the decisions are based on data and analytics.

Catanzaro studied mechanical engineering in Buenos Aires, Argentina, launched businesses in consumer products and engineering in Peru, and then came to MIT to pick up a degree in business. While doing so, he also got a degree from the Aeronautics and Astronautics department at MIT (known as AeroAstro), and worked at NASA headquarters as a researcher; which makes him a certified rocket scientist. After graduation he then became a management consultant for a few years before cofounding DataXu. Working with DataXu cofounder (and AeroAstro PhD) Bill Simmons, Catanzaro developed the core algorithms that make DataXu's marketing decisions, and he is constantly working with his team to improve them.

In that sense, Catanzaro epitomizes a combination of stepping-up and stepping-forward roles. He doesn't do a lot of algorithm or system development anymore himself, but he oversees a lot of both activities.

On a typical day, Catanzaro might meet with his team to discuss their progress on a new algorithm or improvements to an existing one. He often gives advice to the team on how to scale up a new solution or eliminate its limitations. He does that with his team for about 60 percent of his time. He also spends a lot of time with customers—roughly a couple of days a week. He hears what their needs for new capabilities are, and translates that into data science activity by his team. Whenever he can squeeze it in, he interviews and hires new data scientists, and meets with other DataXu executives.

When he hires other data scientists, Catanzaro looks for three types of skills, only one of which is technical. The first is "data science smarts"—being good with big data technologies, statistics, and so forth. He's not so much interested in knowledge of a particular set of tools, but rather the "raw horsepower" to be able to master new tools.

The second trait is business understanding—knowing the problems of marketers, and being able to translate that into how DataXu makes money. Catanzaro always believes in starting with the business problem, then going to the technology and data that will solve it.

Finally, Catanzaro seeks management and collaboration skills in his data scientists. He wants people who can work effectively with a team and create an effective outcome for the organization. And in all of these areas, he looks for a "sharp understanding of reality."

Researchers

—Given that the field of automated decision systems is—in most areas of inquiry, at least—relatively new, there is still important research that needs to be done to advance the state of knowledge. Researchers who step forward may take several forms. They may do basic scientific research in artificial intelligence (usually in universities), applied research in general AI (usually in a corporate research lab, such as the "deep learning" research at Google), or applied research in a specific nonvendor setting.

One prominent example of the latter type is the many physicians and scientists who undertake clinical trials within hospitals and medical schools. This sort of work usually applies to new drugs and medical devices, but it also sometimes involves automated systems. Dr. Rachel Brem, a radiologist and professor at George Washington University, has undertaken research on automated identification of possible breast cancer lesions for many years. She's the director of breast imaging and intervention at GW Medical Faculty Associates, and she works closely with vendors of imaging technology vendors in developing and testing their new systems. Her 2007 research on automated computer-aided detection (CAD) of breast lesions was instrumental in the Food and Drug Administration's approval of that technology in 2008.

Dr. Brem is highly supportive of human review of mammography—the use of imaging devices to detect breast cancer—but she knows the weaknesses of human mammogram reading as well. One of those is a high incidence of false positives—spotting a potential but noncancerous lesion that leads to other imaging or even biopsies. She feels that CAD holds the potential to reduce the number of false positives, so she has been overseeing a variety of clinical trials to understand how to achieve that potential benefit. She's currently conducting a trial to understand the potential of ultrasound-based CAD in dense breast tissue—the most difficult type to assess.

When we asked Dr. Brem why she became interested in CAD, she said that she'd always been interested in new technology—in her medical practice and her personal life. And she believes that the problem of false positives is too important not to address. She works closely with manufacturers of breast imaging systems because she believes the technology is typically many years ahead of what has been approved by the FDA.

Brem isn't particularly worried that CAD or other cognitive tools will replace radiologists. Thus far, she says, it's been more like a spellchecker—pointing out small errors that a human might have overlooked. She hasn't seen any smart machines that rival the abilities of human radiologists yet, but she doesn't discount that they might be available at some point. In the meantime, she believes it's very important for practitioners in her field to understand the strengths and weaknesses of automated diagnosis systems, and she hopes that her clinical research will help facilitate that understanding.

Product Managers

—Automated systems are software products, and software products need product management. Product management in software is a critical function; its role is to ensure that the software has the features and functions that customers need, and that it comes to market with the necessary speed and quality. It often involves persuading and herding individuals who don't actually report to the product manager, so it can be a challenging role.

Jim Lawton, whom we also mentioned in Chapter 2, is chief product and marketing officer at Rethink Robotics, a "collaborative robotics" manufacturer in Boston. Rethink was founded and is led by Rodney Brooks, a former MIT professor, who also plays the role of chief technology officer. He handles the vision and the research. It is Lawton's job to understand what customers want from robots and translate that into product capabilities. He's also an evangelist for the idea that robots and people can collaborate with each other. Rethink's robot models, which now include the cutely named Baxter and Sawyer, don't require a lot of detailed programming. They learn their movements by having a person guide them. Unlike many robots, they don't pose a danger to humans and don't have to be isolated in cages. Rethink's robot appendages move slowly and stop immediately when they touch something unexpected.

So in addition to ensuring that the product gets out the door, Lawton is on a mission to build demand for a new kind of cognitive technology. He blogs prolifically, speaks widely, and visits customers often. Since it's early days for this new kind of robot, Lawton is trying to help the world figure out where it fits into manufacturing and production processes.

Lawton was an electrical engineering major in college but considered a career as a concert pianist. Instead he enrolled in a new program at MIT called Leaders for Manufacturing. The goal of the program was to create a new generation of leaders to revitalize American manufacturing; it addressed technical, managerial, and organizational perspectives on the field. Lawton then also got an MBA from MIT. He then worked at Hewlett-Packard in manufacturing, and at several startups in e-commerce and supply chain management. He's still trying to revitalize manufacturing and feels strongly that Baxter and Sawyer, working closely with humans, can help in the effort.

Marketers

—Marketing is a particularly important function with automated systems and cognitive technologies, primarily because many people don't understand them, and many of those who do are worried about them. A marketer in this area has to be a missionary and an explainer of how these systems work. He or she doesn't have to understand the technical details of automated systems, but there is a requirement to understand how the systems work in general, and what their strengths and weaknesses are—even if the latter are not widely shared.

Daniela Zuin is our automation marketing poster child. She lives in the London area but leads marketing for IPsoft, a New York–based company that offers automated solutions for IT operations (IPcenter) and a general automated virtual agent "wizard" called Amelia.

Zuin is not a highly technical person, though she has worked in a variety of technology services and software marketing roles. She majored in English literature in college and wrote her dissertation on Gabriel García Márquez. She then taught English as a second language in Italy, and later got an MBA. She's worked for Accenture, Electronic Data Systems (EDS), and other systems integration companies before joining IPsoft in early 2014.

She was attracted to automation software and IPsoft because her previous jobs had dealt with conventional technologies. This was the first time, she felt, that she had a really exciting and innovative product to market.

IPsoft has a fifteen-year history of working in IT operations. Its "virtual engineers" receive and interpret messages from a variety of IT devices—servers, storage devices, network controllers—and either take action when necessary, or determine which human needs to be consulted. Even then it brings all the information to the human and can recommend an action. It seems to us an obvious application of automation—who would be more likely to accept a software-based helper than IT engineers? But Zuin says that there are still examples of IT people putting up roadblocks to IPcenter or slowing down its implementation.

Amelia is a broader technology and has the potential to transform human-computer interaction across a variety of settings. It works with IPcenter but it can also automate (or augment) a variety of call center and customer support applications. It's great that it has such broad capabilities, but that makes marketing it a little tougher. One of Zuin's challenges is figuring out where to focus Amelia, given that the possibilities are almost limitless. Learning what areas it works best in, and working with consulting partners to tailor it to different industries and business processes, is an important task for the entire IPsoft organization.

Some customers and settings are better than others, from Zuin's standpoint. As a marketer, she's naturally more interested in customer applications that increase their revenue, rather than those that just cut back-office costs. Operational efficiency is fine, but customers get more excited about increasing the top line.

With Amelia in particular, Zuin and her colleagues have to do a lot of communication with potential customers and the market in general about the automation topic. There are extremes in what people perceive; some fear the loss of control, for example. Zuin counters, however, that organizations increase control over the process with Amelia because they have consistent, compliant interactions. Some companies, particularly in Europe, worry about the impact on jobs, or the perception of the impact on jobs. Others are concerned about being early adopters of a new technology. It's the step-forward marketer's job to quiet such fears and to turn the conversations toward opportunity.

Zuin has already succeeded to some degree in getting the media to focus not just on the downside of automation and on the possibilities for augmentation. In one British publication (*Information Age*), for example, an article titled "The Day I Met Amelia" mentioned IPsoft's British CEO, Richard Warley:

With 20 percent of the workforce working in the kinds of "mid-level knowledge worker" jobs Amelia wants to take on, and with her ability to supposedly cut response time from four minutes to a matter of seconds, the implications for the global economy are clear. But Warley insists it won't be a case of machines taking over—AIs like Amelia will free up humans from the more mundane tasks, he says, allowing them to concentrate on higher-level processes.

What Zuin and her IPsoft colleagues would like best would be if customers and the market would shift toward the positive opportunities furnished by automation software. They would rather companies focus on the potential in freeing up skilled employees from doing lower-skill tasks—such as answering the same boring questions from customers all the time—and giving them higher-level opportunities. They could imagine, for example, companies that really care about their customers proactively reaching out to contact them about problems and issues before the customer seeks help. Zuin knows that the first wave of automation probably will involve taking some people out of business processes, but she hopes for a second wave involving reshaping business processes and work designs to take advantage of technologies like Amelia and IPcenter. In short, she's pulling for augmentation rather than just automation.

Entrepreneurs

—We don't think that entrepreneurs in the automated decision software space are necessarily different in systematic ways than any other type of technology entrepreneur. But we know they are essential. Many of the companies who are stepping these systems forward are startups, and they need entrepreneurs to found and lead them. There will undoubtedly be a lot more, but to give you an idea of the genre we'll describe one who's been at this for a while.

Tim Estes is a young CEO, but he's not as young as he used to be. He was really young in 2000, when he graduated from the University of Virginia and immediately started his company, Digital Reasoning. There his major was not computer science or engineering, but philosophy. Yes, he studied Plato and Wittgenstein, but he also studied the more formal and language-oriented aspects of philosophy. He started Digital Reasoning in the unlikely location of Nashville, Tennessee, with the original intent of creating software that learns. But after September 11, 2001, it became clear to Estes—and many other people, some in Washington, D.C.—that analyzing language in order to understand what terrorists and potential terrorists are thinking and doing would be a very useful capability. With his background in language and categorization, this became a natural focus for the company. And he was inspired by the need to help his country's intelligence analysts know more about terrorists' plans without having to read every communication among them.

Estes's company secured its first contact with U.S. Army intelligence in 2004 and received an injection of cash from In-Q-Tel, the strategic investment arm of the U.S. intelligence community, in 2010. Estes doesn't comment on any specific intelligence community customers or their specific uses of the software, but In-Q-Tel often invests in companies that serve intelligence agencies. And published reports suggest that for the first twelve years of its history, Digital Reasoning's only customer was the U.S. intelligence industry.

But in 2012, financial services companies began to see the virtues of ingesting and digesting text—in emails and other communications—to understand which employees might be perpetrating fraud—SEC violations, market manipulations, and bribes or favors. The focus of Estes's business shifted from just finding evildoers among terrorist organizations to also finding them in large banks and investment houses. Basically the software predicts how likely an employee is to be doing something wrong; if he or she is talking about free tickets with a supplier, for example, that's a pretty good sign that something is amiss. If the predicted level of suspicion is high, human security investigators can investigate further.

Digital Reasoning is now focusing on all types of "predictive compliance" in several different industries, including financial services and health care. The company works with a foundation that reduces human trafficking of minors for prostitution rings. It is also beginning to focus on more opportunity-oriented applications, including customer relationships and understanding the dynamics of financial markets. In 2015 the company raised $24 million in a venture capital round with backers like Goldman Sachs and Credit Suisse, who are also customers.

Estes is passionate about helping to fight terrorism and to eliminate financial fraud. He believes that there is a great opportunity to use data, analytics, and artificial intelligence tools to change the world. He tries to transfer this passion throughout the company; as the company's website notes: "Digital Reasoning is a place where people come to work every day determined to make the 'impossible' possible. From entry-level employees to senior-level software engineers, we have a real passion for what we do and that passion runs through our offices like electricity. . . . We're working to create technology that can read and understand human communication like never before."

Consultants

—These days, when companies need to build or install any type of new system, it's very likely they will call on consultants. We've already mentioned Michael Bernaski, who as a consultant to the insurance industry implemented lots of automated underwriting systems (and changed the career trajectories of a lot of underwriters). Today even highly capable automated systems like IBM's Watson require a very high degree of customization to the specific industry and decision set to which they are being applied.

Even though consulting about automated systems (at least those beyond rule-based systems in insurance) is relatively new, it's a rapidly growing field with several different types of consulting. Some specialize in developing big data and analytics-oriented applications. Others, particularly some of the Indian outsourcing firms, are focused on what they call "robotic process automation"—automating routine back-office processes. Others focus on helping their clients decide where automation initiatives are appropriate, and tailoring the systems to fit the business process and decision.

This latter category of consulting is the focus of Rajeev Ronanki, a principal at Deloitte Consulting. Ronanki is the co-leader of Deloitte's cognitive computing practice. He and his colleagues work with a variety of cognitive and artificial intelligence systems, as well as analytics and big data. Ronanki helped to tailor and implement IBM's Watson at its first commercial customer, a large health insurer.

We asked Rajeev how he came into his position at Deloitte. He admitted that some luck was involved: "I had done my master's degree in computer science with a focus on AI, but there wasn't much consulting in the area at the time, so I moved on to other things. Twenty years later IBM sold a Watson engagement to my insurance client. And Watson needed a lot of tailoring to fit the industry and application, which was insurance preauthorizations. So I was in the right place at the right time." Ronanki gives credit to IBM for bringing about a renaissance in artificial intelligence through their development of Watson and their effective marketing.

He says there are typically three steps involved in working with a client on cognitive systems. Things start with a "cognitive value assessment." The client tells Ronanki and his colleagues what aspects (processes or customer touch points) of the business to look at in terms of their readiness for cognitive technologies. Then each one is evaluated on a variety of different factors that are combined in a "heat map." The variables might include the strength of the business case, investment levels and likely returns, and the ease of using existing technologies in the area. The output of this step is a business case and approach, plus a high-level solutions architecture. This is also the step at which planning for what humans will do in the post-automation context is carried out, which would be done in conjunction with the client's "step-up" executives.

Ronanki says that almost all clients want to try a pilot as the second step, because the technology is new (at least to them) and they're not sufficiently confident to forge ahead with a full implementation. The pilot might be used on a subset of the business process or involve a thinner slice of functionality. That typically requires four to six months.

The third and final step in a consulting project, then, involves scaling the pilot into production. This step involves programming the system, doing system integration to connect it with data, assembling the "corpus" (the body of knowledge from which the system will learn), training the system with a training data set, and testing it. At this third stage, Ronanki says, he and his colleagues work with "superusers" (a term we previously compared to the "step-in" role) who understand the business process and are able to help configure the system and help other users to perform their work with it. For this role they seek the most expert and successful frontline resources, so that the system is learning from the best. In some cases such superusers eventually move into more permanent step in roles involving working closely with the system; in other cases they just go back to their old jobs.

Neither Deloitte nor any other firm yet has a large number of automation consultants, but the number is growing. Ronanki says that Deloitte looks for people in four different skill categories:

data science engineers with the ability to create or at least customize machine-learning algorithms;
graduates with general computer science backgrounds;
people with artificial intelligence backgrounds, though Ronanki says they are particularly hard to find;
people with "big data" technical skills such as Hadoop, Spark, and in-memory computing.

Ronanki says that nontechnical skills are also very important, including functional expertise in the processes being automated. These don't often come in conjunction with the technical skills. "It would be great to find an expert in both insurance claims overpayment and machine learning, but that would be extremely rare." Deloitte has a nascent change management practice in the cognitive systems area, but Ronanki expects it will become much larger and more important as automation initiatives grow in scale and number; "then you will have huge people issues," he stated.

Internal Automation Leaders

—Automation/augmentation projects aren't only developed by startups and consultants; they also get developed by individual companies to address their own internal processes. Some of these involve "classical" artificial intelligence; others—perhaps more common—involve embedding analytical decision-making tools into operational systems.

We described the size and scale and complexity of Schneider's trucking and transportation business in Chapter 6. You've probably seen the company's big orange trucks and containers. What you don't see are the data, algorithms, and rules that help to manage all the complexity of the business.

Zahir Balaporia, whose team developed the system used by Travis Torrence as described in Chapter 6, played an important role in initiating and developing these automated (or at least semiautomated) systems at Schneider for eighteen years (he recently left there and is now doing similar work at FICO). His last job at Schneider was director of advanced planning and decision science. He's held various other jobs at Schneider in engineering, technology, and process improvement, but as we have spoken with him over the years his focus was always on creating more efficient and effective operations for the company.

Balaporia (his colleagues simply call him "Z") has an undergraduate degree in computer engineering and a master's degree in industrial engineering, and is pursuing another master's degree in system dynamics. But he's hardly a total geek. He knows that an automated "system" actually consists of people and processes and computers, all working in tandem—at least when things go well. We would call that an augmented system, of course.

The most complex automated system that Balaporia's team has developed is Short Haul Optimizer (SHO). As we mentioned earlier, that's the system used by Travis Torrence that connects Schneider's truck drivers with container loads at rail ramps, often in big cities. The drivers pick up and deliver containers between customers and rail ramps multiple times a day. In some cities, this "drayage" activity may involve hundreds of drivers and more than five hundred daily pickup and delivery container moves. Balaporia and his team developed an automated optimizer that maximizes driver productivity and minimizes costs to Schneider. It's a complex system that uses "set-partitioning formulation and column-generation heuristics," but the sophisticated math still can't do it all. There are still important roles for humans in the process—including "dispatch analysts" like Torrence who monitors the system's recommendations and sometimes override them.

Although Balaporia tries to automate as much of this complex decision-making as possible, he doesn't believe that humans will be out of the picture anytime soon. The data and the models always need improvement. Furthermore, while at Schneider he and his team were constantly adding new capabilities to their automated system—making additions for city-specific regulations and fees, traffic conditions, and weather. The need for human augmentation may not grow as rapidly as Schneider's shipments do, but it's not going away. He commented to us while still at the company:

"My team has often concluded that augmentation—combining smart humans and smart machines—is a more pragmatic approach than automation. Our original strategy on SHO was an automation strategy. But as we got into the implementation, the operations research team got closer to the operational details and data quality issues by working closely with dispatch analysts. Understanding those details made it more practical to pursue an augmentation approach. But we continue to look for ideas to automate, which will allow the dispatch analyst to focus on broader systemic issues."

Job Implications of Stepping Forward

The establishment and growth of all these automation employment opportunities will add up to a large number of jobs, not all of which are highly technical in nature. Who knows how many it will add up to? The step-forward category probably won't replace all the jobs eliminated because of automation, but it will be a fast-growing and important segment of the tech economy. Gil Press, a columnist for *Forbes*, makes the optimistic case for this by referring back to a 1963 article by John Diebold on the impact of automation. Diebold predicted a level of automation for repetitive work, but only within limits: "Certain functions, such as filing and statistical analysis on the lower management levels, will be performed by machines. Yet very few offices will be entirely automatic. Much day-to-day work—answering correspondence and the like—will have to be done by human beings."[2]

Press comments (using our favorite terminology), "Two years after publishing the book that popularized the term 'automation,' Diebold 'stepped forward' in 1954 (when he was twenty-eight), not by developing the next generation of computers, but by establishing one of the first consulting companies advising businesses on how to adopt this new technology. An entire new industry and entire new breed of knowledge workers followed in his path. 'Automation' has created a lot of new jobs and there is no reason why robots will not create even more knowledge worker jobs—in consulting, servicing, help-desking, observing, counting, talking, analyzing, researching, marketing, selling, etc." We think Gil Press is right about this, of course.

No one can anticipate the exact size of the step-forward job market, but since most people don't know that it exists, there probably won't be much competition for a while. If you want a job in this budding industry, pick one of the categories that we've described, or think of another one that's likely to take off. Then begin to prepare yourself with the types of skills necessary to help the world step forward.

How Are the Forward-Steppers Spending Their Time?

Learning what those who step forward are spending their time and efforts on will give you a sense of what's coming with automated and augmented systems and what it's like to work in this domain. Although every automated system is somewhat different, there are definitely some common themes across the projects their creators and leading users are addressing.

Usability and Transparency by Business Users
—One of the problems with automated systems in the past has been that they have been difficult to understand and modify. They've sometimes been a "black box"—inputs go in, outputs come out, but it's not clear why the system came up with the answer or decision that it did. Increasingly, however, users of these systems aren't content with black boxes. They won't trust the results if they don't know what went into them. If they don't trust them, they won't let them make important decisions. And it makes it very difficult for people to step in to work with cognitive technologies if they can't understand or change the systems they are tending.

The first type of systems that made this sort of transparency possible were rule-based systems in insurance. Vendors and consultants implemented these systems for their customers, but insurance companies wanted to be able to understand the rules and change them to get better outcomes over time. For most companies today using such systems, underwriters and actuaries are able to monitor and change the systems in English-like language and graphic decision paths without help from a vendor or consultant. Rule-based underwriting in insurance has also been expanded to new areas—for example, medical and life insurance underwriting—from its initial base in property and casualty insurance.

Another domain of automation in which transparency and ease of use are increasing is robotics. We mentioned the company Rethink Robotics (and their head of product and marketing, Jim Lawton) earlier in this chapter. That company and several others focus on the "collaborative robots" segment, in which humans and robots can work closely alongside each other. Whereas with a traditional robot, changing the pattern of movements and actions would require changes to a complex programming language, changing the behaviors of collaborative robots typically involves simply demonstrating the required movements to the robot. Any changes to the robot's software are done through a visual user interface. And collaborative robots move slowly and stop when they touch something, which means they aren't dangerous to work alongside and don't have to be put in cages to prevent injuries to humans.

A third type of transparency is well suited to step-up managers who want to have some control over the entire automated process. Aaron Kechley, the senior vice president of products at DataXu—the digital marketing automation company that Sandro Catanzaro cofounded—told us that their system may recommend thousands of different changes within a digital marketing campaign. They have created a button for their customers that says "accept changes," but they give the customers the ability to see (literally—the system gives a visual display of the changes being made) what changes are being made if they want the details. It turns out that most people directly accept the changes, and may not actually use the visualization or participate in the detailed decision process, but they like the feeling that they could.

Unfortunately, other types of automated systems are not yet as transparent and easy to change as rule-based systems in insurance, collaborative robotics, and digital marketing. Some machine-learning algorithms are inherently complex, and as yet there is no easily understood or modified approach to them—although some academics, including Cynthia Rudin at MIT, have called for this capability.[3] Some language-oriented systems can show graphically how different terms are related to each other within a system, and how a user question is broken down into its constituent parts. Systems such as IBM Watson can show the percentage likelihood that an answer, decision, or diagnosis is correct. Some other vendors, such as Digital Reasoning, that use training data to improve the accuracy of an automated system are making it possible for users to do their own training on new data sets, rather than having to call on a vendor or consultant. While these aids to transparency can sometimes be difficult to interpret, they are a step in the right direction.

Broadening the Base of Methods

—As we discussed in Chapter 2, the technologies used to automate decisions are generally quite narrow and rely on a single type of artificial intelligence software. Now, however, several vendors are trying to combine multiple approaches into a broader artificial intelligence "platform." Vendors like IBM, Cognitive Scale, SAS, and Tibco are adding new cognitive functions and integrating them into solutions. Deloitte is working with companies like IBM and Cognitive Scale to create not just a single application, but a broad "Intelligent Automation Platform."

Even when progress is made on these types of integration, the result will still fall short of the all-knowing "artificial general intelligence" or "strong AI" that we discussed in Chapter 2. That may well be coming, but not anytime soon. Still, these short-term combinations of tools and methods may well make automation solutions much more useful.

Broadening Application of the Same Tools

—In addition to employing broader types of technology, organizations that are stepping forward are using their existing technology to address different industries and business functions. IBM is the master of this with Watson, applying it to health-care diagnosis, insurance approvals, technical support, shopping applications, pharmaceutical development, and many other domains. The fundamental technologies within Watson (at least the original version of it) are text digestion and understanding and logical reasoning, and that can be applied broadly. However, Watson's customers have sometimes underestimated the time it takes to train the system on a new set of terminology and issues.

We've already mentioned several companies in this chapter that are applying their technologies to new domains. Digital Reasoning is moving its technology, originally used for analyzing the communications of potential terrorists, to studying regulatory compliance in financial services employees, and then to human trafficking and understanding investment opportunities. DataXu is applying its digital marketing automation software to video ad buying. IPsoft is moving its question-answering capability from IT management to customer service to outbound customer contacts.

Moving across areas in this fashion obviously provides the opportunity for revenue growth for these companies. But it can also be a distraction from improving the basic technology that underlies different applications. It also may be difficult for companies to find the expertise in new areas that is required to tailor the system to a new application.

Reporting and Showing Results

—As we spoke with people who are stepping forward—the vendors of automation software in particular—we were surprised by how often they said they were working on better and more extensive reporting about just what their systems were accomplishing. Now that we think about it, it shouldn't be so surprising. If companies are spending a lot of money and energy on an automated solution, they want to see that they are getting their money's worth.

Remember, for example, Andrew Daley, the vice president of member acquisition at on-demand car rental company Zipcar. We discussed him as a step-up practitioner in Chapter 4. Andrew buys a lot of digital ads using automated "programmatic buying." We wrote in that chapter that Zipcar has twenty-six different markets, each with a different budget. "At the end of the month he has to go to each market and tell them what they have achieved." That means lots of reports, sliced and diced in different ways for different people.

Aaron Kechley at DataXu told us that improving reporting has been a big deal for his company for several years now. He said, "We learned the hard way that you can't preconceive what people will want in a report—people want to process information in different ways." As a result, DataXu has been investing heavily in the latest "business intelligence" tools—new metrics, custom dashboards, and tailored reports.

In fact, one of DataXu's primary offerings these days is a tool that actually shows marketers whether their digital ads are working or not. This approach, which goes beyond reporting, has been done for a while with traditional statistical analysis. Now, however, DataXu has worked out a way to use rigorous and frequent—but still small—experiments to see if an ad or promotion is working. Some people will receive the ad, and others won't, which makes it pretty easy to tell the difference the ad or promotion makes to online sales.

Embedding Automation Functions into a Workflow

—Remember Microsoft's Bob? It was the paper-clip-like "wizard" that always seemed to get in the way of doing your work. Marten den Haring, the head of product at Digital Reasoning, said that the fear of creating another Bob has motivated his company to fit its offerings into a smooth user workflow. "We don't want to be invasive or intrusive," he commented. "If our tools help people in a sensible, easy-to-use way, they will be much more likely to adopt and get value from our system."

This need to fit into the user's workflow is important no matter what the type of worker. UPS has worked mightily to fit its automated driver routing algorithm, ORION, into the jobs of its drivers. Schneider National has gone to a lot of trouble to ease its dispatch systems into the jobs of dispatch analysts. Companies who work with automation of legal and medical functions report that their potential users—lawyers and doctors—are highly resistant to change, despite (or perhaps because of) their high incomes and IQs.

We are confident that in the future we'll see automated decision functions built into a wide variety of business transaction systems. Your company's ERP system will automatically determine whether a particular customer is worthy of a discount or an expedited shipment. The system that takes online job applications will automatically determine whether a particular applicant is worthy of an interview. You may even see instantaneous and automated feedback on whether your college application is successful or not. As the technology research firm Gartner has noted, analytics and system intelligence will increasingly become "advanced, pervasive, and invisible"—embedded within all our systems and business processes.

Adding New Sources of Data

—Another sure bet is that new sources of readily available data will become more readily available all the time. If you're part of a step-forward organization, part of your job will be incorporating new sources of data into automated decision systems.

Name the industry, and we can probably tell you a new source of data that's become available and incorporated into smart machines. Insurers, for example, are rapidly adding satellite images and geospatial data into their property and casualty underwriting systems. They no longer need to drive to a potential customer's location to check the size of the parking lot or the presence of trees close to the house; they can determine that remotely and with automated detection. Financial advice firms used to be restricted to knowing about the customer's financial assets that were invested with their firm; now they can get online information about the average assets in the customer's postal code, or (with the customer's permission) access to the information in the customer's other investment and banking accounts. Health-care providers and insurers can find out what drugs you take, how much you walked yesterday, and—before long— probably even what you had for breakfast (at least if you posted it to Instagram). Your car insurer will—if it doesn't already—know how far and how fast you drive, and at what times of day you do it.

Some of these data sources, of course, will raise privacy concerns. But in many cases they will be "opt-in" information that customers provide in exchange for discounts and increased insights. Firms like Progressive (car insurance) and Kabbage (small business loans) already engage in this sort of exchange with the explicit permission of their customers. Those individuals and businesses that want to maintain their privacy will increasingly be faced with a choice: Give it up or pay more for remaining a mystery to the rest of the world.

Working on the Math

—Many of the firms we interviewed say that they are not only going broader into new AI tools and methods, and new applications of their existing systems. They're also improving and fine-tuning the algorithms and models that make decisions for their customers. Some of this involves automated modeling through machine learning. When machines are doing the modeling, the models can be much more numerous and fine grained. A digital marketing company like DataXu, for example, may need thousands of models a week to help it decide what digital or video ad to place on what site. In companies, like Digital Reasoning, that do language processing, the types of models that digest and interpret language are still evolving rapidly. These companies are always scanning the research literature and hiring new math geeks to help them refine their models.

Some of this greater mathematical and statistical sophistication, of course, may work against the goal of transparency and modifiability by business users. Just as we get transparency of one type of black box, another new one comes along that offers greater predictive or explanatory power, but less visibility and interpretability. Companies and researchers can only continue to work along both fronts and try to maintain a balance between these two objectives.

Focusing on Behavioral Finance and Economics

—Firms that step forward are also beginning to "step aside" a bit—taking on the aspects of their customer relationships that automated decisions can't fully address. For example, where financial decisions are being automated, as with the "robo-advisors" we've discussed earlier, many leading financial firms are adding capabilities to better understand and act on investor behavior. You may have heard about "behavioral economics," which brought the revolutionary (if seemingly obvious) conclusion to economics that humans are not always rational. Financial investment firms have a version of this for personal investing that is called "behavioral finance." It means that no matter how good automated decision-making can be about what financial assets to buy and sell at what times, irrational humans may override the advice—whether human or automated—and make bad decisions.

Some of the common ways that investors make poor decisions include "loss aversion"—caring more about not losing a dollar than gaining a dollar—and "familiarity bias"—being more willing to invest in familiar assets, like the stocks of companies in their home country, than those in companies they've never heard of. These irrational decision criteria lead to such woeful investor behaviors as "buying high and selling low."

Robo-advisor-only companies, such as Betterment and Wealthfront, and large financial advisor companies that have adopted some automated advice capabilities, such as Vanguard and Fidelity, have begun to employ behavioral finance approaches to try to understand and improve investor behavior. In some cases they provide education and other per-suasive methods to try to correct behavioral finance problems. In others they simply program rational behavior into their automated systems and hope that the irrational investor doesn't override their recommendations by taking their money out. We'll describe a bit of how Vanguard is using these ideas in conjunction with a semiautomated online advice system in the next chapter.

Stepping Forward, in Summary

One thing should be clear by now: This will be a vibrant category of the economy. If you think you have some of the necessary skills, it's not too early to start preparing for a career in it.

And as we've said about some of the other steps you can take to preserve your job in an era of very smart machines, stepping forward will require being a lively stepper as well. The technologies for building and imple-menting automated systems are changing rapidly; the development of these systems itself is even becoming more automated. The people who want to work in the automated systems industry will have to be particularly adept at learning new skills and updating their resumes to reflect their new skills. Their reward will be a valuable one, however: working in an exciting indus-try, and drawing a good paycheck from it over many years.

What Those Who Step Forward Look Like

You're a candidate for stepping forward if . . .

- You have a deep understanding of some type of information tech-nology (not necessarily cognitive) and you are willing to explore some new tools;
- You are already comfortable and skilled in playing some form of support role relative to IT;
- You are passionate about cognitive technologies and are willing to undergo a substantial amount of learning;

- You are an expert in your field and would like to explore the role of cognitive technologies in it;
- You have or want the job of exploring new technologies and how they fit into your company's strategy and operations.

You can build your skills for stepping forward by . . .

- Taking computer science and math/statistics classes in college;
- Studying machine learning and AI in online courses;
- Taking courses, listening to webinars, and reading white papers from cognitive technology vendors who sell into your industry;
- Attending conferences about cognitive technology or its underlying components (for example, analytics, machine learning);
- Exploring existing cognitive technology tools by downloading free or inexpensive versions of them or trying them out in the cloud.

You're likely to be found in . . .

- A vendor of cognitive technology solutions;
- A business that is exploring or implementing cognitive technologies.

9

How You'll Manage Augmentation

Sixty-nine days is a long time to spend underground, trapped in a mine and wondering if you'll ever see the light of day again. But the ordeal of the Chilean miners could have been much worse had Codelco not become involved. You probably remember the story: On August 5, 2010, a copper and gold mine owned by the San Esteban Primera Mining Company, near Copiapó in northern Chile, experienced a major underground collapse, leaving thirty-three miners trapped in a shelter 2,300 feet deep. A major international rescue effort began immediately, with substantial assistance from Codelco, the Chilean national copper mining company. Several different rescue holes were drilled to get fresh air and provisions to the miners. Finally, on October 13, the miners were winched to the surface, one by one, in an operation viewed live by some billion people around the world. The triumphant banner was raised: "Misión cumplida Chile."

But something else Codelco did that year, without the world noticing much at all, would ultimately do even more to save miners. In the same year in which the Copiapó accident took place, Codelco launched its new integrated operations center, designed to control a variety of robotic and autonomous mining machines. With its investment in these intelligent machines, Codelco could protect its human employees in the best way: by not sending many of them deep into the mine in the first place.

Codelco didn't only start exploring smart machines in 2010; it had been experimenting with automation since the 1990s, when it first used remote "telecommand" of rock hammers in underground mines. By 2003 it embarked upon a broad "Codelco Digital" initiative that had automation and remote control of mining equipment at its core. The project involved a broad review of available automation technologies and key business processes at the company with an eye to how they might fit together.

Under the Codelco Digital banner, various automation initiatives were launched. Autonomous trucks were introduced in 2008; truck loading is also increasingly automated. Underground mine trains are increasingly autonomous. Smelting and crushing operations run under advanced control systems. In some new underground mines being developed now, 100 percent of the mining equipment will be automated or robotic.

There are still 3,400 miners going underground into Codelco mines today, but the company knows where each worker is at all times and what the current health and environmental conditions are for each miner. Codelco expects to complete automated mining in underground mines in 2016.

Miners aren't "knowledge workers" by any strict definition of the term, but the Codelco example teaches some important lessons for how augmentation gets done right in any environment. To start with, we like the fact that it sprang from a pro-people orientation. Marco Orellana, the company's chief information officer and the leader of Codelco Digital, told us: "The processes of mining work have very high risk and unfavorable environmental conditions in underground mines and smelters. We needed better safety conditions for the workers, and we needed to create a more attractive business for the new workers who don't like working inside the mines and inside the tunnels."

Codelco was also interested in the productivity benefits of automation, of course. But the primary focus was worker safety. Chile has had a socialist government for much of the last decade, and Codelco is a 100 percent state-owned company. Automation initiatives designed primarily to eliminate labor in a state-owned company would not have been politically viable.

It's also instructive that the use of intelligent machines began as an opportunistic and narrowly scoped project (the remote-control hammers) but soon took shape as a broad strategy (Codelco Digital) to enable people doing core work to produce more value. Workers and skills across Codelco have become dramatically different over the past decade. Truck drivers have become joystick drivers, and are now selected in part on the basis of video gaming skills. Control operators understand how automated systems work, and learn about the variables and information they manage in simulations. Fleet managers optimize the use of trucks. Other workers specialize in the maintenance of robotic equipment. Codelco professionals create conceptual design requirements and specifications for needed capabilities, and work with Chilean and international equipment providers to source automated equipment and systems.

The Codelco transformation is an exciting tale of an emerging strategy for human–machine augmentation, which the rest of the business world would do well to watch. The combination of automated technology, centralized monitoring and control, and remote operation means a future in which workers will never—or at least only rarely—have to go underground to extract ores. Copper mining has been transformed from a dangerous and labor-intensive process to one driven by innovation, knowledge, and technology.

Mining the Lessons

Codelco is relatively unusual in developing an augmentation strategy so early in the game, but of course the company had more motivation than most firms in its need to keep employees safe. Most organizations don't have the dirty and dangerous work that Codelco's miners do. And it was aided by a series of external providers of equipment and automation services that were pretty far along in automating their offerings. They knew that, while Codelco was an early and aggressive adopter, many other mining companies would ultimately implement automation and augmentation approaches.

Similarly, the moment is arriving for many other kinds of organizations to think more expansively about how machines and humans will work together, and formulate augmentation strategies. The technologies are maturing rapidly, and big vendors like IBM are signing deals and issuing press releases about them at a rapid rate. One or more of your organization's competitors probably has a project under way. In some industries, like insurance (which is right up there with mining in its early adoption), automated decision-making is already becoming pervasive and commoditized. So it's time for serious thinking above the level of the "one-off" application about what can be done with these tools, how people will work alongside them, and how to achieve the maximum level of organizational advantage from them.

Throughout this book, we've laid the emphasis on equipping individual knowledge workers themselves to adjust to and prosper in a world of smart machines. But we've also repeatedly said that large employers and their managers must create the organizational context for augmentation. So now we are addressing you, dear reader, not as individual contributor but as manager. Under your guidance, your organization can help its knowledge workers make far more, or far less, successful changes. You can encourage people to develop new skills and give them the time and opportunities to do so. You can design business processes to make augmentation an important priority. And you can let your vendors and consultants know that augmentation is a key organizational objective.

Reasons to Augment Your People

We aren't expecting that employers will embrace augmentation strategies just to keep their employees happy—although there does seem to be a growing movement toward making that more of a priority. (HCL Technologies' longtime leader, Vineet Nayar, for example, passionately believes in it, as detailed in his book *Employees First, Customers Second: Turning Conventional Management Upside Down*.) Rather, most companies will come around to augmentation as they begin to understand it is the only path to sustainable competitive advantage.

That process might start as they recognize the self-defeating nature of replacing people with machines. In simplest terms, opting for an automation-oriented strategy means entering yourself in a race toward the zero-margin reality of commoditized work. If you're using automation to do the same things your people were doing, only faster, chances are good that your competitors will follow suit. And vendors and consultants will be only too happy to provide automated solutions to the entire industry. You will end up offering the same products and services as your competitors.

Your costs will go down, but so will everybody else's. Sooner or later some-one will decide that they can pass some of the savings along to customers, and everyone's profits will fall.

You can also expect that an automated process will be more brittle and inflexible than one with some people in it. We've hinted at this already in our references to various technologies that fail to impress, from automated call centers, to online "wizards," to robots who fall down in mid-dance. We give the smart machines their due, as teammates that keep getting better all the time, but the input of humans is still essential to that learn-ing process. Switch to too much robotic autonomy and you'll condemn your customers and employees to a lot of frustration.

Some organizations pursuing automation are doing it while keeping the roles of people in mind (which we'd really describe as augmentation). Others are hoping to get rid of as many people as possible but are not really talking about it in that regard—it doesn't make for good PR. When Canadian oil extractor Suncor, for example, included a slide in a 2013 Pow-erPoint deck for investors about its exciting new "Autonomous Haulage System," it carefully added a bullet point saying the "technology creates opportunity for workers to upgrade technical skills." But comments by the company's chief financial officer, Alister Cowan, to investors at a 2015 RBC Capital Markets conference in New York seemed to more clearly indicate why the company is working to replace its fleet of heavy haulers with automated trucks: "That will take 800 people off our site," Cowan explained. "At an average [salary] of $200,000 per person, you can see the savings we're going to get from an operations perspective."[1]

Some companies don't even bother to talk out of both sides of their mouths. When Martin Ford was doing the research for his alarming book, *Rise of the Robots*, he encountered a company, Momentum Machines, with an automated solution for producing gourmet hamburgers and was able to report this comment from the cofounder, Alex Vardakostas: "Our device isn't meant to make employees more efficient. . . . It's meant to completely obviate them."[2]

Hard-core automation also sometimes locks organizations into a spe-cific production or operations approach. Think about it this way. Whether you have a hamburger production line or a services process like insurance, it takes a lot of investment and organizational change to create an automated approach to it. Once you have that automation in place, you will be less likely to want to change it. Building a new or substantially different automation system is going to be challenging. If you had designed a more augmented approach with smart people working alongside the smart machines, adaptation of the process might be easier.

And a final, related problem with aggressive automation is that, along with the people, you lose the understanding of how the process worked in the first place. If the jobs that remain aren't fulfilling, the best of them will leave you, and they won't be around to improve the process, fix any bottlenecks, or do the work manually when the system fails for some reason. Augmentation-oriented work designs face a smaller risk in this regard; it's usually the more knowledgeable people who remain within an organization. But even firms that adopt augmentation approaches do face an issue when those expert workers decide to leave or retire. If they haven't built an ongoing pipeline of workers at various stages in their careers, the well of expertise will eventually run dry.

Automation-oriented approaches create all these problems because they focus primarily or exclusively on cost reduction. Thus, even when the cost savings materialize, they may come at the long-term expense of revenues and profit margins. Augmentation approaches tend to be more likely to achieve value and innovation. We don't think that any competent organization will be able to ignore the advantages of the intelligent machines that we describe in this book. But coupling them with intelligent people is, we believe, a better bet for the long run.

Meanwhile, it is more than possible to achieve huge benefits in efficiency and productivity while pursuing an augmentation strategy. At Facebook, for example, enormous and rapid growth has led the organization to focus on automating IT-oriented tasks such as management of its huge number of servers. In an interview, Jay Parikh, Facebook's vice president of engineering, made it clear that this is an augmentation case. He told us: "[T]he point of all of this automation is that it allows us to take very simple but time-consuming tasks and move them off the plates of our really smart people. We'd rather have them thinking about the next two years coming than the last two years of stuff we've already built."[3]

When we met Parikh, we were familiar as users with Facebook's basic products, and as avid readers of the business news we had also heard regularly about ambitious new areas Facebook was venturing into. But we had never actually contemplated the sheer scale of its operations. In Parikh's words, "We have an infrastructure that spans hundreds and hundreds of thousands of computers all around the world, we're serving 1.44 billion people on the main app and hundreds of millions of people on the other apps, and there are thousands of engineers writing software that's getting deployed all the time."

The relentless "pace of product development," he explained, is the most important thing to sustain, and the clearest rationale for continued investments in automation. Enabling people to do the very interesting, important, and indisputably human work of conceiving new social solutions means not only freeing up their time, but also taming the operational complexity that comes with service proliferation.

Yet Facebook also gains real bottom-line efficiencies even as it keeps its eye on top-line growth. For example, noting that "things do break in a data center," Parikh described the degree to which Facebook has automated the maintenance of both software and hardware, and for some fixes even made the repair decision and process autonomous. So much work has been done in this regard that now, Parikh says, "we only need one technician in the data center for every 25,000 servers. That is a ratio that is basically unheard of. Most IT shops have ratios of one to 200, or one to 500."

Parikh also reminded us that, while the rest of the economy might not hold as many opportunities, in Silicon Valley there is still a war raging for talent. It would be difficult to hire and retain high-quality engineers at Facebook if the work weren't interesting—and keeping it so depends on figuring out how to take out the less interesting tasks. This heavy emphasis on automation for the sake of freeing up people and keeping them engaged in their jobs sure sounds like augmentation.

With the augmentation approaches we've described in this book—combining people who step in, step up, and step forward—you can get the best of people and machines. There are probably also important roles in your organization for people who have stepped aside or stepped narrowly. If you recognize and reward these people, you can be viewed as a desirable employer of smart humans, attracting people who have gone to the trouble of learning what smart machines can do and how to add value to them. In addition to being more flexible and responsive to change, you can gain some advantages of productivity while not being locked into an inflexible solution. Human beings may find it somewhat difficult to tell you that they are not doing a good job and should be replaced by someone else, but computer systems are incapable of that. Until they acquire that capability, you should combine them with humans. In the next section we'll describe how to go about planning and implementing your augmentation strategy.

Putting Augmentation into Action

Let's say that you're persuaded that humans and smart machines working in combination are the only viable approach to thriving in the future. How should you proceed as a manager? In particular, given the rapidly evolving areas of technology involved, how can you make plans today for the application of technology that may be very different next year?

Don't worry—while things will continue to evolve, the general outlines of what cognitive technologies can do to augment humans are pretty clear and won't change much anytime soon. The key in planning for augmented systems is to have clear views of both what technology can do (at a high level) and what you need to be done.

We'll illustrate the process of planning and developing an augmented solution with a variety of examples, but for each step in the process we describe for you, we'll also point you to one particularly instructive example—Vanguard Group's initiative to support its financial advisors with an intelligent system capable of formulating fast, accurate responses to clients' asset management questions. Vanguard is known for looking out for investors with low costs and index funds, but here it also did a good job of combining smart people and smart machines.

Step 1: Know Your Highest-Impact Decisions and Knowledge Bottlenecks

Unfortunately, it is possible to spend a lot of time implementing intelligent technologies that aren't actually a fit for your business or don't solve a very important problem. So it's a good idea to start with a very simple question: If you could wave a magic wand and give some select professionals in your organization superpowers, in what way would you expand their capacity? In particular, what decisions would you help them make better? In what areas do they lack the knowledge they need to do their jobs more effectively? Many managers like to think in terms of "leverage points" in the enterprise—that is, places where a small improvement in operational performance will yield large gains in market performance or fulfillment of the organization's mission.

At Memorial Sloan Kettering Cancer Center, for example, nothing could have more impact than helping its doctors come up with better answers to the question they face every day: What is the best way to treat this particular patient's cancer? Automated diagnosis and treatment decisions have not yet penetrated the oncology specialty to a significant degree, but there is plenty of evidence that they will before long. The field is becoming just too complex for the unaided human brain to grasp. It's now estimated, for example, that there are more than four hundred types of cancer; new forms are being discovered all the time. The number of drugs to treat cancer is also proliferating dramatically. For breast cancer alone, there are some seventy-five drugs approved to prevent or treat the disease, alone or in combination. At the same time, it's becoming obvious that an individual's genetic makeup influences both the cancers they are likely to get and their response to specific treatments. Phillip Sharp, a leading cancer researcher at MIT, says the sequencing of human tumors "has revealed hundreds of oncogenes [genes that contribute to cancer] and tumor suppressor genes in different combinations."[4] We're just beginning to scratch the surface of understanding these genetic influences.

Personalized treatment options involve a patient's genome, proteome (protein makeup), biome, and metabolic function data. Tests and markers for all these are increasingly available, which means data, data, and more data. So it's wholly appropriate for Memorial Sloan Kettering (and MD Anderson Cancer Center in Houston, and a few other institutions) to be working to augment its diagnosis and treatment decisions with tools like IBM's Watson.

Of course, an organization won't have just one of these application domains. Most, in fact, have many different knowledge bottlenecks that hinder effective decision-making and action. At MD Anderson, for example, while clinicians are pursuing a "moon shot" (their term for it) in the form of a Watson application for treatment guidelines on various cancers, Chief Information Officer Chris Belmont is pursuing a "let a thousand cognitive flowers bloom" strategy. Using technology from Cognitive Scale, Belmont has already developed several applications for issues like guiding patients to local resources, determining which patient bills are most likely to be at risk of nonpayment, a "cognitive help desk" for key enterprise applications, and many more. Belmont and his team have already identified more than sixty use cases for cognitive applications, and he expects many more.

At the Vanguard Group, management knew when launching their new advice service that the heart of the company's success was the trusting relationship between advisor and client. Trust, however, is a psychological contract with more than one dimension: Clients need to be confident not only that their advisor will always act in their best interests, with sympathetic understanding of their goals and situation, but also that the advisor has the competence to advise them appropriately. The latter side of the trust equation is what Vanguard knew it could augment with a smart decision-making tool.

Consider, for example, a typical question that is posed to advisors by clients who are newly retired or nearing retirement: How much of their assets can they safely withdraw each year? The time-honored answer to this decision has been a generic one: 4 percent each year. But such a simple rule of thumb doesn't always apply. A much more useful and safe (which is to say, trustworthy) answer would involve a complex calculation factoring in current expectations about annual return levels, interest rates, inflation, the client's particular financial situation, and more—in other words, it would require a computer program.

The important point we want to underscore about the offering Vanguard devised—which it eventually named Personal Advisor Services—is that it was conceived from the start as a combination of people with a valuable skill set performing a critical role, coupled with a new and sophisticated technology. As Karin Risi, the executive in charge of Vanguard Advice Services (the organization charged with creating Personal Advisor Services), noted in announcing the services, "we believe in the value of the [human] adviser. We've been advising clients for nearly 20 years, so we have seen, through multiple market cycles, the value of the adviser. We still think that's really important to marry those two."[5]

Not only does the Personal Advisor Services arrangement equip advisors to give better advice; it also gives them the capacity to serve more clients. By removing the burden of such manual calculations, Vanguard enables them to focus more of their time and attention on the empathetic coaching that is their forte—and that means more clients can have access to it. Through augmentation, Vanguard was able to lower the cost of its previous human advisor offer, Asset Management Service, to 30 basis points (0.30 percent of invested assets annually)—lower than it previously charged, and lower than the vast majority of other investment advisors. It dramatically broadened the base of customers it could confidently offer such hand-holding; Vanguard's minimum asset requirement for advisor services dropped from $500,000 to $50,000—again, far lower than many other advisors. All of this is very much in line with Vanguard's strong culture and clear mission of providing high levels of service. (The pledge to "Put our investors' interests first at all times" is first on its list of several commitments it makes to clients.) It also makes the advisor role a job in which more people can thrive and feel fully engaged.

To do the equivalent for your organization, your first objective should similarly be to identify those valuable people making the decisions that really move the needle on enterprise success. Another question to surface these opportunities might be: Who are some people you are currently compensating highly, yet only wish you could hire more of? To Jay Parikh's point at Facebook, augmenting them will not only help you keep paying them well, but also help you attract more of them.

And perhaps this is too obvious a point to even state, but we'll do so anyway: Talk to those people. Go straight to the source and ask the workforce: What do they wish they could do better for their customers, if only they had the computational power? Where are they wasting their time and the company's money by doing work that doesn't require or benefit from their talent? If they were able to offload routine tasks they have mastered, how would they propose to use the time instead? The best way to get people to use a new tool is to give them the tool they ask for.

In an ideal world, you might already have a clear map of the most consequential decisions and processes in your organization, and therefore a full taxonomy of opportunities to apply cognitive technologies. Probably, however, you do not. That's fine. It's enough at the outset to have a basic understanding of your business model to identify the key decisions and activities that should appear on your augmentation wish list. As you begin to explore those, you can keep working to map the rest.

Step 2: Track Technology Developments

Sometimes, with a clear idea of what decision or activity to target, it's easy to identify the cognitive technologies that would apply. At other times, however, breakthroughs in the technology itself suggest possibilities for augmentation you would not have imagined. So it's useful to stay abreast of developments in areas like machine learning, natural language processing, robotics, and artificial intelligence and to keep asking the question: How could we make use of that? To be clear, this is exactly the question that can get companies into the trouble we noted above: applying technologies because they are "so hot right now" and not because they address the highest-value opportunities in a company. We don't mean to override Step 1 here. But with that strong caveat noted, it's important to keep feeding the knowledge base that will help you make connections between problems your organization has and the solutions that are out there.

For example, it's been a very recent development that computers have learned to read and make inferences from fast, vast digestion of textual content. If you weren't part of the AI community, you might have first learned of this when IBM's Watson won *Jeopardy!* To come up with each response, Watson (specifically its "Discovery Advisor") read whole encyclopedias and untold Internet pages. How could you use that power? At the Baylor College of Medicine in Dallas, they used it to read through more than 70,000 scientific articles, looking for accounts of any protein that could modify p53, a protein that regulates cancer growth. Most scientists would struggle to identify one such protein in a year; Watson took only a few weeks to find six (although, to be fair, it took several years to prepare Watson to do this).[6] Other organizations are using similar technologies to glean insights from natural-language content that exists in enormous volume.

Or think about the "Internet of things"—the ability to place small sensors on objects in the physical world and have them communicate readings in real time. The rise of this technology has been governed by the rise of computers with the processing power to deal with the immense amounts of data produced; unaided humans could not conceivably monitor and control the vast sensor networks used to, for example, detect if a tsunami is brewing far offshore. It has probably not yet occurred to your organization, therefore, to ask: How could we improve our business if we did have that ability? It should probably occur to you to ask that now.

At Vanguard, the enabling technology behind Personal Advisor Services was on the firm's radar screen because of its previous partnerships with technology vendors, including a company called Financial Engines, which pioneered a financial simulation that could show how likely a retiree was to run out of money under different conditions. There was no off-the-shelf cognitive software product to buy, but there were models out there in "robo-advisor" startups such as Wealthfront, which had already launched online advisory businesses.

Step 3: Consider the Constraints Placed on Machine Autonomy

The degree to which a business automates a process isn't always left up to the company. Law, regulations, and union contracts can strictly limit a firm's use of promising technologies—and even the sense that such rules might be imposed can put a damper on development. It's important to note, however, that the same rules that constrain automation in your industry can end up serving you well, if your own strategy aims for augmentation.

For example, developers of automated transportation solutions—think self-driving cars—face something between a thicket and a morass of regulations. Although it's now pretty clear that the technical capabilities for driverless cars, trucks, and golf carts are already mastered or masterable, it's not at all obvious when the regulatory structure will allow them on highways and fairways. Companies like Google and Tesla, as well as automotive industry mainstays Ford, General Motors, and Mercedes, could find that they have put a lot of energy into developing vehicles that drive themselves but are stuck with regulations that require an alert driver with hands on the steering wheel and feet on the pedals. If that happens, perhaps a company whose strategy all along has emphasized augmentation, not automation—and especially a company that has given careful thought to how to redeploy the human attention that is freed up by the technology—will win big. It will gain the benefits of augmented performance without having to fight the severe pricing pressures of having competitors in the same market with purely automated solutions.

Vanguard Group operates, of course, in a highly regulated sector of the economy. The financial services industry is also one in which any whiff of "robo" has terrible associations, thanks to the fraudulent robo-signing by mortgage lenders that contributed to the 2010 foreclosure crisis in the United States. While no significant barriers have been erected with regard to how "robo-advisor" systems are built and implemented, the Securities and Exchange Commission and the Financial Industry Regulatory Authority (FINRA)—the primary U.S. regulators of financial services firms—have issued a joint alert that customers of financial firms should be wary of these systems, some of which charge nonobvious fees or limit investment options.[7] It's not a regulation per se, but it's an educational bulletin the regulators felt compelled to issue. Vanguard, with its augmented arrangement, steers further from the dangers that a purely automated service might present.

To understand both the restrictions on your business and the opportunities inherent in them, you should stay on top of recent rulings and attuned to the conversations that are shaping the rules to come. This is particularly true if your envisioned solution involves the use of personally identifiable data on your customers. If you live in "Old Europe," as former U.S. defense secretary Donald Rumsfeld once referred to it, you might well find that despite the fantastic capabilities your company has to personalize emails or Web ads to individual customers, you are barred from sending or serving them. Even in the United States, you might be able to make great recommendations for how a patient should deal with a disease or choose a doctor but be unable to offer them without violating HIPAA regulations on medical privacy.

We're not lawyers, and we don't hang around K Street (regulatory lobbying heaven) in Washington, D.C. But we can advise you not to invest too heavily in smart machines without carefully assessing such risks. Find yourself an attorney who knows all there is to know about the legal ramifications of automating key decisions in your space. And be prepared to pay some hourly fees. As you can imagine, an esoteric legal specialty like this one is far from automated yet!

Step 4: Build Your Augmentation Solution

With all this information you've gathered and digested about your business and its decisions, evolving technologies, and the legal constraints placed on automation, you should now be seeing clear opportunities for augmentation arrangements that fit your mission and strategy. You're ready to go after a good initial target for these technologies—in other words, an application.

Our prediction is that you will be torn between possibilities of two main types: moon shots and small steps. Moon shots offer potentially huge rewards to change how the most core, high-impact work of the organization is done—but because of that, they also feature the high visibility that makes any failure a much bigger setback. Small steps allow you to learn and gain confidence out of the spotlight—but may not have enough impact on overall enterprise success to inspire follow-up investment.

There is no single right answer to this dilemma; what is best for your context probably depends on the appetite and expectations for such innovation. At Memorial Sloan Kettering, it was easy to see the potential value of a system that supports cancer treatment recommendations; it's a very complex set of diseases, and the information and science involved are far too difficult for a human to keep in mind. But people there also understand how that increases the complexity of solving the problem. The cancer center's Watson project is well behind schedule, as are all the other cancer-oriented AI projects we know about. It turns out to be a lot harder to battle cancer with smart computers than anybody anticipated.

That's the upside and the downside of a "moon shot" target, in a nutshell—it is a very valuable and important problem to solve, but it's really hard to do. Such ambitious projects will cost a lot and will probably take longer than anyone anticipated. They may even fail altogether. So you have to balance the value of achieving an ambitious goal with the higher likelihood that it will be difficult or impossible to address successfully.

The opposite strategy is to choose some area of your business that is less strategic, but in which you see easier ways to use intelligent machines to augment the work of valuable professionals. As we've mentioned, MD Anderson has adopted this strategy in addition to a moon shot. Often this means targeting "back-office" activities—those tasks and processes that aren't mission-critical or strategic, but where you still want to benefit from innovation and continuous improvement. This is a lower-risk, lower-reward approach to targeting an application of cognitive technologies.

In many cases in the past, this type of work was outsourced to offshore providers that could do it for lower labor costs. Many of the tasks that were outsourced and sent offshore were those that could be specified and monitored easily. When work was hard to specify it was also difficult to write contracts for its completion, so it didn't get outsourced. Take, for example, administrative banking transactions. Banks could specify the workflow and processing logic clearly, and it could be orchestrated via technology. The location of the work no longer mattered, so it went to countries with low-cost labor and good English skills—most frequently India.

Offshore outsourcing became a thriving industry. Today, however, automated systems and process automation are performing structured administrative tasks. Both software startups—companies like Automation Anywhere, RAGE Frameworks, and IPsoft in the United States, and Blue Prism in the United Kingdom—and large outsourcing firms like Wipro, TCS, and Infosys are creating artificial intelligence platforms to automate administrative tasks.

Blue Prism customers O2 and Xchanging (the outsourcing company spun out of Lloyd's) have already brought back home some of their offshored work to be done now by "robots" (actually computers programmed with software flexible enough to be taught by knowledge workers to perform their repetitive tasks). Automation Anywhere focuses on pulling information together from a variety of different systems, as in electronic medical records. RAGE Frameworks has focused on automated processes for financial services firms. IPsoft has focused primarily on automating IT management processes thus far but is broadening that focus with its "Amelia" intelligent interaction system.

We spoke with one company, KMG International (a substantial international oil company based in Romania), that has already used IPsoft's product IPcenter to automate many of its IT management tasks. Marcel Chiriac, the company's chief information officer, said that he led an effort in 2013 to restructure an out-of-control outsourcing agreement. One aspect of it involved working with IPsoft to automate many straightforward IT tasks, such as network and infrastructure management and gas station technology monitoring. There are automated scripts running on a couple hundred "automatas" (hey, it beats calling them robots) that do things like disk space monitoring and file deletion, automated rebooting of frozen PCs, and setting up new employee email accounts. He showed us a report that 73 percent of recent trouble tickets were resolved without human intervention. Chiriac says his company has saved some money by automating some previously outsourced services (even given the low labor costs in Romanian outsourcing firms), but his primary concern is the quality of the service. And that's been high; not only do trouble tickets get resolved quickly and automatically, but his IT infrastructure has had no unplanned outages in the last fifteen months.

Obviously this is a very different kettle of fish than the cancer treatment work being done by Memorial Sloan Kettering. It's low risk, involves administrative workers rather than high profile knowledge workers, and there are several vendors with well-established solutions in the area being automated or augmented. But if done on a large scale, this augmentation of back-office workers could produce a tectonic shift in how and where work is done, and the effects on the over $100 billion a year outsourcing industry could be dramatic. It could mean that work once sent offshore for low-cost labor could return home—on machines.

To come back to Vanguard, we've already noted that the company picked its advisors as the professionals to augment, and that the identification of the right technology to help them dispense sound financial advice to aging boomers was not difficult. Still, the company had tough choices to make in its application of those tools. For instance: Should it develop its own "advice engine," or use existing products? Should it allow for direct use of the system by clients, or only with advisors in the process? Did the system need to handle "Q&A" interactions like Watson, or could it just rely on traditional online interfaces? And what were the most important aspects of financial advice that the system should include?

Vanguard decided to develop its own capabilities. Since the human advisor was key to the company's augmentation approach, the system was designed to be used collaboratively by the client and the advisor. No Q&A function was deemed necessary at this point, but Vanguard did feel the need for an improved user interface. And the key components of the system were simulation (for the mathematically inclined, Monte Carlo–type simulation) of wealth throughout retirement, balancing and rebalancing of portfolios, and tax loss harvesting. The project took three years to develop, with substantial involvement by Vanguard's IT developers, several expert financial advisors, and analytics professionals.

Step 5: Manage the Change

Throughout your work to augment people with smart machines, you need to be thinking about their perspectives on the change. You might have made the all-important decision to augment their work—by giving them computer teammates and allowing them to focus more on what they as humans do best—but that doesn't necessarily mean that they fully trust your intention. You need to keep reinforcing and demonstrating your conviction that the success of the enterprise depends mostly on its humans.

Sometimes the automation of tasks will be disruptive enough that people will need to be moved into very different roles. More often, their jobs will have to be recalibrated to allow them to apply more valuable human strengths than they have in the past, while handing over some computation-based work to the machines. In either case, the process of helping people adjust their skill sets should start as early as possible.

In Chapter 3, we described the five steps knowledge workers could take in their workplaces to increase their own value while making room for machines. We took one kind of professional—the insurance underwriter—through each option to show how they differed. It's equally imaginable that the underwriter's employer could help her understand those options. By raising awareness of the steps that are available, managers could help people choose their own best paths.

Two key components of this step are education and communications. Whether their role is to step in, step up, or step forward (or step out of the way), people need to be trained on how the cognitive system works and its strengths and weaknesses. Most people won't need to leave the workplace and get another degree; on-the-job training is usually enough. This isn't nuclear physics. It does, however, require a willingness to engage with a system and to look under its covers a bit.

The other key activity involving humans is to communicate with them. If the terms "automated," "robot," or "artificial intelligence"—even "cognitive"—are bandied about with regard to a new system, people will be justifiably worried about their jobs. We recommend an early declaration that no one will lose his or her job to a machine. That will immediately ease the nerves of the workforce and make it much more likely that they are open to the new virtual colleague. Some stories about early implementations—both the triumphs and the challenges—in a newsletter or company-wide email would also help employees to feel positively about the system and support its use.

At Vanguard, there was never any doubt that the approach taken to financial advising would be augmentation, not automation. Financial advisors were informed about the system from the beginning of its development, and told what it would and wouldn't do in the client relationship. Most advisors welcomed the system because they hoped (and this turned out to be true) that it would allow them to serve their clients better, while relieving them from some of the less fulfilling aspects of their jobs. Advisors with a technology-oriented focus were part of the project on a rotational basis, so they could help to shape how it worked.

Some training was given to the advisors on the system and its capabilities. But with a lot of the basic information transmittal tasks now being handled by a machine, Vanguard executives felt that human advisors would have more time to work with clients on important financial behavior issues. As we pointed out in the previous chapter, the area of "behavioral finance" has developed (as something of an adjunct to "behavioral economics") over the last decade or so. Vanguard embarked upon a strategy to equip its advisors with more behavioral coaching abilities.

According to Karin Risi, "The new system gives advisors more freedom to interact with their clients. Many of them are now using face-to-face video for these meetings, since all of the informational details are in the system. The advisors are also doing behavioral coaching when they interact with their clients—it's very common, for example, for them to be a voice of reason when clients want to get out of the market in a downturn. Some of our clients turn to advisors for help because they know they lack the discipline to contribute steadily and take a long-term approach. It's not unlike using a personal trainer to help you exercise."

Vanguard has an Investment Strategy group that helped both to develop the advice to put in the system and to incorporate behavioral finance approaches whenever possible—to gently nudge clients, for example, into increasing their 401(k) contributions.

Step 6: Embark on a Project, but Envision a Platform

Most organizations are too new to cognitive systems to embark upon a full-fledged "platform" for the technology at the beginning. Rajeev Ronanki, the Deloitte consultant we wrote about in Chapter 8, says that virtually all of his clients want to start with a pilot or "proof of concept." In his words, "They want to make sure that it's not science fiction before they really commit to the technology at full scale. So the first project is typically a pilot that takes four to six months to develop."

Proofs of concept (PoC) typically involve selection of technology, development or implementation of a solution, and then some testing and measurement to assess the performance and value of the system. It's really not much different from any other new technology adoption process.

If the pilot or PoC is successful—and most are unless they are overly ambitious, or the wrong technology has been selected—organizations then realize, usually pretty quickly, that there are a lot of opportunities for cognitive technology in their businesses. If they had success in automobile insurance underwriting systems, for example, they want to apply it to home insurance, or small business insurance. It's best, then, to think about this technology as a potential platform rather than a single application project. As we suggested in Chapter 2 that some vendors are enabling, make sure that you assemble a variety of cognitive capabilities, not just one. That will make your platform much more flexible and useful. You also want to make sure that your cognitive technologies can scale, that they fit with your existing technology architecture, and that you can find people who can work on the number of projects you are likely to take up.

At Xchanging, for example, platform thinking was in place from the beginning. The company didn't just identify one business process that it could support with its chosen technology, a "robotic process automation" tool from Blue Prism—it identified ten. Each of the first ten was relatively straightforward and structured, and all were in the company's sweet spot of the British insurance market (the company outsources processes in several other industries as well, even though it was spun out of Lloyd's).

Xchanging moved rapidly through an initial proof of concept, completing it in a month or so. In fact, the company started in June 2014 and had four processes up and running on Blue Prism by the end of August of that same year. Blue Prism's technology is relatively easy to use, and Xchanging's processes—as an outsourcing company—were already pretty structured and well documented. Xchanging wanted to be able to configure the technology itself, so it trained about fifteen people in the discipline of "model development." In fact, they haven't needed anyone from Blue Prism to help them since the day the first process went live.

We've already described some of the aspects of Vanguard's Personal Advisor Services development implementation. Because it had experience with aspects of the advising system already, it didn't feel the need to do a proof of concept. It jumped in full throttle and took three years to develop and fully install the system. The most likely move to a "platform" might be to extend the existing system to retail investors with lower asset levels and perhaps to employ a more self-service approach. Vanguard is also working on pulling in data from its clients' investments outside the company when the client wants a full picture of net worth or retirement assets.

Step 7: Put Someone in Charge

The last piece of advice we have for your organization's augmentation strategy is that you should put someone in charge of it. As with any other organizational imperative that crosses internal siloes, it's extremely valuable to have someone tightly focused on it, collecting the lessons of experience, accountable for showing progress, and making strategic plans for the future.

The duties of the "automation leader" are still emerging—there aren't too many of these people in place yet—but they have much in common with the step-up role we defined in Chapter 4. There are some common themes and tasks that are emerging. One is to survey the organization and decide on the best opportunities for this technology. Another is to identify the best technologies and vendors. A third is to lead the projects to implement cognitive technologies across a business. Finally, it's important to take leadership of communications, education, and change management initiatives. In short, virtually all of the organizational steps we've described in this section of the book require leadership.

Not surprisingly, the people who perform these roles need to be familiar with both the business and the technology. A great example of this combination is Justin Myers, the first "automation editor" at the Associated Press (we described Lou Ferrara, Myers's boss at the AP, in Chapter 4 on "stepping up"; we think Myers's own role is a combination of stepping up and stepping in). It's Myers's job, as he puts it in his description of it, to "identify and evaluate opportunities to automate the creation and production of news content (what we've classified as a step-up role), and . . . write Ruby applications and libraries to implement new automation processes (a step-in role to our minds)." Ruby is a programming language that is well suited to artificial intelligence applications.

Myers has an unusual background at the intersection of information technology and journalism, which is a perfect one for his job. He had a double major in electrical engineering and journalism at the University of Missouri, a journalism powerhouse. He's been a news editor, a producer of interactive and data-driven news sites, and an academic researcher on how people consume content. If you want an automation leader for your organization, you may have to find a similar "unicorn" with an unusual combination of backgrounds.

Of course, different emphases in an organization's automation or augmentation programs require different types of people. At Xchanging, the highly process-oriented nature of the work means that the head of "Robotic Automation," Paul Donaldson (he has since moved to a similar job in a different company), needed a strong process focus. Fortunately, he's a Six Sigma Black Belt.

Donaldson says that his key responsibilities included directing the overall operation of robotic process automation, deciding which processes to apply it to, education, coordinating with IT, and setting the direction for where to go with the technology. He also worked closely with a systems manager in Xchanging's IT organization who handles the technical aspects of the system and the interfaces with other systems.

Back at Vanguard, we've mentioned Karin Risi, who heads Advice Services for the organization. She is not a technology person but worked in partnership with Vanguard's IT group to develop the human-augmented advice service. She's held a variety of different jobs at the company, working with high-asset investors and investment advisors and being an investment analyst herself. So she clearly knows the key issues and the context for providing computer-based advice to Vanguard's clients. The company is a collegial organization, so Risi can easily collaborate with the company's functions for technology, investment strategy, and risk and compliance.

The Inevitable Headaches

Companies are geared to do one thing: compete. They invest in what will give them a winning edge.

Part of this edge comes from efficiency—their ability to do more with less—and of course this provides the incentive for higher and higher levels of automation. Some months ago, for example, Tom had a conversation with the CEO of a large automobile insurance company. The subject was the firm's current and planned uses of big data and analytics. The CEO mentioned the possibility that some types of claims adjustment—for example, assessing damage when cars are exposed to hailstorms—could be made using automated analysis. A photograph of the damaged car could be analyzed to assess how many and how deep the hail-caused indentations are, and the result could be automatically converted into a cost to repair the car. He said, "We have done some pilot projects in this area, and the machines are more reliable than the human adjusters." When Tom asked what might be the implications for the adjuster role—a job whose holders often have great people skills on top of their repair-cost knowledge—he said, "We won't need nearly as many of them. I need to reduce the labor-intensiveness of the claims process, and this is a way to do it."

This CEO apparently does not yet find it an interesting question to wonder what his firm could do next for customers, once his adjusters on the front lines have the capacity to do more. Much less does he see it as his problem to preserve their jobs. He understands his quest as cutting costs and achieving consistency. Perhaps the majority of CEOs in publicly traded firms would have replied in the same way, if not more baldly. When Foxconn chairman Terry Gou was asked why he hoped to build a million robots for his production facilities, he replied: "As human beings are also animals, to manage one million animals gives me a headache."[8]

This thinking will have to change, ironically, as we move more fully into the age of machines. Managers will increasingly understand that the key to their firms' competitiveness is not the efficiency that automation provides but the distinctiveness that augmentation allows. For that, they will see, they will have to attract highly capable people, engage them, and retain them.

For firms, then, just as for individual workers, the coming years will be a time of difficult transformation—but there simply isn't an alternative. In this chapter we've described organizations that get it, and some of the individuals who have helped them see the light about augmentation. We encourage you as a manager to become one of those individuals. But you need help from your organization. If you see no likelihood of that happening—if your CEO is firmly committed to an automation future that reduces reliance on people—do us all a favor and look elsewhere for employment. You'll make more headway toward an augmented future, and chances are your old firm will not be prospering anyway.

10

Utopia or Dystopia? How Society Must Adapt to Smart Machines

Our main mission in this book has been to give you a sense of agency and to help you begin to make decisions for yourself about how to deal with advancing automation. Until now the discourse about automation and AI has been too much at the level of macroeconomics, and has created too much of an impression that individuals are helpless in the sweep of events and at the mercy of higher-level decision-makers.

That said, however, it would be silly to deny that social and economic policy have big roles to play in shaping the environments in which humans will continue to thrive. In this chapter we'll look at how governments, other convening bodies, and the experts who advise them are, or should be, thinking about the needs of society in an age of smart machines—and we will suggest some priorities they should adopt to advance an augmentation agenda.

Let's start by observing that many smart people are thinking about the robot-filled society of the future, and that they are widely distributed on the basic question of whether we are all going to hell in a handbasket. Our news culture being what it is, we tend to hear the opinions of celebrity thinkers and innovators the most, and particularly when they are willing to thrill us with a good scare. Thus the statement by Elon Musk that AI represents "our biggest existential threat" was probably the most repeated quote of 2014. Right on its heels was Stephen Hawking's warning that "the development of full artificial intelligence could spell the end of the human race," and Bill Gates's musing that "I don't understand why some people are not concerned."

Many thinkers, however, are less famous and less frightened (and therefore give up any headline-grabbing impact or opinion). Artificial intelligence expert Joanna J. Bryson, for example, dismisses the scare-mongering by insisting that AI is "just another artifact." Humankind, she notes, has used tools since the time of *Homo habilis*, and this is simply the latest. The fact that AI has, like many of its predecessors, exceeded prior tools in its usefulness does not mean that we will suddenly become its servant. Even as AI exceeds our powers of cognition, we shouldn't be afraid that whichever is smartest somehow "wins." Bryson points out, "We already have calculators that can do math better than us, and they don't even take over the pockets they live in, let alone the world."[1]

As we've described earlier, there are passionate prophesiers of "superintelligence" like Nick Bostrom of Oxford. Bostrom's colleague Stuart Armstrong published a report calling for a whole new category of risks to be recognized: risks of potentially infinite impact. Among a number of global challenges "threatening the very basis of our civilization" (including nuclear war, climate change, and global pandemics) they included artificial intelligence, because of what is known as "the control problem."[2] Once machines can outthink humans, their ability to decide and make things happen might be beyond our power to rein in.

Bostrom and Armstrong paint apocalyptic scenarios, but you don't have to buy into a future of robot overlords to believe we need society-level decision-making in the face of advancing AI. Many forward-thinking people are convinced that, at the least, it will mean a precipitous fall in human employment. We hear this debate at every conference we attend and find experts to be deeply divided about the net impact. If you need more than our convenient sample, consider a recent Pew survey, part of its Future of the Internet project. Pew asked 1,986 experts, including research scientists, business leaders, journalists, and technology developers, whether they believed AI and robotics will have displaced more jobs than they have created by 2025. Respondents were almost evenly split, with the optimists slightly edging out the pessimists, 52 to 48 percent.[3]

Most everyone agrees that the growing ability to automate knowledge work will cause (indeed, *is* causing) labor dislocations that are painful in the short run; they disagree, however, about the long term. Economists steeped in the history of productivity improvement tend to point out that it's always bad in the messy middle of a transformation, but everything works out for the better in the end, as productivity gains give rise to investments in new ventures that provide jobs that were never imagined before. At least historically that has always been true. But others insist that this time, history won't rhyme.

For example, Larry Summers is one of the most distinguished economists in the United States, having served as Treasury secretary and the Director of the National Economic Council in the Obama White House. He's also known for speaking his mind, which got him into a bit of trouble as president of Harvard University. He said in a 2013 speech at the National Bureau of Economic Research that when he was an MIT undergraduate in the early 1970s, many economists scorned "the stupid people [who] thought that automation was going to make all the jobs go away. Until a few years ago, I didn't think this was a very complicated subject: the Luddites were wrong, and the believers in technology and technological progress were right. I'm not so completely certain now."[4]

As evidence, consider the very sluggish post-recession recovery we've been experiencing. In 2014 the OECD assessed the progress of recovery in its member states, the most developed economies in the world. It found 45 million people out of work—12.1 million more than before the global financial crisis hit in 2008–09. The conclusion of the report was that the persistent unemployment could no longer be called a cyclical phenomenon. It reflected a structural change, in part due to the growing sophistication of automation.

Put us in the camp expecting the outcomes of smart machines to be mainly positive—but at the same time, wishing for a greater sense of urgency around making the decisions that will ensure that is the case. We don't believe, as Bostrom seems to, that momentous choices must be made at once because "this is a problem that we only ever get one chance to solve." But we do know that the changes required to make this period of transformation minimally destructive are the kinds of changes that usually take a long time. We like how Stuart Russell, an AI professor at UC Berkeley, responded recently when he was asked whether superintelligent computers would be a threat to humanity. He pointed out that it's not like the weather, something we can only watch while hoping for the best. "We choose what it's going to be," he insists. "So whether or not AI is a threat to the human race depends on whether or not we make it a threat to the human race."[5] This doesn't make him sanguine—it makes him think we need to get to work.

The Goal Should Be Augmentation

If you've read this far, you know what we've advocated: workplaces that combine sophisticated machines and humans in partnerships of mutual augmentation. That's something we believe knowledge workers should embrace personally and employers should pursue for competitive reasons. It's also something societies should encourage in ways big and small.

Because scientific discoveries and technological breakthroughs get so much credit for changing the world, it can be easy to overlook the importance of social policy-making in ensuring that times of transformation turn out overwhelmingly for the good. We were reminded of this by John Frank Weaver, an attorney in Boston who works on artificial intelligence law. Reflecting on the social impact of the industrial revolution in the United States, and particularly the emergence of its all-important middle class, he is careful to point out that Americans had more than steam power and machinery to thank. "The technology certainly made that middle class possible, but the legal innovations that we created following the Industrial Revolution made possible the widespread prosperity of the mid-20th century American middle class: minimum wage laws, child labor laws, laws protecting unions, regulations governing workplace safety and environmental protection, etc." Without such laws, he stresses, average Americans don't benefit much from technological breakthroughs.[6]

The corollary to this truth might be a little harder to swallow for some: Market forces alone won't get the job done. This is the point that Columbia University economist Jeffrey Sachs wants to drive home. He worries that while smart machines may raise productivity and output on average, the effect of market forces will be "to concentrate the gains among a fraction of the population—those with high skills and wealth—and leave behind the rest, notably the young, the poor, and the workers displaced by the machines." The rise of inequality in the United States is, in all likelihood, already partly driven by the early impacts of automation (some economists attribute half of the decline in U.S. economic output going to workers' wages to it). To ensure that the gains to society are broadly distributed, we'll need government intervention in those markets.

What, then, might be the legal innovations we need today to ensure that the benefits of this fresh wave of technological disruption are broadly shared? We'll share some thoughts, but the first thing we hope to do here is to get readers focused on the question. The same legal levers Weaver cites are still available to us, although they are certainly complicated by globalized markets. There is also that other great lever of the past that Weaver doesn't mention: education policy. And governments have other tools for bringing about change short of lawmaking. They can invest in programs and capabilities, fund research, conduct real-world experiments, disseminate knowledge and intellectual property on how to work well with machines, and use their convening power to enable players from various sectors to arrive at shared goals and work collaboratively.

All of these levers could collectively make an enormous difference if they were all pulling together in the same direction. For that to happen, however, there must be some shared philosophy or principle guiding them all. We think the case for augmentation we've been making could provide that philosophy. There are certain things you might do, for example, in public education settings if your plan were to prepare a workforce to work in greater complementarity with smart machines. Your thinking about income taxation and social welfare programs will be quite different depending on whether you foresee few or many opportunities for humans to create economic value. (A future of augmentation sees many.) The expectations you have of employers and what it takes for firms to earn the "license to operate" will take certain forms in societies that seek augmentation, and other forms where the aim is to suppress or accelerate the takeover of human work by machines.

Is STEM Education the Only Answer?

Let's start with how we educate our kids. Clearly, as artificial intelligence advances by leaps and bounds, the calls for the educational community to respond are mounting. Some of these calls have to do with how schools themselves make use of these technologies to fulfill their educational missions. For much of the content that students are taught and tested on today, smart interactive systems would make excellent tutors. They are capable of serving up lessons based on real-time awareness of which material has been mastered and which a student still struggles with—and to do so in formats best suited to a student's learning style. Greater reliance on them would help to reorient schools originally built around the fact of only-human teachers having to advance batches of perhaps thirty students to generic next levels within a year's time. Instead of their design being driven by teachers' needs to accomplish that task, they could be driven by learners' needs. As we reached the point where all students had the benefit of individualized education plans, we might even finally see the end of the tremendously problematic school calendar—an anachronism inherited from a time when farming families needed children in the fields all summer, and when some religions' holidays were respected more than others'.

It's important to apply AI to change *how* content is taught. But at least as important is reforming *what* content is taught to prepare students to succeed in a world transformed by AI. Note that schools are free to the public because society has a strong interest in maintaining a well-educated population. This is true not only in democratic systems, where we want educated people casting votes; it's true for every polity that wants its citizens to enjoy decent standards of living in a globalized economy. We need people who can, in the context of the current economy, add enough value to earn living wages. And when something like a major new technology changes the economy, what society needs people to know is also changed.

This was the whole reason, recall, that the public provision of education began. At the time of the industrial revolution, business and political leaders both recognized early on that the potentially dramatic gains from automation would be denied to them if a workforce did not exist that was capable of working with the machines. Prepping that workforce meant not only changing its knowledge base to include many subjects that hadn't been vital on the farm, but also changing its daily habits of exertion and production. It is no coincidence that (with the exception of that summer-long concession to agrarian ways) schools made it their business to inculcate habits of steady production of rote work at unvarying workstations, with learners complying unquestioningly with the orders of a single superior in the room. Going to school effectively established the soft skills required for work in factories.

By the end of the nineteenth century, the notion of orienting schools toward technological education took hold. Five industrializing cities in the United Kingdom founded new, "red brick" universities concentrating on science or engineering courses by 1909. Many more towns created night schools called Mechanics' Institutes, where adult working men could acquire the skills factory owners needed to expand their production facilities. The mills at Lowell, Massachusetts, took a similar approach to educating women (although not every female factory worker had the energy to attend lectures after a twelve- to fourteen-hour workday).

Fast-forward to today, and the same kind of solution is being promoted—now with calls for more "STEM" education, referring to science, technology, engineering, and math. It's a tried-and-true response to a time of broad-based, technology-driven change. And perhaps it is an even more powerful one today since, much more than in the past, education is subject to more clear and centralized direction. Governments are able to influence education standards, methods, and facilities to a degree they never could before.

For example, in the United Kingdom today, a new approach to teaching kids about computers has been adopted. It focuses on some familiar skills like coding and using productivity tools. But the bulk of the training seems to us well suited to developing some of the skills needed to engage with smart machines. For example, according to a BBC News article, five- to seven-year-olds are learning to:

- understand what algorithms are, how they are implemented as programs on digital devices, and that programs execute by following precise and unambiguous instructions;

- create and debug simple programs;
- use logical reasoning to predict the behavior of simple programs.[7]

Whether a student ends up stepping in, up, or forward, this type of knowledge would be useful.

But if we have managed to convince you that there are five viable "steps" that knowledge workers can take vis-à-vis machines, you might have already realized that the push toward more STEM education makes sense for three of them, and therefore perhaps only half of the population of workers. Computational and analytical training is quite useful for those who step in to use smart machines daily, step up to evaluate their impact, and step forward to build new systems. Yet many educational prescriptions advocate STEM education for everyone.

If we were going to reengineer public education for the value-creation prospects of all augmentation workers, we might focus as well on stepping-in or stepping-aside knowledge and skills—but again, there is no need given the availability of individualized learning tools to focus on any one of these steps. Rather, public education should recognize that all five exist and be designed to help students explore them and gravitate toward the pathways that suit them best.

Stepping narrowly, for example, is an option that schools have not served very well in the past, but could do much more for. As well as letting students pursue narrow lines of interest, with smart machines still ensuring they were doing so with sufficient rigor and making fast enough progress, education systems could facilitate apprenticeships with current masters of a specialty to pass along the tacit aspects of their trade, including the passion they bring to it.

Schools could also work better with employers to create pools of talent with particular narrow strengths. In the Boston area, for example, given the regional cluster of robotics manufacturers, vocational high schools typically include robotics courses and concentrations. These programs are shaped heavily by the input of hiring managers in the nearby firms. But there is no absolute requirement that a school's specialized programs relate to its particular geography. Also in the Boston area, Northeastern University has created a program designed to mint the next generation of cybersecurity professionals, with funding from the federal government.

This is a program that could be located anywhere (cyberattacks, after all, emanate from everywhere) but benefits from having a physical location where students and instructors working on the leading edge can learn in real time from each other's experience.

Increasingly, we think, employers will also take on more of the burden themselves of educating their human workers to work in concert with smart machines. Just as smart employers in the industrial revolution developed approaches to training "a sufficient supply of mechanics, mill managers, and weavers" (according to *Learning by Doing* author James Bessen), wise employers in the twenty-first century will provide the contemporary equivalent of augmentation skills. In the last chapter, we explained that they will have ample rationale for making this investment, as human capacities become more and more their source of competitive advantage.

We also expect that corporations' efforts to keep human workers employable will become part of their "social license to operate"—the responsibilities governments and citizens place on them in return for their use of publicly funded infrastructure. This will probably not be a formal responsibility, but rather one involving expectations and exhortations.

In the same way that in the industrial revolution's aftermath employers were forced to enact safety standards (because the machines presented a threat to the bodily strength that was a worker's source of value), perhaps today employers should be compelled to enact education standards— because the threat is to the cognitive strengths that are today's knowledge workers' sources of value. If this sounds extreme, note that—just as in the prior era, with safety and living-wage standards—it is only what enlightened firms are doing already. By enlightened, we don't mean altruistic but oriented toward the long term and convinced that their ultimate competitive advantage lies in developing human capital (even if free-riding competitors poach some of it along the way). Since much of the relevant knowledge content will be held by some employees more than others, smart organizations will facilitate their education of each other. Google, for example, has a program called Googlers-to-Googlers (G2G), in which Google employees train each other. More than half of the company's educational offerings are taught by employees. The content ranges from technical topics (data visualization, Python programming) to Spin and parenting classes.

It's easy to see how this tendency of the world's leading firms could eventually become the social expectation of all firms—as it should. After years of seeing the benefits of productivity increases accrue more to owners of capital than to labor, it is not unreasonable for societies to declare it is not wholly their problem to deliver up labor that can be productive on day one. On-the-job training has always been a powerful tool, and companies need to embrace it to facilitate augmentation.

Education Should Stress Augmentation

More than anything, schooling needs to put more emphasis on teaching students *how to augment their strengths with machines*. In a recent essay, technology blogger Shelly Palmer pointed out that some knowledge workers have naturally embraced the forms of artificial intelligence available to them to become more capable:

> If you move numbers from one cell in Excel to another for a living, or if you move markers on a Gantt chart to track production progress and manage projects, you've probably created some macros to help minimize the tediousness of your job. In practice, you've already created a man-machine partnership. If you're great at it, you may be more productive than other people who compete with you. Efficient man-machine partnerships are "the" key component to modern productivity. If you're better using your tools, you will almost always be better than your competition.[8]

He's right, and therefore we must raise the obvious, uncomfortable question. Is anyone teaching you or your kids how to be better at creating such human–machine partnerships, to avoid getting trounced by those smarty-pants?

As parents of kids who have recently made their way through good school systems, the two of us can attest to at least one dramatic way in which American pedagogy has changed since we were young: It puts greater emphasis on collaborative team projects. Students today are more likely than in our day to hear that the "lone inventor" is a myth, and much more likely to have portions of their grades depend on the efforts of others with whom they might or might not have chosen to work. This is often painful to straight-A students and their tiger parents, motivated to attain the level of perfection that will get Ivy League admissions officers to consider their applications. But it is undeniably aligned with the reality of workplaces. In modern workplaces, almost all achievement must happen in the context of diverse teams.

Looking forward, schools might want to push this emphasis on teamwork even further, by recognizing that the teams students will join in workplaces will include machines. They could teach from an early age what it takes to forge an effective human–machine partnership, which has each partner effectively complementing the strengths and weaknesses of the other. Such offerings could be the contemporary version of "shop class," in which boys learned to cut wood and metal. Our otherwise well-educated kids did not experience this in their own educations, which is unfortunate.

Something Joi Ito, who heads the MIT Media Lab, said in a recent TED Talk connects well to this thought. Talking about education, he wondered why teachers continue to insist that students be able to perform certain tasks with no technological support when, in the real world for which they are being prepared, all those supports exist (primarily on the Internet or as smartphone apps). Would you, for example, ask a seventeen-year-old to resort to long division in the midst of a chemistry test when calculators are ubiquitous? Permitting the calculator means the teacher can ask more challenging chemistry questions. The same could be said for any cognitive support tool—and the future will bring many. If the goal in the end is to teach humans to find the best ways to augment their strengths with machines, the way to achieve that is not by refusing to let kids do so till they walk out of school.

Education should also focus much more on teaching wise decision-making—with the aid of smart machines or not. Students need to learn what kinds of decisions are best made by machine and which ones require human intervention. There will always be judgment calls that have to be made by humans, because they concern themselves with the unknowable future. The latter kinds of decisions are often about setting a course that others can support sufficiently to advance with their efforts—so that a decision can *become* the right one by virtue of everyone's having agreed to make it work.

Instruction in what goes into good decision-making is a long-established discipline in fields like foreign policy and business management; few students in such fields make it through a degree program without taking related coursework (although the courses don't often include any references to artificial intelligence). Lately, some experts in decision-making such as Daniel Kahneman (with his book *Thinking, Fast and Slow*) have broken beyond those fields and achieved some crossover appeal to lay readers. We'd like to see the awareness of decision-making as a skill pushed more broadly and further down into earlier levels of education. We'd also like to see decision-making discussed as something that can be facilitated or performed by computers. Why? Because people's decision-making capabilities, already shaky, are at risk of worsening if they get less practice at it—as they will when artificial intelligence tools take many decisions off their hands.

For all of time, people have learned to make hard decisions by first making a lot of easy ones. They gain skills and confidence in simple situations where it can be determined post hoc whether they made them well. As computers take over these no-brainers and leave only the highly ambiguous situations for humans, we need to make sure that we don't turn decision-making into a lost art. If fewer people understand how to diagnose the kind of decision that must be made by humans, and know how to make it well, where will we be? Christian Reimsbach-Kounatze, an OECD analyst, made an ominous prediction at a recent meeting convened by that organization's Committee on Legal Affairs. He worried we might soon find ourselves under a "dictatorship of data" in which less educated or less concerned decision-makers automatically follow the decisions of machines.[9] That won't always be a bad thing, but it will be sometimes. We humans need to know which is which.

One last set of soft skills we'd encourage educators to cultivate are the skills of ongoing learning. The traditional expectation of students has been that they would focus in their schooling on learning a certain body of knowledge rather than on *learning how to learn*. The former may suffice in eras of slow change, but in today's rapidly advancing world, where the content one learns in school may be obsolete—or thoroughly mechanized—within a decade, the latter is far more valuable. Virtually no one out of school—or currently in school, for that matter—learned anything about cognitive technologies or deep-learning networks, but knowing how they work will be essential in the near future. And as we argued in our chapter on stepping narrowly, no one is likely to learn the narrow skills necessary for this role in school, either. It simply wouldn't make sense to teach such narrow topics to large groups.

John Seely Brown, known best for his longtime leadership of research at Xerox PARC, refers to the need to encourage "entrepreneurial learners." He's not talking about teaching entrepreneurship but rather about teaching students to be more venturesome in adding to their knowledge. Entrepreneurial learners, he says, are "constantly looking for new ways, new resources, new peers and potential mentors to learn new things."[10]

Teaching students to create human–machine partnerships, to make wise decisions, and to become entrepreneurial learners could be considered some of the vital "soft skills" training of the machine-augmented worker. And the idea of teaching the soft skills required for employment seems to be gathering proponents. There are, increasingly, organizations focusing on teaching basic "hygiene" attributes like showing up on time, being courteous to customers, and following established protocols, mainly to entry-level workers who were raised in settings where unemployment was the norm. At a higher level, soft skills training can help workers build on the human strengths that will continue to be their greatest source of value: their abilities to empathize with customers and colleagues, influence others to pull together, solve problems, communicate, and manage relationships—and above all, to keep learning. Whether we want to keep up with smart machines by working with them directly or doing something they can't, we will have to work hard to succeed at it.

Job Creation Policy Should Encourage Augmentation

If education policy is a long-term strategy for minimizing automation's threat to employment levels, a more near-term set of moves can be classed under the heading of job creation policy. Traditionally in times of labor dislocation, governments have used a variety of strategies to encourage private sector investments that will boost employment. These have included reducing interest rates to make investment less risky; committing to purchases of goods and services by government agencies; funding infrastructural upgrades that require private sector labor; subsidizing the hiring of some workers; and providing federal credits for hiring.

More directly, many governments have simply expanded their own payrolls to keep people gainfully employed. Most famously, in the United States, job creation in the time of the Great Depression took the form of the Works Progress Administration (WPA). Established by President Franklin D. Roosevelt's executive order in 1933, it was a federal assistance program that put unemployed Americans to work directly on government-funded infrastructure projects and other community-improving efforts. Part of the WPA included a series of programs focused on arts and cultural programs, which nurtured the careers of artists and writers like painter Jackson Pollock and playwright Arthur Miller. In total, WPA jobs provided income to 3 million of the 10 million workers rendered jobless by the Depression. Other Depression-era job creation programs included the Civilian Conservation Corps, a program for young men focused on planting trees and building parks.

It's important to be clear that the Depression was the result of a massive failure of the financial system and not due to the automation of work that was proceeding apace in the nation's factories. Still, the potential threat to jobs that automation also posed had certainly been noted. John Maynard Keynes, most famously, diagnosed in his 1930 essay "Economic Possibilities for Our Grandchildren" what he called a "new disease" in the world's largest economies. He called it "technological unemployment" and explained that it was "due to our discovery of means of economizing the use of labor outrunning the pace at which we can find new uses for labor." And a clever YouTube video, "No Humans Need Apply," points out that it wouldn't be that difficult for automation to lead to the same levels of unemployment—about 25 percent in the United States—found in the Depression.

Today we're seeing governments and their economic advisors contemplating all these kinds of moves to protect jobs from the onslaught of smart machines. And that is appropriate—all options belong on the table. Our stance, however, would be to encourage them, by their use of any of these tools, to think in terms of human–machine augmentation. They should encourage the creation of jobs that put people in complementary roles with smart machines, and equip them to work in better collaboration with machines in the future. Depression-era programs often improved the employability of workers with government jobs, and this should be true of future programs involving automation or augmentation.

In China's booming cities today, one often encounters an arresting sight: In front of the construction site of some glistening skyscraper, and amid the crowd of office workers checking smartphones as they bustle along to their business meetings, there is often a worker dressed like a peasant sweeping the street with a straw broom that looks positively medieval. This is make-work, of course, and we summon the image only to mark the absolute antithesis of the job creation we are advocating. Not only is this poor worker performing a task that could be better done by a machine, but she is gaining no ability to work in any better capacity by doing it.

In dramatic contrast, look at the set of policies Finland has used to deal with the dislocation of laid-off tech workers after the failure of Nokia. As the *New York Times* reports, when Nokia started laying off employees in droves, "politicians started providing government grants, entrepreneurship programs and other training to help the thousands of laid-off tech workers start their own companies." Beyond that, Finland has encouraged other global companies to open offices there to take advantage of this newly available talent pool, and compelled Nokia to do more than it would have otherwise to support its former employees. This help goes far beyond the normal outplacement services. According to the *Times*, it "includes one-off grants for new business ventures and allowing former employees to use some of the companies' intellectual property, like unwanted patents, almost free of charge."[11]

In terms of our framework, we would call this a political strategy to encourage "stepping forward"—equipping tech-trained workers to build the next set of enabling technologies (in the case of Nokia, mobile ones more than automation ones) and bring them to market. And it is a strategy likely to pay dividends far into the future, both to the knowledge workers involved and to the economy of Finland.

Closer to home—and closer in spirit to the WPA—we noted a jobs skills program that seems ideal for a stepping-aside path. Called HOPE, for "Hands On Preservation Experience," the program was launched by the National Trust for Historic Preservation in 2014 to train thousands of young people in the hands-on skills required to maintain properties and sites of historical significance to their communities.[12] These entry-level workers are simultaneously learning the techniques of careful preservation and gaining a deeper appreciation of something central to humanity: their cultural heritage. We'd guess that they, more than many in jobs training programs, are honing the sensibilities that will make them effective complements to increasingly smart machines.

What other programs could be designed to build the right skills and sensibilities for the various "steps" we've outlined in this book? With some imagination, it would not be hard to identify the kinds of jobs that would place people in productive partnerships with smart machines and then create incentives for employers to create more of them. In general, we think, the right use of public funding is to encourage the job creators, more than to create jobs or to redistribute gains. We're in agreement here with Silicon Valley entrepreneur Jerry Kaplan, author of a book memorably titled *Humans Need Not Apply*. In a recent interview, he said, "[T]he answer isn't to expand our social safety net with more welfare and handouts to the disenfranchised—this is simply stirring up the pot in the hope of preventing it from boiling." A better strategy is to equip people with the skills and tools that will enable them to keep creating economic value in an age of extreme automation. For that, Kaplan says, "[w]e need to train future entrepreneurs and capitalists, not laborers and clerks."[13]

Government investment in jobs creation often gets criticized when it effectively puts policy-makers in the position of "picking winners"—but that might not be an issue in this case. As more people become concerned with the "race against the machines," surely not many will object to a government that picks winners who are human, or at least helps those humans to win.

The Idea of Guaranteed Basic Income
Misses the Point

One key fact of economic life in capitalist societies is that most people who don't work don't make any money. Some social and economic policy wonks have argued, then, that as automation improves our productivity we can afford to pay people a living wage, whether they work or not. As we write, a real-world experiment is beginning in Holland to see what happens when people in a community are simply granted a basic income, effectively breaking the bond that has always existed between income and work. The concept is not a new one (it was discussed, for example, as early as the Nixon administration in the United States) but it has picked up support from various quarters as new levels of automation fuel expectations that unprecedented productivity will create more than enough wealth to sustain us all. Unfortunately it will land in only a very few bank accounts—that is, unless government steps in with some extraordinary form of redistribution.

The question, of course, is whether the provision of income with no strings attached will create too much disincentive to work for recipients' own good and the good of society. Proponents of unconditional income believe the impulse to create value is innate in humans, and if anything is channeled into less socially valuable activities then the point must be to gain payment for one's work. University of London professor Guy Standing, who coined the term "precariat" to describe a working class increasingly stressed by precarious work arrangements, says that, even more important than a redistribution of wealth, guarantees of basic income would constitute a "redistribution of security."

Opponents of the idea are much more inclined to think humans are naturally lazy, and that if given the opportunity to do nothing for their income, will do exactly that. While such critics are legion, we would put, for example, *New York Times* columnist David Brooks in this camp. Brooks has said that, as part of a job creation agenda, the government should "reduce its generosity to people who are not working but increase its support for people who are."[14]

To find out who is right, the city of Utrecht, Netherlands, in partnership with researchers from the University of Utrecht, has taken the portion of its residents who are already on welfare, and who are currently obliged to fulfill certain requirements to keep receiving it, and divided them into three groups. Some get the income unconditionally, meaning that they are not subject to any rules; indeed, even if they start working at a paying job or otherwise gain income, the monthly disbursements will still be made. The second group is subject to some rules, albeit different ones than the city has today. And the third group, as the experiment's control group, continues receiving benefits according to current law, which requires them to engage in job hunting and to lack other sources of income.

The results, as they begin to come in, will be fascinating to see, and we applaud Utrecht for its willingness to experiment. But for our part, we feel no strong stake in seeing the unconditional income idea vindicated. There are a couple of reasons for this. Work has value in itself as a way to find meaning in life. As we've noted, in global polls having a good job is the most desired thing in the world. Freud said, "Love and work . . . work and love, that's all there is." Many studies have found that unemployed people are less happy, and that compensating them anyway doesn't make them as happy as putting them back to work.

How about the idea that unemployed people will resort to creative and recreational activities? Unfortunately, the data don't bear that out. As Derek Thompson notes in his provocative *Atlantic* article "A World Without Work," time studies suggest that people who don't work tend to sleep more, watch more TV, and browse the Internet. So much for taking up painting.

Even if severing the tie between work and income led to happy people, our perspective is that it is unnecessary to contemplate such drastic redistribution unless you have given up on the possibility of widespread employment in well-paying jobs. If you are convinced, as we are, that human strengths will continue to enable humans to produce economic value, and to be paid for that value, there is no reason to forcibly decouple work from income. Instead the focus of government action should be on job creation. Without ruling out that some change in the tax structure may be necessary to correct for the "winner take all" effects many predict from further productivity-improving automation, we're in favor of governments enabling the creation of more meaningful work for their citizens, not requiring less of it.

Why not, for example, fund projects that support more people's desires to engage in artistic production (as in the WPA's Federal Art Project)? Most poets, painters, and playwrights today don't hold steady jobs. Changing that to give them incomes matched to their efforts would seem no more difficult than administering a bureaucracy of handouts—and would yield much surer returns to society. Why not pay people for many of the tasks that are now done on a volunteer basis, for the good of communities? Volunteer service does generally lead to greater happiness. We do believe that the huge gains in productivity will mean we could afford, as a society, to go in either direction. But guaranteed jobs, in our book, still beat guaranteed incomes hands down.

More to Worry About than Jobs

At a 2014 gathering in Boston, PayPal cofounder and venture investor Peter Thiel observed that the arrival of general artificial intelligence would be as momentous as the arrival of some new species of intelligent being on earth. And, he added wryly, "I think, if aliens landed, our first question wouldn't be: what will happen to *jobs*?" Throughout this book, we've been talking about how to ensure continued employment, but even we have to admit that jobs are not the only things threatened in a world where machines become more capable of making decisions and acting on them. Most of the people we hear expressing fears of AI aren't talking about their livelihoods but their lives.

What else might these aliens do, beyond beating us on *Jeopardy!* and taking away our work? In the near term, what scares many people is the prospect of machine-waged war. As militaries around the world consider developing and deploying autonomous weapon systems—weapons, that is, that can select and engage targets without human intervention—it is not hard to imagine how things could go very, very wrong. Both the UN and Human Rights Watch are calling for international treaties to ban these lethal autonomous weapons systems. And most AI scientists appear to stand with them. When Max Tegmark and his colleagues at the Future of

Life Institute wrote an open letter to world military powers urging them not to start an arms race in AI weapons technology, hundreds of their colleagues readily added their signatures.

Almost invariably, when the governance of autonomous AI is discussed, the three laws that science fiction author Isaac Asimov set forth in 1942 are cited. If you're an AI aficionado, you can repeat them by heart. But assuming you are not, his first law states, "A robot may not injure a human being or, through inaction, allow a human being to come to harm." The second: "A robot must obey orders given to it by human beings, except where such orders would conflict with the first law." And the third: "A robot must protect its own existence, as long as such protection does not conflict with the first or second law."

Plenty of people have pointed out that the laws are problematic, because social situations are complex. Legendary investor Warren Buffett, for example, raised a common question about autonomous vehicles during a forum hosted by the National Automobile Dealers Association. What if, he asked, a toddler runs into the street in front of a self-driving car, and the robot's only option not to hit that child is to swerve into the path of an oncoming vehicle with four people in it? After that split-second decision is made and fatal accident results, said Buffett, "I am not sure who gets sued." More deeply, "[I]t will be interesting to know who programs that computer and what their thoughts are about the values of human lives and things."

Or think of end-of-life decisions that are not so hasty; as we increasingly depend on AI to specify, monitor, and to even administer individualized health care, will we trust a machine to say when a patient has suffered long enough and it's time to cease heroic measures, move her to a hospice setting, and let her die in peace? What about AI-driven decisions to remove children from unsafe homes, or elders from settings where the signs of elder abuse are present or can be predicted? So many situations represent gray areas and offer no objectively "right" decisions beyond the decisions we can live with.

This moves us into a set of questions that Geoff Colvin, editor of *Fortune* magazine, engages with in his book *Humans Are Underrated*. Colvin cites the discomfort of such questions as evidence that we need to look at the threat of AI differently. Many thinkers have set themselves the task of figuring out what computers will never be *able* to do as well as or better than humans—but that is the wrong question to ask (and a difficult one to answer as well), Colvin says. Instead, we should ask what we will *allow* them to do, acknowledging that there will always be some activities and decisions we will simply not tolerate being handled by computers, however capable. Thus many important decisions and tasks will remain in human hands even when we have been shown that machines are better at them in some strict sense. "The issue isn't computer abilities," says Colvin, "it's the social necessity that individuals be accountable for important decisions."

Colvin has raised an interesting point, but we're not sure that all humans would always choose human decision-makers for all decisions. Colvin suggests, for example, that no one would want to be judged by a computer in a courtroom. But a minority defendant given the choice between a probably prejudiced jury, a possibly prejudiced judge, and a race-blind machine might well choose the latter option.

In addition, not everyone agrees that we humans will remain in a position to dictate which decisions and actions will be reserved for us. What would prevent a superintelligent machine from denying our commands, they ask, if it thought better of the situation? To prepare for that possibility (familiar to those who remember HAL in *2001: A Space Odyssey*), some insist that computer scientists had better figure out how to program values into the machines, and values that are "human-friendly," to color the decision-making that might proceed logically but tragically from their narrowly specified goals. (The example often given is that an AI instructed to protect humans would think it an ideal solution to pen people up in concrete bunkers.) Programmed-in values would allegedly save the machines from extreme goal pursuit by forcing some balancing with other considerations important to humans. In other words, even a decision-maker that is not "conscious" might be made to operate with a conscience.

Is it possible to imbue a machine with human values? And assuming it is possible, is it truly advisable? Perhaps it would only create more, and more troubling, potential for unintended consequences. Edward Moore Geist, at Stanford University's Center for International Security and Cooperation, dismisses the suggestion as "propounding a solution that will not work to a problem that probably does not exist."[15] Yet there is no question that, as AI advances and humans' roles in decision-making are supported and in some ways diminished by it, there will be profound ethical and policy implications—and that they will be hard to make, let alone enforce—within the borders of individual nations. Even as it raises new questions for humankind, it will force us to find new ways of answering such questions.

Who Gets to Decide?

Hard questions relating to AI will arise with increasing frequency as smart machines become more ubiquitous—and they will have to be addressed by decision-makers at many levels. Take, for example, the debate now brewing about whether it is a good or bad idea to endow machines with emotions. Is that a question for an individual developer's organization (university or private enterprise) to address, or for a consortium, or for national governments, or perhaps the UN? Or take "rogue" uses of AI in workplaces. Soon enough, the idea will occur to some ambitious knowledge worker that she could delegate portions of her job to a personal robot and be twice as productive as her colleagues. It's arguably a logical extension of the "bring your own device" movement. Should her employer forbid that (or encourage it)? Is it something the Department of Labor or its Occupational Safety and Health Administration needs to rule on?

Sitting a layer above our need to answer such questions is our need to figure out how they should be answered, and by whom. Speaking at a 2014 MIT event, Elon Musk said, "I'm increasingly inclined to think that there should be some regulatory oversight, maybe at the national and international level, just to make sure that we don't do something very foolish." But issues of governance will arise in every setting where smart machines take over tasks from humans, and we doubt they can all be answered by governments. And in the meantime, of course, Musk's company continues to program autonomous driving capabilities into Teslas.

Albert Wenger is a venture capitalist in New York who likes to do early-stage investing not only in new businesses but also in ideas for social innovation. We came across him as we looked into the "unconditional basic income" movement discussed above; he's helping to fund some of the experimentation to discover its merits. We bring him up here because of his conviction in general that government need not, and does not, have a monopoly on enacting major social change.

An example Wenger cites is crowdfunding, which enables creative people whose ideas do not offer enough value-creation potential to make them exciting to venture capitalists, to raise funds in the form of many small contributions from ordinary folk who would just like to see their ideas realized. It's a completely new mechanism for funding projects, and Wenger points out that it constitutes an important social innovation that was wholly conceived and built outside the government's purview. Joi Ito of MIT mentions another one, now called Safecast, in the TED Talk we referred to earlier in this chapter—a bottom-up, volunteer-based approach to mapping the spread of radiation in Japan after the 2011 tsunami. Online education is another one, given the social benefits of having education easily accessible for free or at a very low cost that previously would have cost thousands or tens of thousands of dollars. "I don't think we need to wait for somebody in Washington, D.C., to decide this is something that needs to happen, or Berlin or wherever," Wenger says. "These are things we can start to work on just as we are today."

Perhaps in a problem space that knows no geographic boundaries, the most important first steps toward regulation will emanate from nongovernmental bodies. Max Tegmark's group, for example, called the Future of Life Institute, was formed with the intent of creating consensus in the AI community itself about what it should and should not do with the technology. (Musk has also supported the institute's approach, in the form of a $10 million donation to fund research.) In an open letter which it invited others to sign, it said:

> The progress in AI research makes it timely to focus research not only on making AI more capable, but also on maximizing the societal benefit of AI. Such considerations . . . constitute a significant expansion of the field of AI itself, which up to now has focused largely on techniques that are neutral with respect to purpose. We recommend expanded research aimed at ensuring that increasingly capable AI systems are robust and beneficial: our AI systems must do what we want them to do.

As of our last check, nearly seven thousand people had affixed their signatures. It was based on that evident enthusiasm that the group next asked others to join in its call for a ban on autonomous war machines.

Tegmark's group is in the spirit of what Vannevar Bush argued in his famous 1945 report to President Roosevelt, *Science: The Endless Frontier.* This was in the immediate aftermath of the Manhattan Project's development of, and Truman's decision to drop, the atomic bomb. With the technology proven to devastating effect, the nation faced the huge question of what to do with it. More broadly, the stunning scientific achievement of the Bomb raised the question of how science and technology should be governed in general. While Bush, as a scientist himself, wanted government to dramatically boost its spending on science, he defended the scientific community's ability to be self-governing and said it should be free from much public oversight.

Ultimately, of course, the products of science can't be outside the power of societies to govern. Yet it is also true that seventy years after the use of the atomic bomb, there is no global agency or organization with the power to regulate the use of nuclear weapons. (Even the International Atomic Energy Agency holds sway only over those countries that have signed the Nuclear Non-Proliferation Treaty.) Is it possible that, seventy years from now—deep into that time frame when AI experts expect machine superintelligence to exist—no global mechanisms will exist to contain a technology that Elon Musk calls "potentially more dangerous than nukes"?

We're encouraging the many convenings that are happening already to surface the decisions that must be made about artificial intelligence and its impacts—and the more international they are, the better. When a major business-oriented conference like the Global Drucker Forum focuses on a theme like "Claiming our Humanity in the Digital Age," that can only be for the good. When Google's Vint Cerf and technology thinker David Nordfors found a group called i4j (Innovation for Jobs) it can only get more people thinking about the changes that could be made to ameliorate the negative impacts of automation.

In both these cases and other settings, another important thing is going on: Experts from the social sciences are adding their perspectives to those working on the technologies themselves. In the face of prior technology revolutions—from the advent of the automobile to the development of nuclear capabilities to the arrival of nanotechnology—social scientists have often been slow to conduct related research and weigh in from their social perspectives. In recent decades, however, the social sciences have become much stronger disciplines with more rigorous tools of analysis and proven tools of influence. Throughout this book, we have referred to social scientists' writing and research in relation to artificial intelligence. Even when some of it strikes technologists as naïve or uninformed, it is valuable activity. Collectively it puts issues out on the table that technologists haven't themselves been addressing. And it is doing so in ways that are accessible to lay readers. That will prove invaluable as the general public comes to terms with a set of AI technologies that are developing faster than many would believe possible. Ultimately, every one of us should be able to form opinions on the right way forward for a machine-augmented humanity—while it is still up to us to decide.

Governing Itself Needs Augmentation

We need to bring better governance to AI. But at the same time, we should probably be bringing more AI to governance. Decision-making in matters of public policy is of enormous consequence and usually requires many considerations to be factored in. If there is any realm in which we would want the best possible decision-making, surely it is for the good of society.

Oxford's Stuart Armstrong said: "Humans steer the future not because we're the strongest or the fastest, but because we're the smartest." He added: "When machines become smarter than humans, we'll be handing them the steering wheel." Would that be so bad—at least for some decisions? Throughout this book, we've offered examples of algorithms making far better decisions than humans could make, because they are able to process immense amounts of input and consider choices without bias. Even in the context of his report on "12 Risks That Threaten Human Civilization," Armstrong calls AI a unique case, because "on a more positive note, an intelligence of such power could easily combat most other risks in this report, making extremely intelligent AI into a tool of great potential." Jerry Kaplan, the author of *No Humans Need Apply*, has even defended autonomous weapons. He argues, for example, that a smart mine on the ground might be able to identify noncombatants and not blow up.

There have already been some forays by government agencies into using AI to augment human decision-making (outside of the intelligence sector, where it's already pretty pervasive). In Australia, for example, the agency in charge of administering the intellectual property rights, IP Australia, has just begun an exploratory project with IBM to find ways to apply Watson to its various operations. And in Singapore, journalist Joshua Chambers reports on the "Risk Assessment and Horizon Scanning System" in use by the government, which it created using software from DARPA's Total Information Awareness Office. Urban planners there value its ability to pick up "weak signals" from masses of data sets and point them to areas of civic need. For example, geolocation data taken from mobile phones adds up to a picture of citizen behavior throughout the city. Using that, "urban planners can see crowded areas, popular routes, lunch spots and more, showing where to build new schools, hospitals, cycle lanes and bus routes."[16] So far, the decisions such data point to are being left to humans, but the agency sees that as a matter of choice. Some decisions could be left to autonomously acting computers—and perhaps will be in the future.

Not surprisingly, we're going to argue for an augmentation approach. Policy will be better when it is made by powerful pairings of people and machines. We have always had "technocrats" and they have been the "hard" complement to the "soft" skills of politicians and most government employees. This is a classic combination that can be preserved, except that the latter side can and should be increasingly machine augmented.

In the rise of intelligent machines, we are confronting one of the greatest challenges of the twenty-first century. Central to that challenge is ensuring the future of human work. Technological progress has always displaced workers, but it has also always created new opportunities for human employment in excess of the jobs it took away. This time, with automation encroaching on the realm of knowledge work, it is easy to imagine that pattern being broken. In the face of such uncertainty, it is irresponsible to adopt a "wait and see" attitude, hoping for the best. There are actions we can be taking now—and perhaps must take before too long—to ensure that the world of work remains a hospitable one for humans.

At all levels of our society, the pursuit of mutual human–machine augmentation can serve as a motivating and actionable goal. For governments, it is the way to ensure that the people they serve continue to work productively, and enjoy the many rewards of doing so. Policy-makers aiming for greater levels of augmentation will nudge enterprises to provide for it in workplaces and equip citizens to acquire and build the skills they need to thrive. They will use their unrivaled communications powers to educate and inform.

For enterprises, an augmentation agenda is the way to ensure the ongoing innovation and flexibility required to survive in a fast-paced, competitive economy. Only with deep human skills, well leveraged by powerful machine analysis, can they continue to offer solutions that resonate with their all-too-human customers. When employers invest in augmentation, they create settings in which knowledge workers are empowered to do more, not asked to do less—and where as a result more value accrues to them as well as to the business's customers and owners.

For individuals, augmentation represents the antidote to automation and the removal of a threat to their ability to have positive impact in the world. It is the invitation to take five kinds of steps, at the least, that they might not have recognized as options before. It's the invitation to either add value to what these machines do, or have the machines add value to their work.

Today, many knowledge workers are fearful of the rise of the machines. We *should* be concerned, given the potential for these unprecedented tools to make us redundant. But we should not feel helpless in the midst of the large-scale change unfolding around us. The steps are there for us to take. It's up to us, individually and collectively, to strike new, positive relationships with the machines we have made so capable. With our powers combined, we can make our workplaces, and our world, better than they have ever been.

ACKNOWLEDGMENTS

For ideas and feedback on the topics and format of the book, we'd first like to thank everyone who gamely submitted to an interview and appear in the text. They are all illustrative of what it takes to win in the age of smart machines. In addition, we'd like to thank some other smart humans in the editorial process who aren't mentioned inside these covers, including Hollis Heimbouch, our editor and old friend despite her traitorous move to New York, and other hard workers on our behalf at Harper Business including Stephanie Hitchcock, Brian Perrin, and Nick Davies. Clare Morris of the Clare Morris Agency helped us confirm quotes and company mentions.

Smart comments and insights were provided along the way by Alastair Bathgate, Erik Brynolfsson, Lynda Chin, Sameer Chopra, Geoff Colvin, Forrest Danson, Chetan Dube, Sue Feldman, Matt Greitzer, Matt Haldeman, Kris Hammond, Rob High, Davey Ishizaki, Yuh-Mei Hutt, Mark Kris, Chris Johannessen, Stephan Kudyba, Vikram Mahidhar, Melinda Merino, Brigitte Muehlmann, Judah Phillips, Joan Powell, Manoj Saxena, Adam Schneider, Rasu Shresthra, Richard Straub, Chris Thatcher, Mike Thompson, Miklos Vasarhelyi, Dean Whitney, and Floyd Yager. None of them will be automated any time soon!

NOTES

Introduction

1. Michael Kan, "Foxconn to Speed Up 'Robot Army' Deployment," *PC World*, June 26, 2013, http://www.pcworld.com/article/2043026/foxconn-to-speed-up-robot-army-deployment-20000-robots-already-in-its-factories.html.

2. Gartner Inc. press release, "Gartner Identifies the Top 10 Strategic Technology Trends for 2014," October 8, 2013, http://www.gartner.com/newsroom/id/2603623.

3. James Manyika et al., "Disruptive Technologies: Advances That Will Transform Life, Business, and the Global Economy," McKinsey Global Institute, May 2013, http://www.mckinsey.com/insights/business_technology/disruptive_technologies.

4. Thomas H. Davenport, *Thinking for a Living: How to Get Better Performance and Results from Knowledge Workers* (Boston: Harvard Business School Press, 2005), 4.

5. Paul Beaudry, David A. Green, and Benjamin Sand, "The Great Reversal in the Demand for Skill and Cognitive Tasks," National Bureau of Economic Research, Working Paper No. 18901, March 2013.

6. William H. Davidow and Michael S. Malone, "What Happens to Society When Robots Replace Workers?" *Harvard Business Review*, December 10, 2014, https://hbr.org/2014/12/what-happens-to-society-when-robots-replace-workers.

7. Ben Hirschler, "World Economic Forum Warns of Dangers in Growing Inequality," Reuters, January 16, 2014, http://www.reuters.com/article/2014/01/16/davos-risks-idUSL5N0KP0QO20140116.

8. Bruce Weinberg, Eric Gould, and David Mustard, "Crime Rates and Local Labor Market Opportunities in the United States: 1979–1997," *Review of Economics and Statistics* 84, no. 1 (2002): 45-61.

9. "The Great Decoupling," interview with Robert Schiller, *McKinsey Quarterly*, September 2014, http://www.mckinsey.com/insights/public_sector/the_great_decoupling.

10. Dan Schwabel, "Gallup's Jim Clifton on the Coming Jobs War," *Forbes*, October 26, 2011, http://www.forbes.com/sites/danschawbel/2011/10/26/gallups-jim-clifton-on-the-coming-jobs-war/.

Chapter 1: Are Computers Coming After Your Job?

1. David Foster Wallace was famous not only for his convoluted sentences, but also for his extended and frequent footnotes and endnotes. We include this one not only to

honor that tradition, but also to point out that while at the moment it may be impossible to ask a computer to compose prose in "David Foster Wallace mode," we would not bet against that capability being available in the near future. As we will argue later in this book, computers can already write prose, and can even be instructed to write it in a snarky fashion.

2. "Systems-Based Practice: The Role of the Case Management Physician Advisor," *Medical Staff Leader Insider*, September 1, 2011, http://www.hcpro.com/MSL-270392-871/Systemsbased-practice-The-role-of-the-case-management-physician-advisor.html.

3. Dan Townend, "Study Shows 40 Per Cent of Brits Rely on Autocorrect for Spelling," *Daily Express*, October 5, 2014, http://www.express.co.uk/news/uk/519111/Brits-rely-on-autocorrect-for-spelling

4. Christopher Niesche, "The New Flavours of Auditing," IntheBlack.com, April 11, 2014, http://intheblack.com/articles/2014/04/11/the-new-flavours-of-auditing.

5. Catherine Rampell, "Want a Job? Go to College, and Don't Major in Architecture," *New York Times* Economix blog, January 5, 2012, http://economix.blogs.nytimes.com/2012/01/05/want-a-job-go-to-college-and-dont-major-in-architecture.

6. Frank Levy, "How College Changes Demands for Human Skills," OECD Working Paper, March 2010, http://www.oecd.org/edu/skills-beyond-school/45052661.pdf.

Chapter 2: Just How Smart Are Smart Machines?

1. Ray Kurzweil, *The Singularity Is Near* (New York: Viking, 2005), 206.

2. Thomas H. Davenport and Jeanne G. Harris, "Automated Decision-Making Comes of Age," MIT Sloan Management Review, Summer 2005, http://sloanreview.mit.edu/article/automated-decision-making-comes-of-age/.

3. Patrick May, "Q&A: Surgeon, Inventor Catherine Mohr Pushes Robotic Surgery to New Heights," *San Jose Mercury News*, June 13, 2014, http://www.mercurynews.com/business/ci_25959851/q-surgeon-inventor-catherine-mohr-pushes-robotic-surgery.

4. Farhad Manjoo, "Will Robots Steal Your Job?" *Slate*, Sept. 27, 2011, http://www.slate.com/articles/technology/robot_invasion/2011/09/will_robots_steal_your_job_3.html.

5. Thomas H. Davenport, "Analytics 3.0," *Harvard Business Review*, December 2013, https://hbr.org/2013/12/analytics-30.

6. "Gartner Identifies the Top 10 Strategic Technology Trends for 2015," press release, October 8, 2014, http://www.gartner.com/newsroom/id/2867917.

7. Karen Tillman, "How Many Internet Connections Are in the World? Right. Now," Cisco blogs, July 29, 2013, http://blogs.cisco.com/news/cisco-connections-counter.

8. "An Updated Survey of Health Insurance Claims Receipt and Processing Times," AHIP Center for Policy and Research, February 2013, http://www.ahip.org/survey/Healthcare-January 2013/.

9. Mary Lacity, Leslie Willcocks, and Andrew Craig, "Robotic Process Automation

at Telefonica O2," London School of Economics case study, April 2015, http://www.umsl.edu/~lacitym/TelefonicaOUWP022015FINAL.pdf.

10. Interview with Paul Donaldson, then of Xchanging, and Leslie Willcocks, Mary Lacity, and Andrew Craig, "Robotic Process Automation at Xchanging," London School of Economics case study, June 2015, https://www.xchanging.com/system/files/dedicated-downloads/robotic-process-automation.pdf.

11. Jordan Novet, "South Korea's Team KAIST Wins the 2015 DARPA Robotics Challenge," VentureBeat, June 6, 2015, http://venturebeat.com/2015/06/06/koreas-team-kaist-wins-the-2015-darpa-robotics-challenge/.

12. Anna Solana, "The Next Frontier for Artificial Intelligence? Learning Humans' Common Sense," ZDNet, July 17, 2015, http://www.zdnet.com/article/the-next-frontier-for-artificial-intelligence-learning-humans-common-sense/.

13. Tom Walsh, "U-M Alum Takes IBM's 'Jeopardy!' Champ to New Worlds," *Detroit Free Press*, February 23, 2015, http://www.zdnet.com/article/the-next-frontier-for-artificial-intelligence-learning-humans-common-sense/.

14. "Fanuc to Build Brainier Robots with Startup," *Nikkei Asian Review*, June 11, 2015, http://asia.nikkci.com/Business/Companies/Fanuc-to-build-brainier-robots-with-startup.

15. Byron Reese, "Interview with Stephen Wolfram on AI and the Future," Gigaom website, July 27, 2015, https://gigaom.com/2015/07/27/interview-with-stephen-wolfram-on-ai-and-the-future/.

Chapter 3: Don't Automate, Augment

1. Royal Astronomical Society, "Using Artificial Intelligence to Chart the Universe," *News & Press*, September 24, 2012, https://www.ras.org.uk/news-and-press/219-news-2012/2171-using-artificial-intelligence-to-chart-the-universe.

2. Aaron Krol, "Berg and the Pursuit of the Body's Hidden Drugs," Bio-IT World, August 28, 2014, http://www.bio-itworld.com/2014/8/28/berg-pursuit-bodys-hidden-drugs.html.

3. Steve Jobs, in "Memory & Imagination: New Pathways to the Library of Congress" (TV movie), directed by Julian Krainin and Michael R. Lawrence, 1990, Accessed on YouTube, October 29, 2015, https://www.youtube.com/watch?v=ob_GX50Za6c. Jobs was referring to the article "Bicycle Technology," by S. S. Wilson, in *Scientific American* 228, no. 3 (1973).

4. Douglas C. Engelbart, "Augmenting Human Intellect: A Conceptual Framework," SRI Summary Report AFOSR-3223, prepared for Director of Information Sciences, Air Force, Office of Scientific Research, Washington 25, DC, Contract AF 49(638)-1024, SRI Project No. 3578 (AUGMENT,3906), October 1962, http://insitu.lri.fr/~mbl/ENS/FONDIHM/2012/papers/Englebart-Augmenting62.pdf.

5. Norbert Wiener, *The Human Use of Human Beings: Cybernetics and Society* (New York: Da Capo Press, 1988), 159.

6. Maddy Myers, "Google Glass: Inspired by Terminator," Slice of MIT, May 30, 2013, https://slice.mit.edu/2013/05/30/google-glass-inspired-by-terminator/.

7. David Scott, remarks at the opening of the Computer Museum, June 10, 1982,

transcript accessed October 29, 2015, http://klabs.org/history/history_docs/ech/agc_scott.pdf.

8. David A. Mindell, Digital Apollo: Human and Machine in Spaceflight (Cambridge, MA: MIT Press, 2008).

9. John Maynard Keynes, *Essays in Persuasion* (New York: Norton, 1963), 358–73.

10. David H. Autor, "Polanyi's Paradox and the Shape of Employment Growth," prepared for the Federal Reserve Bank of Kansas City's economic policy symposium on "Reevaluating Labor Market Dynamics," September 3, 2014, http://economics.mit.edu/files/9835.

11. Tyler Cowen, *Average Is Over: Powering America Beyond the Age of the Great Stagnation* (New York: Dutton, 2013).

12. CareerSearch, "Career Advice on How to Become an Insurance Underwriter," http://www.careersearch.com/careers/real-estate-and-insurance/insurance-underwriter/.

13. Mike Batty and Alice Kroll, "Automated Life Underwriting: A Survey of Life Insurance Utilization of Automated Underwriting Systems," prepared for the Society of Actuaries, 2009, file:///C:/Users/jkirby/Downloads/research-life-auto-underwriting.pdf.

14. Thomas Arnett, "How Technology Displaces Teachers' Jobs," Clayton Christensen Institute for Disruptive Innovation, November 19, 2014, http://www.christenseninstitute.org/how-technology-displaces-teachers-jobs/#sthash.PyjrVrNk.dpuf.

15. David Port, "Reckoning with Robo-Advisors," LifeHealthPRO, December 31, 2014, http://www.lifehealthpro.com/2014/12/31/reckoning-with-robo-advisors.

Chapter 4: Stepping Up

1. "Statement of Ronald J. Cathcart," Hearing Before the United States Senate Permanent Subcommittee on Investigations of the Committee on Homeland Security and Governmental Affairs, April 13, 2010, https://www.hsgac.senate.gov/downloads/stmt-cathcart-ronald-april-13-2010-psi-fin-crisis-hrg.

2. John Cassidy, "Mastering the Machine: How Ray Dalio Built the World's Richest and Strangest Hedge Fund," *New Yorker,* July 25, 2011, http://www.newyorker.com/magazine/2011/07/25/mastering-the-machine.

3. Richard Feloni, "No, Bridgewater Didn't Just Build a Team of Robotic Traders—They've Had Robot Traders for 32 Years," *Business Insider,* March 12, 2015, http://www.businessinsider.com/bridgewater-artificial-intelligence-development-2015-3.

4. "Systems Intelligence Self Evaluation," Systems Analysis Laboratory, Aalto University, Finland, http://salserver.org.aalto.fi/sitest/2012/.

Chapter 5: Stepping Aside

1. Walter Kirn, "The Tao of Robert Downey, Jr.," *Rolling Stone,* May 13, 2010.

2. Tricia Drevets, "How to Make Money Living off the Grid," *Off the Grid News,* June 25, 2014, http://www.offthegridnews.com/financial/how-to-make-money-living-off-the-grid/.

3. Heather Plett, "What It Means to 'Hold Space' for People, plus Eight Tips on How to Do It Well," Heather Plett blog, March 11, 2015, http://heatherplett.com/2015/03/hold-space/.

4. Steve Wozniak, "Does Steve Jobs Know How to Code?," response to email posted on Woz.org, http://www.woz.org/letters/does-steve-jobs-know-how-code.

5. Dan Ariely, *Predictably Irrational: The Hidden Forces That Shape Our Decisions*, revised and expanded edition (New York: Harper Perennial, 2010).

6. Howard Gardner, *Frames of Mind: The Theory of Multiple Intelligences*, 3rd ed. (New York: Basic Books, 2011).

7. Peter Salovey and John D. Mayer, "Emotional Intelligence," *Imagination, Cognition and Personality* 9, no. 3 (March 1990): 185–211.

8. John Markoff, "Skilled Work, Without the Worker," *New York Times*, August 18, 2012, http://www.nytimes.com/2012/08/19/business/new-wave-of-adept-robots-is-changing-global-industry.html?_r=0.

9. Michigan News, "Empathy: College Students Don't Have as Much as They Used To," May 27, 2010, http://ns.umich.edu/new/releases/7724-empathy-college-students-don-t-have-as-much-as-they-used-to.

10. Jean M. Twenge and W. Keith Campbell, *The Narcissism Epidemic: Living in the Age of Entitlement* (New York: Atria Books, 2010).

11. Kyung Hee Kim, "The Creativity Crisis: The Decrease in Creative Thinking Scores on the Torrance Tests of Creative Thinking," *Creativity Research Journal* 23, no. 4 (2011): 285–95.

12. Marc A. Brackett and Susan E. Rivers, "Transforming Students' Lives with Social and Emotional Learning," in *International Handbook of Emotions in Education*, 1st ed., edited by Reinhard Pekrun and Lisa Linnenbrink-Garcia (New York: Routledge, 2014), 368–88.

13. Association for Talent Development, staff report, "$164.2 Billion Spent on Training and Development by U.S. Companies," December 12, 2013, https://www.td.org/Publications/Blogs/ATD-Blog/2013/12/ASTD-Releases-2013-State-of-the-Industry-Report.

14. Alex Silverman, "Suns' Ryan McDonough Discusses Unorthodox Path to GM, NBA's Rise of Analytics," *Sports Business Daily*, October 29, 2013, http://www.sportsbusinessdaily.com/Daily/Issues/2013/10/29/NBA-Season-Preview/McDonough.aspx-http://www.sportsbusinessdaily.com/Daily/Issues/2013/10/29/NBA-Season-Preview/McDonough.aspx.

15. Dan Shaughnessy, "For Suns GM Ryan McDonough, Sports Is in His Blood," *Boston Globe*, November 18, 2014, https://www.bostonglobe.com/sports/2014/11/18/for-suns-ryan-mcdonough-sports-his-blood/CeJzozAV7MGErB44Gn2ihK/story.html.

16. Eugene Sadler-Smith, "Using the Head and Heart at Work: A Business Case for Soft Skills," research report prepared for the Chartered Institute of Personnel and Development, November 2010, http://www.cipd.co.uk/NR/rdonlyres/18616949-CF66-47F8-A088-7C8FF2D864E0/0/HeadandheartguideFINAL.pdf.

17. D. P. Weikart, D. Deloria, S. Lawser, and R. Wiegerink, "Longitudinal Results of the Ypsilanti Perry Preschool Project," Monographs of the High/Scope Educational Research Foundation (Ypsilanti, MI: High/Scope Press, 1970).

18. Peter Gray, "Early Academic Training Produces Long-Term Harm," *Psychology Today*, May 5, 2015, https://www.psychologytoday.com/blog/freedom-learn/201505/early-academic-training-produces-long-term-harm.

19. William Zinsser, *On Writing Well: The Classic Guide to Writing Nonfiction*, 30th Anniversary Edition (New York: Harper Perennial, 2006).

20. National Endowment for the Arts, "Artists and Arts Workers in the United States: Findings from the American Community Survey (2005–2009) and the Quarterly Census of Employment and Wages," NEA Research Note #105, October 2011, https://www.arts.gov/sites/default/files/105.pdf.

21. George Anders, The 'Soft Skill' That Pays $100,000+," author's LinkedIn blog, June 26, 2013, https://www.linkedin.com/pulse/20130626195513-59549-empathy-and-jobs-that-pay-100-000.

22. Thomas O'Neill, "Don't Sack Your Copywriter Yet, but Are Machines Set to Take Over?," *Drum*, May 14, 2015, http://www.thedrum.com/news/2015/05/14/dont-sack-your-copywriter-yet-are-machines-set-take-over.

23. Todd B. Kashdan, "What Really Makes You a Happy Person?," *Creativity Post*, October 29, 2015, http://www.creativitypost.com/technology/the_art_of_computational_creativity%20-%20sthash.HDvoEzx9.dpuf.

24. "IBM's Watson Is Out with Its Own Barbecue Sauce," NPR, July 1, 2014, http://www.npr.org/sections/thesalt/2014/07/01/327204491/ibms-watson-is-out-with-its-own-barbecue-sauce.

25. Lewis Segal, "Merce Cunningham Dies at 90; Revolutionary Choreographer, *Los Angeles Times*, July 28, 2009, http://www.latimes.com/local/obituaries/la-me-merce-cunningham28-2009jul28-story.html.

26. Eleanor Tucker, "How Robots Are Helping Children with Autism," *Guardian*, February 1, 2015, http://www.theguardian.com/lifeandstyle/2015/feb/01/how-robots-helping-children-with-autism.

27. Thomas Claburn, "Artificial Intelligence Will Put Us Out of Work," *Information-Week*, January 30, 2015, http://www.informationweek.com/it-life/artificial-intelligence-will-put-us-out-of-work/d/d-id/1318875.

28. Paul Colford, "A Leap Forward in Quarterly Earnings Stories," Associated Press blog, June 30, 2014, https://blog.ap.org/announcements/a-leap-forward-in-quarterly-earnings-stories.

29. Geoff Colvin, *Humans Are Underrated: What High Achievers Know That Brilliant Machines Never Will* (New York: Portfolio, 2015).

30. Will Oremus, "The Prose of the Machines," *Slate*, July 14, 2014, http://www.slate.com/articles/technology/technology/2014/07/automated_insights_to_write_ap_earnings_reports_why_robots_can_t_take_journalists.html.

31. Philip Auerswald, "The Bifurcation Is Near," author's blog, May 19, 2015, https://medium.com/@auerswald/the-bifurcation-is-near-f60633de45b3#.3wvhop154.

Chapter 6: Stepping In

1. David R. Meyer, *Networked Machinists: High-Technology Industries in Antebellum America* (Baltimore: Johns Hopkins University Press, 2006).

2. James Bessen, "Will Robots Steal Our Jobs? The Humble Loom Suggests Not," *Washington Post*, January 25, 2014, https://www.washingtonpost.com/news/the-switch/wp/2014/01/25/what-the-humble-loom-can-teach-us-about-robots-and-automation/.

3. James Bessen, *Learning by Doing: The Real Connection Between Innovation, Wages, and Wealth* (New Haven, CT: Yale University Press, 2015), 17.

4. Thomas H. Davenport, *Mission Critical: Realizing the Promise of Enterprise Systems* (Boston: Harvard Business School Press, 2000).

5. "Dr. Doris Day with Melafind on Fox 5," Fox News New York, August 13, 2012, https://www.youtube.com/watch?v=Lw70cKKhft4.

6. Ralph Losey blog, http://e-discoveryteam.com/.

7. Leslie Mitler, "Entry-Level Jobs Are No Longer Entry-Level," SimplyHired, August 13, 2013, http://www.simplyhired.com/blog/jobsearch/career/entry-level-jobs-longer-entry-level/.

Chapter 7: Stepping Narrowly

1. "Rat Attack!," *Nova*, Season 36, Episode 12, PBS, November 2009.

2. Craig Lambert, "The Art of Subtraction," *Harvard Magazine*, July–August 2013, http://harvardmagazine.com/2013/07/the-art-of-subtraction.

3. "Unusual and Highly Specialized Practice Areas," New York City Bar, http://www.nycbar.org/career-development/your-career-1/spotlight-on-careers/312-unusual-and-highly-specialized-practice-areas.

4. See, for example, Michael J. A. Howe, *The Origins of Exceptional Abilities* (Cambridge, MA: Blackwell, 1990).

5. K. Anders Ericsson, Ralf Th. Krampe, and Clemens Tesch-Romer, "The Role of Deliberate Practice in the Acquisition of Expert Performance," *Psychological Review* 100, no. 3 (1993): 363–406, http://graphics8.nytimes.com/images/blogs/freakonomics/pdf/DeliberatePractice(PsychologicalReview).pdf.

6. Mihaly Csikszentmihalyi, *Creativity: The Psychology of Discovery and Invention* (New York: HarperCollins, 1996).

7. McKinsey Global Institute, "Disruptive Technologies: Advances That Will Transform Life, Business, and the Global Economy," May 2013, file:///C:/Users/jkirby/Downloads/MGI_Disruptive_technologies_Full_report_May2013%20(2).pdf.

8. Syd Field, *Four Screenplays: Studies in the American Screenplay* (New York: Delta, 1994).

9. Edward Dolnick, *The Clockwork Universe: Isaac Newton, the Royal Society, and the Birth of the Modern World* (New York: Harper Perennial, 2012).

10. Greg Farrell and Andrew Martin, "How Goldman Banker Became NFL's Go-To Stadium-Finance Guy," *BloombergBusiness*, January 29, 2015, http://www.bloomberg.com/news/articles/2015-01-29/how-goldman-banker-became-nfl-s-go-to-stadium-finance-guy.

Chapter 8: Stepping Forward

1. Thomas H. Davenport and D. J. Patil, "Data Scientist: The Sexiest Job of the 21st Century," *Harvard Business Review*, October 2012, https://hbr.org/2012/10/data-scientist-the-sexiest-job-of-the-21st-century/.

2. Gil Press, "How Knowledge Workers Can Save Their Jobs in the 'Bring Your Own Robot' Age," *Forbes*, June 12, 2015, http://www.forbes.com/sites/gilpress/2015/06/12/what-should-knowledge-workers-do-in-the-age-of-bring-your-own-robot/.

3. Cynthia Rudin, "Algorithms for Interpretable Machine Learning," proceedings of the 20th ACM SIGKDD international conference on knowledge discovery and data mining, 2014, 1519.

Chapter 9: How You'll Manage Augmentation

1. Geoffrey Morgan, "How Canada's Oilsands Are Paving the Way for Driverless Trucks—and the Threat of Big Layoffs," *Calgary Herald*, June 8, 2015, http://business.financialpost.com/news/energy/how-canadas-oilsands-are-paving-the-way-for-driverless-trucks-and-the-threat-of-big-layoffs.

2. Martin Ford, *Rise of the Robots* (New York: Basic Books, 2015), 12.

3. Julia Kirby, "An Inside Look at Facebook's Approach to Automation and Human Work," *Harvard Business Review*, June 12, 2015, https://hbr.org/2015/06/an-inside-look-at-facebooks-approach-to-automation-and-human-work.

4. Anne Trafton, "A New Way to Model Cancer," *MIT News*, August 6, 2014, http://news.mit.edu/2014/new-technique-to-model-cancer-0806.

5. Kirsten Grind, "Vanguard Launches Robo Adviser, Sort Of," *Wall Street Journal*, April 6, 2015, http://www.wsj.com/articles/vanguards-partly-automated-service-just-dont-call-it-robo-adviser-1428375815.

6. Doug Henschen, "IBM Watson Speeds Drug Research," *InformationWeek*, August 28, 2014, http://www.informationweek.com/big-data/big-data-analytics/ibm-watson-speeds-drug-research/d/d-id/1306783.

7. "Investor Alert: Automated Investment Tools," U.S. Securities and Exchange Commission and the Financial Industry Regulatory Authority, May 8, 2015, http://www.sec.gov/oiea/investor-alerts-bulletins/autolistingtoolshtm.html.

8. Henry Blodget, "CEO of Apple Partner Foxconn: 'Managing One Million Animals Gives Me a Headache," *Business Insider*, January 19, 2012, http://www.businessinsider.com/foxconn-animals-2012-1.

Chapter 10: Utopia or Dystopia? How Society
Must Adapt to Smart Machines

1. Joanna Bryson, "Ethics: Robots, AI, and Society," author's blog, http://www.cs.bath.ac.uk/~jjb/web/ai.html.

2. Dennis Pamlin and Stuart Armstrong,"12 Risks That Threaten Human Civilization: The Case for a New Risk Category," Global Challenges Foundation, February 2015, http://globalchallenges.org/wp-content/uploads/12-Risks-with-infinite-impact.pdf.

3. Aaron Smith and Janna Anderson, "AI, Robotics, and the Future of Jobs," Pew Research Center, August 6, 2014, http://www.pewinternet.org/2014/08/06/future-of-jobs/.

4. Derek Thompson, "A World without Work," *Atlantic*, July/August 2015, http://www.theatlantic.com/magazine/archive/2015/07/world-without-work/395294/.

5. Thomas Claburn, "The Threat of Artificial Intelligence," *InformationWeek*, July 3, 2015, http://www.informationweek.com/mobile/mobile-devices/the-threat-of-artificial-intelligence/a/d-id/1321188.

6. John Frank Weaver, "We Need to Pass Legislation on Artificial Intelligence Early and Often," *Slate*, Future Tense blog, September 12, 2014, http://www.slate.com/

blogs/future_tense/2014/09/12/we_need_to_pass_artificial_intelligence_laws_early_and_often.html.

7. Jane Wakefield, "Does a Five-Year-Old Need to Learn How to Code?" BBC News, September 26, 2014, http://www.bbc.com/news/technology-29145904.

8. Shelly Palmer, "What Will You Do After White-Collar Work?," author's blog, August 1, 2015. "http://www.shellypalmer.com/2015/08/what-will-you-do-after-white-collar-work/.

9. Committee on OECD Legal Affairs Working Group on Legal Questions Related to the Development of Robotics and Artificial Intelligence, minutes of the meeting of May 26, 2015, in Brussels, https://polcms.secure.europarl.europa.eu/cmsdata/upload/14082ed0-a408-4d02-868a-05b717349c18/WG_Robotics_26%20May%202015_minutes.pdf.

10. John Seely Brown, "Cultivating the Entrepreneurial Learner for the 21st Century," keynote presentation at the 2012 Digital Media and Learning conference in San Francisco, March 1, 2012.

11. Mark Scott, "After Nokia Layoffs, Tech Workers in Finland Regroup and Refocus," *New York Times*, August 9, 2015, http://www.nytimes.com/2015/08/10/technology/after-nokia-layoffs-tech-workers-in-finland-regroup-and-refocus.html.

12. National Trust for Historic Preservation, "HOPE Crew—Hands-On Preservation Experience: Engaging a New Generation of Preservationists," https://savingplaces.org/hope-crew/#.VjLRoLerTIU.

13. Yale Books Unbound, "Robots in Our Midst: A Conversation with Jerry Kaplan," Yale University Press blog, July 29, 2015, http://blog.yupnet.org/2015/07/29/robots-in-our-midst-a-conversation-with-jerry-kaplan/.

14. David Brooks, "The Working Nation," *New York Times*, October 23, 2014, http://www.nytimes.com/2014/10/24/opinion/david-brooks-the-working-nation.html?_r=1.

15. Edward Moore Geist, "Is Artificial Intelligence Really an Existential Threat to Humanity?," Bulletin of the Atomic Scientists, July 30, 2015, http://thebulletin.org/artificial-intelligence-really-existential-threat-humanity8577.

16. Colin Marrs, "Artificial Intelligence Services," PublicTechnology.net, February 18, 2015, https://www.publictechnology.net/articles/features/artificial-intelligence-services.

INDEX

ABOUT THE AUTHOR

THOMAS H. DAVENPORT is the President's Distinguished Professor in Management and Information Technology at Babson College, cofounder of the International Institute for Analytics, a fellow of the MIT Center for Digital Business, and a senior advisor to Deloitte Analytics. He teaches analytics and big data in executive programs at Babson, Harvard Business School, MIT Sloan School of Management, and Boston University, and is the author or coauthor of seventeen books.

JULIA KIRBY is a contributing editor for *Harvard Business Review*. She is the coauthor of *Standing on the Sun: How the Explosion of Capitalism Abroad Will Change Business Everywhere*.